W9-BZD-267

MISSY AVILA—
An appealing and irresistible young beauty, she was a popular teen with a secret enemy...

KAREN SEVERSON—
Overweight, emotional, Missy's lifelong best friend, she spearheaded the hunt for the killer...

CINDY SILVERIO—
She had seen too much. Tormented by what she knew and scared for her life, she kept a terrifying secret.

LAURA DOYLE—
Angry and tough, a child of a troubled home, she screamed that she'd kill Missy for stealing her boyfriend...

VIC AMAYA—
Missy's loyal friend, he nearly killed the wrong person in revenge.

IRENE AVILA—
Missy's grieving, desperate, very pretty mother, she would unknowingly invite a murderer into her own home...

CATHERINE SCOTT—
The dedicated homicide detective who carried a lock of Missy's hair as a reminder of a crime that had become personal —a crime she had to solve.

"I LOOK AT THE PICTURE OF MISSY AND I CAN'T HELP BUT THINK ABOUT HOW SHE MUST HAVE STRUGGLED."
—Irene Avila, Missy's mom

Homicide detective Catherine Scott made a note of the scratches and bruises around the girl's face and eyes. She'd been beaten up pretty badly before she was drowned. The coroner touched the cold, gray skin of the girl's face and arms. It slid grotesquely from her bones.

"We have skin slippage," he said. "Make a note of it. She's probably been dead a couple of days."

It was then Catherine noticed the hair.

Clumps of dark brown hair lay on a boulder. Catherine walked closer and saw more hair on the ground. "It looks like someone cut her hair before they drowned her," she said.

Quietly, Catherine picked up a small, shiny, dark lock of Missy's hair. She placed it on a piece of paper, folded it into a tiny square, and tucked it inside her pants pocket.

She would never forget this girl. Never give up on solving her murder. And for the next three years, wherever she went and whatever she did, Catherine Scott carried that lock of Missy's hair.

Also by Karen Kingsbury

FINAL VOWS

MISSY'S MURDER

KAREN KINGSBURY

A DELL BOOK

Published by
Dell Publishing
a division of
Bantam Doubleday Dell Publishing Group, Inc.
1540 Broadway
New York, New York 10036

ISBN: 0-440-20771-1

Printed in the United States of America

Published simultaneously in Canada

December 1991

10 9 8 7 6 5 4 3

RAD

ACKNOWLEDGMENTS

I would like to thank the people who made this project possible. First, my thanks goes to Arthur Pine, an incredibly persistent man whose talent, knowledge, and encouragement made a difference. I would also like to thank Irene Avila, Mark Avila, Tamia Hope, and the others who helpfully provided accurate information throughout the writing of this book.

Finally, I want to thank Leslie Schnur for being the most patient editor in the world. I also thank Mercer Warriner for her editorial expertise and Jill Lamar for her creative assistance.

DEDICATED TO

My loving husband,
who has been my best friend ever since we met.
Thank you for changing my life
and being proud of me.

My dad,
who encouraged me
and believed I would accomplish
my dreams.

My mom,
whose excitement and enthusiasm
has kept me going throughout
this project.

My precious daughter,
who inspired me to pursue
the impossible.

And especially my Heavenly Father:
Thank you for answered prayers.

AUTHOR'S EXPLANATORY NOTE

The events described in this book are taken directly from court transcripts and other public records and numerous interviews with many people involved. However, in many instances, in order to better communicate the story and the atmosphere surrounding the events, incidents and dialogue were dramatically re-created based on court testimony and other public records, and interviews with various participants or other knowledgeable individuals.

Except for Missy Avila, Karen Severson, Laura Doyle, Irene Avila, Ernie Avila, Sr., Mark Avila, Shavaun Avila, Chris Avila, Ernie Avila, Jr., Judge Jack Tso, prosecutor Tamia Hope, Victor Amaya, and a few other minor characters, the author has chosen to change the names and disguise the identities of the people involved in this story. This has been done to preserve privacy. Any similarity between the fictitious names used and those of living persons is, of course, entirely coincidental.

1

THE SANTA ANA winds started blowing in the San Fernando Valley on October 1, 1985. Usually, the winds came much later in the month and sometimes not until November. Most people liked the Santa Anas because they were soothing after the stagnant summer. Gentle and warm, they blew away the smog, leaving behind a rare blue in the southern California skies.

On that particular Tuesday afternoon Missy Avila sauntered from the gates of Mission High School and started looking for Bobby's car. Missy loved this kind of weather. It was invigorating and infused her entire day with joy.

Even the school day had been a good one. Missy thought back over it as she stood outside the campus waiting for her ride. She had finished her math homework earlier than usual and her English teacher had read one of Missy's poems aloud, as a fine example of descriptive writing.

With the warm air swirling around her Missy at seventeen felt that the world promised endless possibilities. Her future plans to finish school and work as a physical therapist seemed as sharply focused as the San Gabriel Mountains in the distance. The gentle peaks, covered with bare shrub trees and wild brown grass brittle from the dry summer, formed a ridge that was usually hidden under a veil of smog. That afternoon the sky was so clear, Missy thought she could see each pine tree at the summit. She wanted to hike there, find the perfect rock, and sit for hours writing poetry about her youth and love of life.

But the gorgeous sky and gentle wind were not the only causes of Missy's buoyant mood. Bobby Miller, the tall boy with the sandy-brown hair and heart-melting grin, had been dating Missy for three months, and there were times when Missy wondered what it would be like to marry him. She believed in the possibility of love.

Missy smiled as she saw Bobby drive around the corner in his beat-up Mustang and screech to a stop at the curb where she was waiting.

"Wait a minute," he yelled, jumping out of the car and running around to open the passenger door. "You must allow me, my princess!"

Missy tossed her head, her long shiny dark hair spilling down past her waist, and laughed as only a teenager in love can laugh. A few of Missy's friends walked by and grinned when they saw Bobby bowing graciously to her. She climbed in the car, and he shut her door, then ran back to the driver's seat.

"Let's say we spend the rest of the day together!" He turned to Missy, pulling her close. "We could make a picnic lunch and take it to the park, find a quiet place, just you and me. What do you say, Missy? Can I talk you into it?"

She frowned and looked out the window. It would have been a perfect day to spend with Bobby.

"I can't, Bobby. I promised Laura I'd see her this afternoon."

"Yeah, but you can get out of that. You can be with her anytime. How many times do we have to spend an afternoon like this together? Come on, Missy!"

For a few seconds she considered changing her plans, but Laura had recently broken up with her boyfriend, Vic, and she needed Missy's sympathetic counsel.

"I just can't do it. Laura's counting on me." Missy leaned closer to Bobby, and the look in her green eyes made his heart melt. He understood. After all, he valued Missy's loyalty. He couldn't remember her ever standing up a date. If Missy had made a promise to Laura, then she'd stick to it.

They pulled up in front of Missy's house and Bobby leaned over to kiss her.

"Okay. You win. If I can't be with you, then at least have a good time without me."

Missy smiled and kissed him quickly.

"When Laura gets here, we'll probably go out and do something. But I'll be home this evening." She climbed out of the car and waved. "I'll call you!" Bobby nodded, flashing his handsome grin, before he drove off.

It was one o'clock when Missy walked in the front door of the house she'd lived in all her life.

"Hi, Mom!"

Irene Avila looked up from the square kitchen table where she had been arranging flowers for the past two hours. She rubbed her eyes and smiled at her only daughter.

Irene and Ernie Avila had been separated for some time, but the divorce had become final earlier that year. Irene's sole comfort during those weary afternoons and lonely nights had been her love for Missy. The boys were wonderful, too, of course; Ernie junior, Mark, and Chris, who was years younger than the rest. In fact, her two oldest sons both had good jobs and Irene was proud of them. But Missy was special.

Irene knew it wasn't right to treasure one child more than the others. She even worried that she tempted the fates by doing so. But she couldn't help her feelings. Seventeen-year-old Missy was closest to her heart and always would be.

Irene sometimes speculated on the reasons for the intensity of her love. Perhaps the girl reminded her of her younger self; Missy's loving spirit and happy, carefree heart were so like Irene's before she'd married Ernie.

And surely their late-night talks strengthened the bond. For the past few years Missy and her mother had ended the days together whispering in the darkness of Irene's room before turning in for the night. Irene treasured those moments.

Of course, Irene wasn't always pleased by Missy's confessions; her first sexual experience, for example, or the time she'd tried marijuana with some friends. But Irene was careful not to disapprove too much of her daughter's experiments. She had done similar things when she was young. And Irene sensed that strict mothers didn't have late-night talks with their daughters. They had fights. In her loneliness since the divorce Irene needed Missy too badly to risk losing her friendship.

So Missy got away with an unusually late curfew and more privileges than most of her peers. This freedom, combined with Missy's looks and personality, made her the envy of nearly everyone at Mission High School. If Missy's perfectly formed body—which, at four feet eleven and ninety pounds, had filled out in all the right places—her beautiful brown hair and flashing green eyes, and her popularity weren't sufficient causes for jealousy, then her friends could be a little resentful of Missy's friendship with her mother. Seemingly advantageous, this permissiveness may have worked against her.

That October, Irene wasn't worried about her permissiveness. Missy was her best friend and all she cared about was maintaining that closeness, even if she had to compromise her parental authority. As for Missy, she loved Irene and felt closer to her than most teenage girls felt toward their mothers. Even so, Missy never intended to share all her secrets.

If Irene had considered Missy's life-style, the kind of people who befriended her and the boys she liked to date, she would easily have seen that Missy wasn't telling her everything. But it was so much nicer to believe that one's daughter had nothing to hide, so Irene never probed too far.

That Tuesday morning had been particularly trying for Irene, and as she kicked off her tennis shoes she felt a headache coming on. This wasn't unusual. She spent several hours a day arranging dried flowers on her dining-room table to bring in extra money. Irene never regretted working from home to make ends meet, but she found it exhausting.

Years earlier when she was still preparing tax forms for a handful of clients, she noticed her eyesight weakening. And not long afterward the headaches started. In March 1985 doctors operated on Irene's wrists because of tendon problems. After recovery Irene found the forms were simply too painful for her weak hands to prepare and she finally quit. Irene considered rejoining the work force, but she decided that her kids needed her too much. Rather than taking an office job Irene began making dried floral arrangements.

At forty-four she was still a beautiful woman, with chestnut-brown hair and deep brown eyes. No matter how busy, she always took time to do her hair and nails and to dress nicely. The years of scrutinizing numbers and equations, and now the strain of arranging dried flowers, were, it is true, beginning to leave a network of lines across her face; still, Irene never complained—working at home was preferable to an office job. Irene's two greatest concerns were that her children should have someone waiting for them when they got home and that the family should have enough money to put food on the table. In that order.

Although it had been a long day for Irene, she liked seeing Missy so happy. For months after her parents' separation Missy had moped about the house and then disappeared for hours without saying where she was going. These days Missy was her old self, so Irene forgot the calluses on her fingers and the tired feeling in her eyes.

Irene stood up, pulled a sandwich from the refrigerator, and poured her daughter a tall glass of milk.

"How was school?" She walked over to Missy and hugged her tight, handing her the sandwich.

"Great! Couldn't be better." Missy sat down and started eating. "But I have to hurry. Laura's coming over to pick me up and I want to wash my hair before she gets here."

"Laura Doyle?" Irene looked confused. "I thought she was upset with you."

"Yeah, but we worked everything out yesterday," Missy said.

Irene shrugged. "I'll never understand you girls."

Just a week or so earlier Laura hadn't been speaking to Missy because she thought Missy had instigated the breakup between Laura and Vic. The truth was, even though they had dated a few times before Laura started seeing him, Missy and Vic were merely close friends. In fact, Missy wanted nothing more than to help Laura get over the breakup, and maybe even help the two get back together.

Missy had a way of ignoring the bad feelings if a friend lost her temper because of something she had done. If she found one of her friends upset with her, well, then, maybe the friend had been through a tough time at home lately or had had a bad day or had broken up with her boyfriend. Any of a hundred excuses might do. But Missy had a difficult time believing anyone would be angry with her out of dislike. In fact, were her brothers to compile a list of their sister's faults, at the top would have been this statement: *Missy is too trusting.*

She wanted everyone to like her, and at Mission High School, despite the jealousies, nearly everyone did. Missy was happy, vivacious, and easy to like. Even better, she attracted the boys. That would probably have been reason enough for Laura Doyle to come back looking for Missy's friendship.

Missy had taken her shower and was drying off when the phone rang. "I'll get it," Missy shouted from the bathroom as she grabbed a towel and ran dripping wet into the kitchen.

"Hello?" A small puddle began forming where

Missy stood. "Oh, hi. Yeah. That's great. Yeah, I'll be ready."

As Missy spoke, Irene thought how very beautiful she was, shivering and laughing and fresh from the shower. Missy had been blessed with a lovely complexion and, unlike most of her friends, had never suffered from teenage acne. Now, with the bath towel wrapped loosely around her daughter, Irene could see neither bruise nor blemish; Missy's skin was perfectly clear.

Irene sipped her coffee and leaned back in her chair as the warm liquid made its way through her body. She took a long drag from her cigarette and thought about her plans for the afternoon. She was finished with the day's paperwork and the boys had already taken off with their friends. It was going to be a beautiful afternoon—blue skies, a warm breeze, and the house all to herself.

"That was Laura," Missy said as she darted back toward her bedroom to get ready, her wet hair flying. "We're going to the park. She'll be here at three."

Irene had washed the dishes and was drying her hands when she heard Laura's Volkswagen pull up out front. It was exactly three o'clock.

Irene knew Missy cared about Laura's friendship and she was glad the girls were spending an afternoon together. Irene didn't know that the girls were driving to Stonehurst Park to do a few lines of cocaine. Like her friends Missy was never very serious about doing drugs, but an occasional experiment was generally accepted by her group. In the summer of 1985 the drug of choice was cocaine. They didn't use it often or in large quantities because it was expensive. But that afternoon before Laura arrived, Missy had called her

friend Christy Crawford and told her about their plans
for the afternoon.

"We got some coke and we're going to do a few
lines," she had said. Cocaine was something different
and new, and teenagers had no idea back then of the
ravages the drug would bring in years to come because of those early experiments. Laura had been far
more interested than Missy. But that afternoon the
cocaine lines would be free, and Missy was as willing to
be included as any of her friends.

Laura ran lightly up the front walkway to the Avila
house. She was skinny and angular, not petite like
Missy, and her white complexion never fared well
against her long red hair. She was a child of a troubled
home, and Missy sometimes felt sorry for her. Ever
since the girls had been in high school, Missy had
taken Laura under her wing and the redheaded girl
had begun calling Irene "Mom" whenever she was at
Missy's house. Those who knew Laura Doyle described her as something of a loner, always on the
outskirts of Missy's popular circle. Years earlier Laura's
mother had enrolled her in a modeling course to teach
her the social graces she so apparently lacked.

Laura never completed the course. Her mother
blamed the failure on lack of funds and Laura's friends
blamed it on Laura. The way they saw it, Laura took
the course only at her mother's prodding and never
had any desire to spend her life smiling for a camera.
Laura was perhaps more realistic than her mother
when it came to her looks. Her unattractive mouth
and skinny body made it difficult for her to attract
boys.

"Missy, come on," Laura yelled as she walked into

the house. Then she spotted Irene. "Hi, Mom. Is Missy almost ready?"

Irene smiled. "She'll be right out."

Laura and Irene heard a door slam from down the hall and turned to see Missy enter the room. She was stunning, even in her tan sweatshirt and faded blue jeans. Laura grinned at her and grabbed her wrist. "Come on, let's go."

Missy turned toward her mother as she made her way toward the door. "We'll be at Stonehurst Park. I don't think we're going anywhere else, and I'll be home by six. Don't worry, I'll call if I'm going to be late." She stooped to kiss her mother and flashed her a grin.

"Hey, you have the house all to yourself," she said. "Enjoy it."

Irene smiled as the girls left. Then suddenly, almost as if she'd forgotten something important, Missy turned around and ran back to Irene, waiting on the porch. She looked at her mother intently and smiled, her green eyes warm and sparkling. "Mom, I love you. I just wanted to tell you. I really love you a lot." Missy leaned over and hugged her mother.

This was unusual behavior. Irene and Missy were closer than many mothers and teenage daughters, but Missy wasn't prone to dramatic displays of affection. Still, Irene felt touched that her daughter had been thoughtful enough to share her feelings.

"I love you, too, sweetheart," Irene said. "Have fun."

Irene watched until they had climbed into Laura's red Volkswagen bug and driven away down the street. She stood on the porch for a moment, letting the warm wind blow over her skin.

For the next several hours Irene abandoned all thought of work and sat outside in a folding chair with a glass of iced tea.

She was still there, enjoying the peace and quiet, when the phone rang. It was six o'clock, and Irene thought the caller would be Missy wanting to spend the night at Laura's. She grabbed her iced tea, ran into the house, and answered the phone on the third ring. "Hello."

"Hi, Mom. This is Laura. Is Missy there?"

Irene felt her heart skip a beat.

"Of course not, Laura. She's with you."

Laura cleared her throat. "No, she's not." Irene felt the color begin to drain from her face. There was silence for several seconds before Laura finally continued. "When we left your house we went by Stonehurst Park. Missy saw three guys she knew in a blue Camaro, so I dropped her off to talk to them. Then I went to get gas for the car. When I came back Missy was gone and so were the boys in the Camaro." Laura paused. "I thought she might be home by now." Laura waited. "Mom?"

"Yes, I'm here." Irene forced herself to think. "Did she say anything else, Laura? Do you have any idea where she went?"

"No. She knew I was going to be right back, but I figured she must have decided to go with them."

"Well, who were the boys? Just give me their names and I'll see if I can call and find Missy."

"Umm, I don't know. I didn't know them. Missy said they were friends of hers." Laura cleared her voice again and Irene could hear traffic in the background. "Well, have her call me when she gets home, okay?"

Irene nodded silently and hung up the phone. Her

sons were not due home for three hours and it was already getting dark. Irene's eyes glazed over as she made her way mechanically to the living room and opened the front door. Slowly she backed up and sat on the edge of the sofa, her back stiff. Her mind began racing.

Even as she reassured herself, an oppressive fog settled over her mind, making it difficult to think. Logically, Missy probably had had a very good reason for leaving with the boys in the Camaro and an equally good reason for not calling. But something about the situation bothered Irene and she stared hypnotically out the front door, remembering Missy's words. "Don't worry, Mom, I'll be home by six. I'll call if I'm going to be late."

Irene focused on the clock that hung over the kitchen table. Soon it was seven and still there was no word from Missy. The minutes ticked away one at a time. Eight o'clock. Nine. Ten.

The boys weren't home, either, and Irene knew she should go to bed. There wasn't anything she could do by waiting and worrying. She closed her eyes and listened to the wind. It was stronger now, howling through the trees and nearby mountains. Occasionally an angry gust would shake Irene's screen door and front windows, but she continued to stare outside, having no reason to dread the worst but no way to stop the thoughts that were crowding her mind.

Sometime around eleven o'clock, while she sat and waited and imagined all sorts of terrible things that might have happened to her daughter, Irene Avila began to cry.

2

IRENE VALDEZ WAS twelve years old when her family moved from downtown Los Angeles to Pacoima, a community situated in the eastern San Fernando Valley. It was 1952 and the Valley was a series of quiet communities separated by acres of orange and walnut groves, far away from the dirty streets and fast-paced life the Avila family had lived in Los Angeles.

In those days the San Fernando Valley was just thirty-five minutes from downtown Los Angeles, and developers were getting rich overnight building housing tracts across the Valley floor as quickly as families arrived. This was before the days when smog and gang warfare would invade eastern sections of the Valley, making it a less desirable place to live. Back then the Valley, even the eastern parts like Pacoima, was the ideal home for commuters like Irene's father.

The day the Valdez family moved into their three-bedroom house, Irene noticed a boy her age who lived next door. Ernie Avila hooted and yelled and raced his bicycle up and down the street, trying to attract the new girl's attention. Irene wasn't impressed. Boys her age bored her, and she promised herself that she would never date Ernie Avila.

Irene's father quickly enrolled his children in a local

private school, where they were forced to wear uniforms. After all, he hadn't moved his family to a nice suburban neighborhood to have them go to school with just any children.

Walking to the bus stop each morning, clad in her plaid skirt and white bobby socks, Irene learned to shrug off the constant teasing from her public-school peers. But soon she became friends with several of the girls in her neighborhood. Irene was easy to like. She was petite with beautiful hair the color of mahogany and had a contagious laugh. Each day she walked home with her new friends after school, always avoiding Ernie Avila's house. Ernie never quite knew what he had done to offend the new girl, but they attended different schools and by the time he was fifteen he had given up trying to win Irene Valdez's attention.

That year Irene brought home a friend, Carol White, who attended San Fernando High School. The two girls were sitting outside talking when Ernie came home, parked his bicycle, and went inside his house.

"Hey, that's Ernie Avila!" Carol whispered, and a blush spread across her cheeks. "You didn't tell me you lived next door to him. Every girl in school has the hots for him."

Irene shrugged her shoulders. "He's nothing special," she said.

"Are you kidding? Hey, maybe if I come over here more often he'll notice me and ask me out." The girl glanced toward Ernie's house, and for the rest of the afternoon Irene never felt she had Carol's full attention.

With every girl at San Fernando High interested in him, Ernie Avila's value rose considerably in Irene's eyes. She began walking home at the same time as he did, making a point to pass his house—slowly. Two months later they were an item.

Although smaller than the other girls in her class, Irene grew to be very beautiful, and the romance flourished. Soon, Irene and Ernie had little time for their friends and spent nearly every evening together studying or necking.

Sometimes Irene would spend a night with her girl-friends and the group would go to neighborhood parties. Typically the parties would dissolve when gang kids from Pacoima and San Fernando grew rough. At the peak of a confrontation kids would typically throw beer bottles or bricks at each other's cars.

Sometimes a kid would even pull out a knife. It wasn't a weapon for killing; usually just a switchblade, something to scare off rivals.

The turf wars had grown more frequent in the late 1950s when the kids from Pacoima and San Fernando began forming gangs. Pacoima and San Fernando were two communities separated by the 118 Freeway, which ran along the north side of the San Fernando Valley and hooked up with Interstate 5 at the valley's far eastern end. The freeways created man-made barriers that gave the teenagers a reason to divide the community. Pacoima boys were on the south side of the 118, San Fernando boys on the north side. At that time Interstate 5 ran along the west side of San Fernando and through the middle of Pacoima. There was a slightly better area in Pacoima, with houses that were a few hundred square feet larger and lawns that were more neatly kept. This area changed its name to Arleta in the sixties. It bordered both San Fernando and Pacoima, but it was wedged along the west side of Interstate 5. In those days Interstate 5 was enough to keep most of the tough kids out of Arleta. No one cruised there on weekends; it had no hangouts where kids could compare cars and smoke cigarettes.

Arleta was a perfectly planned community of middle-class houses lined up in perfectly planned rows. From the sky it had the geometric look of a well-planted farm; but instead of crops there were houses.

In Arleta one could feel safe and separated—at least until the late 1970s, when gangs began using handguns and the kids realized a simple cement freeway couldn't stop them from invading an area.

The community leaders hadn't foreseen that the Arleta kids would be bored by their planned neighborhoods. The high school was in San Fernando and they liked the faster life east of Interstate 5.

Before she met Ernie Avila, Irene had enjoyed the fast life too. At one point during her freshman year she even ran with some girls who considered themselves part of a gang. Eventually she found their values immature, and she decided to stop seeing them. At that point she was spending all her spare time with Ernie.

When Irene and Ernie were nineteen, she walked up the aisle of the local Catholic church and promised to love, honor, and obey Ernie Avila until death.

They had been married nearly two years when Irene began getting headaches and constant waves of nausea. A doctor confirmed what Ernie Avila already suspected—Irene was pregnant. The couple were delighted; together they spent hours working on the baby's nursery. When they weren't painting walls and hanging curtains, they were busy reading Dr. Spock's baby-care book. Finally, there was nothing to do but wait.

Then one day Irene was folding laundry and humming lullabies when she doubled over in pain. Ernie rushed her to the hospital, but it was too late. The baby Irene and Ernie had planned and prepared for was dead.

In the weeks that followed, Irene grew depressed and lost weight. The solution was simple to Ernie— they must try again—but it wasn't that easy for Irene, who dreamed at night about her first child.

"Ernie, you'll never understand what it's like to have a child living inside you," she told him one day. "That child was a part of me. I may never have held him, but I will never forget him as long as I live."

Ernie tried to be more compassionate, and two years later Irene was thrilled when the doctor told her she was again pregnant. This time the pregnancy was flawless, and Irene and Ernie pulled out pieces of the nursery they had put away in storage.

Several months later Ernie Avila, Jr., came into the world with a healthy angry cry. When Ernie was nearly three years old, Irene gave birth to another son named Mark.

"We are blessed, my tiny son," Irene whispered, looking down at the six-week-old Mark while Ernie junior played nearby. "You are so beautiful."

Ernie senior agreed. "Our second son looks just like you," he said.

Irene shook her head, and when Ernie looked up he noticed tears in her eyes. "No, Ernie. Mark is our third son. He will always be my third son."

Ernie junior and Mark grew to be healthy, chubby toddlers who loved playing with mud, bugs, and anything that made a mess. No matter what Irene did, they rarely looked clean and hardly ever sat still. She began to pray that her next child would be a girl. She would be tiny and feminine and Irene would dress her in pink, frilly outfits. Unlike her boys Irene's daughter would enjoy sitting still, looking at picture books and savoring her mother's company.

Irene was twenty-six when she got pregnant again.

This time the nausea and headaches were worse than before, and because of her miscarriage doctors ordered strict bed rest from the seventh month on. Although Irene worried about losing this child, she had a feeling that if she could get through the eighth month the baby would survive.

"It's a girl, Ernie, I know it," Irene said one day as she lay on the living-room sofa.

Ernie smiled. "Irene, don't get your hopes up. A boy wouldn't be so bad, now would it?"

"Not at all," Irene said, her voice soft. "But I just know this baby is a girl."

Two months later, on February 8, 1968, Irene looked up at Ernie from a hospital bed as she held her newborn baby. "See. I knew this was my little girl."

It had been a very complicated delivery and doctors had feared they would lose both mother and child. Finally, the tiny girl was born and the danger passed. They named her Michele Yvette Avila, but from the beginning they called her Missy.

She had a shock of dark hair that framed her perfect features, and as Irene held her for the first time she knew her prayers had been answered. When Missy was four months old, the doctor told Irene to increase her feedings because the child was so tiny. By the time she was eight months old it was clear to Irene that her daughter would forever be smaller than her peers. Missy was a strong baby, despite her size, and from the moment Irene and Ernie brought her home she was the constant object of her brothers' attention.

Meanwhile, Irene started preparing income-tax forms and doing accounting for a handful of clients. It was tedious work, especially with three active children to take care of, but it allowed her the privilege of being home.

Much to Irene's dismay Missy learned to crawl, boy-fashion, a toy truck in her hand. And she learned to walk outdoors, while playing with her brothers in the mud. Still, there were moments when Missy was all little girl, just as Irene had dreamed. During those times Missy would smile coyly at her brothers, tilting her head and flirting.

"She's going to be a real heartbreaker when she grows up," Irene's brother warned her one day. "You can see it in her eyes. You're going to have your hands full."

Irene laughed, happy to be the mother of three such healthy children and especially proud of her tiny daughter. "That's a long time from now, Ron. She's got a lot of growing up to do before she's out there breaking hearts."

It occurred to Irene that one day Missy really would grow up. She'd fall in love, have a beautiful wedding, and leave home. On that day, Irene knew, hers would be the broken heart. Irene prayed that day wouldn't come too soon.

Life was hectic in the Avila house. Missy toddled about and Ernie junior and Mark were more active than ever. Irene wondered sometimes how she managed to handle them all as well as she did.

One day in mid-July 1969, when Missy was eighteen months old, Irene was working on a major house-cleaning project when she heard choking sounds coming from the kitchen. She ran to Missy and found her writhing on the floor, an empty bottle of bathroom cleaner sitting nearby.

She swooped up her daughter, grabbed her car keys, and drove to Arleta Community Hospital in five minutes. Missy was rushed into emergency and doctors hurriedly pumped her stomach. Nearly an hour passed before one of the physicians came out in the hallway to talk to Irene.

"Mrs. Avila, it looks like everything is going to be okay," the doctor told her. "Her lungs were partially collapsed and she was getting very little oxygen when you brought her in. But we cleared the poison from her system and gave her an antihistamine for the swelling in her throat. We're going to keep her overnight for observation, but you can go in and see her if you'd like."

Irene thanked the doctor and rushed to the pay phone. She had to call Ernie and let him know everything was all right. Her hands shook as she dialed his work number.

"Ernie, she's going to be fine, I just talked to the doctors," Irene said, tears streaming down her face. "It was my fault, Ernie. We almost lost her because of my carelessness."

Ernie calmly reassured Irene that it couldn't possibly have been her fault. Five minutes later, when Irene hung up the phone, her sobbing had subsided.

Slowly, Irene made her way to the room where her daughter lay sleeping soundly on a hospital bed.

Irene leaned over and nestled her head next to Missy's. "Oh, Missy, I'm so glad you're okay," Irene whispered. "You could have died and I would never have forgiven myself. I couldn't live if anything ever happened to you."

Irene closed her eyes and said a silent prayer. The nurse found her there an hour later, tightly clutching Missy's hand. Later the nurse would tell her husband about the little girl and her mother.

"It was strange, Frank," she said as they sat down to dinner. "She seemed afraid to let go of that little girl's hand, as though something would happen if she didn't hold on."

3

IT WAS NEARLY midnight when Mark and Chris Avila parked in front of their house on Ottoman Street that October first. An afternoon of Frisbee and softball had blended into an evening of chatting with friends over a barbecue. They hadn't planned to be this late and Mark, being the older of the two brothers, felt guilty bringing Chris home at such an hour. After all, it was a school night and Chris was just twelve. Despite nearly eight years that separated them the two boys were very close, and Chris loved spending time with his older brother.

As they strode up the sidewalk, Mark suddenly noticed that the front door was wide open and the house lights were on. That was strange. Arleta wasn't as safe as it had once been, and some of the neighbors had even taken to putting bars over their windows.

They walked lightly up the walkway and opened the screen door quietly so as not to wake their mother. The boys found her asleep on the sofa and Mark laid a blanket over her. The brothers tiptoed off to bed, thankful she hadn't noticed their late arrival.

Hours later Irene sat straight up and threw the blanket off her shoulders. She stood up slowly, eyes wide open, and walked down the hall. She could hear the boys snoring as she made her way to Missy's room. It was empty. Missy's alarm clock glowed in the dark, and Irene felt a wave of panic building as she looked at the time.

Three A.M.

Suddenly anger swept her anxiety away, anger at Missy. The least she could have done was call.

As Irene stood there, watching the minutes on Missy's alarm clock change from 3:01 to 3:12 and then to 3:26, she tried to convince herself that Missy had probably had too much to drink and fallen asleep somewhere. After all, to believe Missy had intentionally avoided calling her was to believe Missy wasn't telling the truth about everything else.

By four that morning Irene was frustrated and more than a little frightened. She considered returning to her bedroom, but more than four years after she and Ernie had divorced, the room still seemed lonely. Especially tonight, with Missy out. She turned off the hall light, walked back out to the couch, and lay down, spreading the blanket neatly.

Sleep would not come and Irene's eyes adjusted to the darkness. She could just make out the oil painting that hung above her. It was a portrait of her children: Mark and his fiancée, Shavaun, Ernie, Chris, and Missy. The picture had been taken three months earlier, and Irene had paid the studio to frame it for the living room. As Irene stared at the picture, her eyes settled on Missy.

"Oh, Missy," Irene whispered. "Just call me and tell me you're okay."

The panic began creeping up again, and Irene felt her heart pounding inside her chest. She sighed. It was useless to think of sleep until Missy got home. She walked to the front window, glancing up and down the street. She was still standing there when Mark woke up three hours later. A recent high school graduate, he was used to rising early, though on Wednesdays he didn't work until the afternoon.

"Been up long, Mom?" he asked her as he walked into the kitchen and poured himself some cereal.

Irene turned her head, suddenly aware of her son's presence. In the back bedroom she could hear Chris getting ready for school. She stared at Mark for a moment and when she finally spoke, her voice was flat. "Missy isn't home yet."

Mark seemed confused by his mother's response. "Home from where? Missy never goes anywhere this early."

Irene tried to respond, but a lump had lodged itself in her throat. She collapsed slowly in their overstuffed chair and began to sob.

"Mom?" Mark stood up and knelt by his mother. "What is it? What's wrong? Where's Missy?"

Irene struggled to explain herself. "She went to the park yesterday with Laura Doyle and she said she'd be home by six or else call." Irene let her head drop into her hands. "I don't know where she is. Oh, Mark, do you think something happened to her?"

Mark offered his mother a tissue and patted her on the back. He didn't like the fact that Missy hadn't called to let their mother know she'd be gone overnight, but it wasn't the first time she had been so inconsiderate. He knew she was running with a faster crowd these days, which didn't make him happy. He had tried to talk some sense into her on several occasions, but Missy had always brushed him off. She had probably partied too hard the day before and crashed at one of her friends' houses. He didn't want to say that to his mother, but he wanted to assure her that Missy would be fine.

"Mom, you know Missy. She probably stayed up late talking to one of her friends and she didn't want to wake you. I'm sure she'll be home any time now." He gently helped her up. "Come on, now. Have something to eat and don't worry so much."

Irene nodded, forcing herself to smile at her middle son. As she followed Mark into the kitchen to make breakfast, she tried to believe that he was right.

For the next three hours Irene refused to let herself think about Missy. She saw Chris off to school and kept herself busy doing housework and paying bills. Finally, at 10:30 that morning, she could no longer concentrate. She called Bobby, Missy's boyfriend. But his mother said he was out with the guys and had come home early the night before. Missy hadn't been with him.

Irene began to cry and found Mark in the living room.

"Mark, we have to do something," she said. "This isn't like Missy to disappear and not even call us."

Mark nodded in agreement but forced his voice to sound calm.

"Why don't you call Christy and see if she knows where Missy is?" he said. "If she isn't there, Christy will know where she is."

"You're right. I'll go over to Christy's."

Faithful Christy Crawford. She and Missy had become close friends at Byrd Junior High, but Christy had moved to Long Beach with her parents before high school. She often came back to Arleta and stayed with her grandmother. During those visits she and Missy were always together.

Thinking about Christy made Irene remember something else. Missy had called Christy just before Laura picked her up yesterday. Irene hadn't heard their entire conversation. She didn't hear Missy tell Christy about doing a few lines of cocaine at the park, but she had heard Missy say something about getting together that evening.

Irene pulled a sweater over her shoulders and quickly headed outside down the street to Christy's grandmother's house. All Missy's friends lived in the neighborhood. Laura Doyle. Karen Severson. Christy Crawford. Irene had always felt comforted knowing that Missy was usually in the neighborhood, and now she fully expected to find her at Christy's.

Five minutes later she stood on the Crawford porch and knocked. Christy opened the door and smiled when she saw Irene, but before the teenager could speak, Irene blurted the reason for her visit.

"Christy, is Missy here?" Irene stared into Christy's eyes.

"No." Christy looked concerned. "Is she supposed to be?"

It was nearly eighty degrees outside, but Irene was suddenly cold. She began to shiver and pulled the sweater tight around her body.

"She left yesterday afternoon to go to the park with Laura Doyle. She was supposed to come home by six but she never did. And she didn't call." Irene gazed down the street, still expecting to see Missy drive up. "I thought she might be with you."

Christy didn't like the sound of Irene's story. She knew Missy sometimes stayed out late, but she never would have let her mother worry this long about her whereabouts. Christy prided herself on being Missy's closest friend. She hadn't known her as long as Karen Severson, but she and Missy were always there for each other. Christy fought back a wild thought. She was sure Irene didn't know about Missy's experiments with cocaine. What if Missy had taken too much cocaine and overdosed? What if something had happened to her?

"Have you asked Laura? She must know where Missy is if they left together."

Irene told Christy how Laura had dropped Missy off to talk to three guys in a blue Camaro.

"I have a few ideas, Mrs. Avila," Christy said, grabbing her car keys from inside the house. "Let's go talk to some people and see if we can find out where she is."

Irene followed Christy to her car. She would rather have visited the police station and filed a missing person's report, but the police had told her they wouldn't take any information until twenty-four hours after a disappearance. It was 11:25 A.M., which meant that for the next three hours Christy was Irene's only hope.

The two women spent the next several hours calling on Missy's friends, but no one knew where Missy was or which boys might own a blue Camaro. At each house they visited, Irene called Mark. Maybe Missy had called. Maybe she was home.

At 3:00 P.M. Irene asked Christy to take her to the Foothill police station.

An officer behind the counter was filing paperwork when Irene burst in and asked for a missing person's report.

"My daughter is gone. She's been gone for twenty-four hours and no one knows where she is. I think something might have happened to her. Can you help me?" Irene sounded frantic.

The officer looked annoyed. *Another hysterical mother,* he thought. *They're all the same. Daughters and sons who haven't learned how to be responsible and parents who haven't learned to let go.* He sounded bored when he finally answered Irene.

"How old is your daughter?"

Irene detected his lack of interest and tried to sound calmer as she answered him. "Seventeen. She's seventeen."

"Look, lady, if she's seventeen she's probably just spending a little time at her boyfriend's house. You two getting along or did you have a fight yesterday?" He had returned to filing papers and Irene was beginning to lose her temper.

"We haven't had any fights and she would have called me if she were at her boyfriend's. Don't you people care about what's happening out there?" Irene was screaming now. "I have a seventeen-year-old daughter who hasn't been heard from in twenty-four hours and you act like I'm reporting a missing wallet."

The officer looked at Irene and handed her a form. "Here. Fill this out and we'll see what we can do."

Irene took the form and began writing as tears streamed down her cheeks. She blinked hard.

The form was routine. Missing person's name. Birth date, eye and hair color. Weight and height. Date and time last seen. Person last seen with.

Then the questions got harder.

Is there anyone who has threatened the person's life recently? Any identifiable birthmarks or bruises on the person's body?

Irene remembered Missy talking on the phone to Laura, dripping wet and wearing only a bath towel wrapped around her body. Carefully, Irene wrote her answer. No birthmarks. No bruises.

Christy read over her shoulder as Irene finished the form. The question about bruises and birthmarks had bothered her too. She knew why they wanted to know. They needed the information in case the missing person had been killed. Bruises and birthmarks would be a means of identifying the body. Christy shut her eyes and swallowed hard. She hoped Irene hadn't figured that out.

4

ALTHOUGH PACIFIC BELL and the U.S. Post Office recognize Arleta as a city, it really is just another suburb in the San Fernando Valley. The Valley areas are technically called communities, and even though they are divided by boundaries, they have no separate legislative representation from their mother city—Los Angeles.

For that matter, the entire San Fernando Valley has only token representation with a handful of Los Angeles council members stationed throughout its boundaries. With the 1990 census the Valley, as people who live there call it, had hit the 1.5 million mark, making it larger than all but a handful of cities in the United States. So there has often been talk among Valley people of making the San Fernando Valley a city of its own.

Such talk is always quickly dismissed, because the San Fernando Valley is simply too valuable for Los Angeles to part with. The Valley brings in millions of dollars in revenue, and its new growth raises the aesthetic value of the aging city.

But most importantly, Los Angeles doesn't want to lose control over the aqueducts, which weave through the Valley floor like so many concrete arteries, carrying an essential supply of water from the Owens Valley to the Los Angeles basin. If those aqueducts should ever become the sole property of a city called the San Fernando Valley, Los Angeles officials know they will lose a great deal of political power in addition to the water rights.

In essence, Los Angeles has become an indifferent stepmother and the San Fernando Valley her unloved stepchild, who just so happens to be providing for the entire family. Even though the mother might see some advantages to giving her stepchild freedom, such a move would destroy the family and so remains out of the question.

It all happened back in the early 1900s, when Los Angeles city officials discovered there wasn't enough water in their dusty basin to keep a major city operating. Researchers didn't take long to realize that nearby Owens Valley, a thriving farm and homesteading community, had abundant water.

In order to be transported to Los Angeles, the water would have to go down hills and across a sparsely populated valley (about twenty miles long by ten miles wide) just north of the city. So, officials quickly devised a plan and presented it to the federal government. The officials acted promptly and in 1906 the chief of the U.S. Forest Service under President Theodore Roosevelt issued an order transforming Owens Valley into a Federal Forest District. Overnight, the homesteaders were ousted and the land became the U.S. government's to use as it pleased. Not too surprisingly, U.S. officials gave Los Angeles permission to construct a water project on the land.

With everything in order Los Angeles approved a multimillion dollar project to build the aqueducts. In the history of the city never was a project finished as quickly and as cost-efficiently.

In 1913, the same year the aqueduct system was completed, the Los Angeles City Council voted to annex the San Fernando Valley (where the valuable aqueducts now lay) as part of the city of Los Angeles. The stepchild had arrived.

In the 1980s Morrow Mayo, a journalist from the Los Angeles area, wrote an article titled "The Rape of the Owens Valley," included in the book *The San Fernando Valley: Past and Present* by Lawrence C. Jorgensen. (Published by Pacific Rim Research.) In it he said that the "Owens Valley went from a wonderful Valley with millions of acres of fruit and alfalfa to a desolate wasteland" because of the aqueduct system. He also noted that it gave Los Angeles "more water so the Chamber of Commerce could drink more toasts to growth, more water to dilute its orange juice, and more water for its geraniums to delight tourists." He added that "meanwhile, giant cottonwoods in Owens Valley have died and it is now a valley of desolation."

Mayo said that after Los Angeles took the water out of Owens Valley, there was a saying that became popular among the farmers who lost their livelihood when their crops dried up. It went: "The federal government of the United States held Owens Valley while Los Angeles raped it."

Once it was done, there was no way any official in Los Angeles was going to release the hold on such a vital resource. In fact, once the valley land became part of Los Angeles, the city officials forgot about it and never made any move to encourage developers or industry. The San Fernando Valley remained an oversized piece of land inhabited by a couple of hundred farmers who had been incorporated into the city of Los Angeles, but were essentially ignored.

Over the next forty years the Valley's population grew slowly. After all, automobiles were still scarce and it was a good twenty or thirty miles over the hill to downtown Los Angeles. No horse-drawn carriage was about to make that kind of commute. But after World War II the automobile had changed everything for the San Fernando Valley. Roads were built connecting the land of the aqueducts to Los Angeles, and by 1950 the Valley had a population of 402,538, most of whom had come to the area since 1945. Even though Los Angeles city officials were pleased and amazed at the sudden glut of people bringing income to the city, this growth was nothing compared to what was to come in the 1950s.

By then the San Fernando Valley had developed itself into about twenty communities, including Canoga Park on the west side, Encino on the south, and Granada Hills on the north, affluent communities featuring more swimming pools and higher per capita income than anywhere else in the country. But in the East Valley, in an area called Pacoima, the residents shared none of this prosperity.

Pacoima, founded in 1887, was originally made up of lucrative farms and orange groves, and inhabited by twelve families comfortably housed in two-story mansions. By 1927 there were still just forty families living in Pacoima, which of course by then was just another part of Los Angeles.

Then after World War II, the Brown Bomber, Joe Louis, entered the picture. Louis, the best heavyweight boxer of his time and arguably the best ever, had recently made a bundle of money winning the heavyweight title. He proceeded to spend much of it buying several acres of land in the heart of Pacoima. In what was thought to be a grandiose gesture at the time, Louis paid for hundreds of small homes to be built on the land. He called them the Joe Louis Homes, and sold them only to blacks, most of whom were still suffering the effects of segregation, prejudice, and unfair wages. To Louis these houses were the perfect solution.

At the same time the aerospace industry was taking off, and many companies were building plants in the northern, western, and southern parts of the Valley. In Burbank, just three miles east of Pacoima, Lockheed Corporation built a plant, making Pacoima the perfect place for many of the assembly-line workers to settle.

During this time, in 1952, the Valdez family moved to Pacoima. Irene was just twelve, but she wasn't too young to know that her father was an important union steward with Lockheed.

By 1960 the San Fernando Valley had become noteworthy enough to attract a team of researchers from Security Pacific Bank for an extensive survey on the area and its people. Apparently, someone high up on the bank's corporate ladder had the foresight to believe the Valley might be a hot spot on which to open a few branches.

The study first noted the population, which had doubled to 840,531, since 1950. It was the greatest growth explosion any area of California had ever experienced —for the past decade an average of 120 people a day had moved to the Valley.

The study went on to describe it as a 234.8-square-mile hotbed of growth, which housed upper-class executives from downtown Los Angeles. The study also noted that, unlike the other parts of the Valley, the eastern region (essentially Pacoima) was almost exclusively the home of blue-collar workers and low-income families. For the most part they worked at neighboring Lockheed, but there were many who were employed by Pacoima's two major factories—Paragon Tool, Die and Engineering; and Whiteman Manufacturing Company. But nobody needed a Security Pacific Bank study to determine the obvious: Pacoima had become the Valley ghetto.

On the day before Valentine's Day 1966, two years before Missy Avila was born, the *Los Angeles Times* ran a piece on the racial problems plaguing the community. "The word *Pacoima* to many Valley residents," it began, "conjures up images of a high crime rate, a slum neighborhood, and the war on poverty." It went on to state, to no one's surprise, that Pacoima was the Valley's lowest income area and that, of the 9,975 blacks in the Valley, only one percent didn't live in Pacoima.

The U.S. postmaster in Pacoima that year was a black woman by the name of Nancy Avery. In her opinion the Joe Louis Homes idea had backfired on the community. She was quoted in the article:

"Pacoima has become a ghetto and it is expanding enough as it is. . . . We don't need any more Negro-only subdivisions."

Another prominent Valley resident observed, "Most of the Valley communities show little difference one to the next. But Pacoima seems to have been bodily lifted from Watts and dropped into the Valley."

The article, along with other bad publicity about Pacoima, prompted a group of mostly white Pacoima residents west of Interstate 5, to get together later that year and petition Avery's post office. They felt their homes and neighborhoods were nicer than most in Pacoima and they wanted their own identity. They wanted to call the new community Arleta.

After a brief struggle with longtime Pacoima residents who saw it as abandonment, the people on the west side of Interstate 5 got their way and Arleta came into being. Meanwhile, Los Angeles city officials were virtually ignorant of the fact that the population explosion in the Valley was causing any identity crisis. They could see no reason why people accustomed to a small town would object to being part of a city many of them had never even visited.

Discussing the partition of Arleta from its parent community, Avery remarked, "It's a racial thing. They think they're somehow better than us and that by changing their name it will raise their property values."

Sometimes when a community splits off and calls itself by another name, property values do rise. In the case of Arleta and Pacoima, that never happened. In fact, old-timers in Pacoima to this day refuse to recognize Arleta as anything other than Pacoima. Perhaps for that reason history books on the San Fernando Valley never mention Arleta but refer to the area only as Pacoima.

Pacoima in the late 1960s and 1970s had other problems that drew attention. The first was an increasing level of crime to go along with the poverty and racial tension. The second, more notorious, problem was the Cattle Slaughterhouse, located near the Joe Louis Homes in the middle of a poor residential area.

Neighbors hated the slaughterhouse. They complained of rank smells, swarms of flies, and blood running in the streets. Its worst offense, though, was the constant sound of screaming cows and of guns firing into the early morning hours—this, near a neighborhood where children played.

In 1967 an article in the San Fernando Valley *Sun* quoted one neighbor as saying the sound of shooting kept him awake almost every night.

Thirteen years later it was still the sound of shooting that kept residents of Pacoima awake at night. Only by then the victims weren't cows.

Because the people of Arleta had managed to separate themselves from Pacoima only on paper, the problems—whether cattle killers or gang members—marred their community as well. By the mid-1980s the San Fernando Valley still had no real identity of its own, and Arleta even less. Even now Arleta is best described by what it hasn't got. It has no major employers, no factories, no aerospace plants, no companies other than those in neighboring Pacoima. The only employment in Arleta comes from places like the local fast-food restaurants, liquor stores, 7-Elevens, barbershops, and a few doctors' offices.

It also has no high school, no movie theater, no roller-skating rink, no bowling alley, no shopping mall, and no real way to escape the shadow of crime and poverty in neighboring Pacoima. So bad is Pacoima's image in the San Fernando Valley that, even as the 1990s dawned, the community's activists were thinking of ways to fight graffiti, gang problems, and poverty—just as they were doing in the sixties.

Here Irene Avila and eventually her children and their friends grew up. There were two reasons Irene and Ernie never dreamed of moving out of Arleta: First, it was all they'd ever known; and second, it was not Pacoima. It didn't matter to them that it was a lower income area than most communities in the Valley or that there were more children whose parents worked, more children roaming the streets after school. In those days Irene was one of the only mothers on her block who made the necessary sacrifices to be at home with her children during the day. It was obvious to Irene that the children in Pacoima and Arleta were tougher than most; she felt that by staying home she could better protect her own children from the harsh world outside and from undesirable influences.

Irene was right. In fact, the children of the East Valley baby-boomers decided finally they had to make some kind of name for themselves, and so in the 1980s gang violence in Pacoima, Arleta, and San Fernando began to increase drastically. These kids were set apart from those in other Valley communities by their nearly unanimous need for identity, and their loyalty to anything they could claim as their own. This feeling carried over into their gang activities, their relationships and friendships. In fact, most of the gang killings in the 1980s were attributed to revenge. If someone came under verbal attack, his friends would stop at nothing to seek revenge. It was a fierce kind of loyalty, but in Pacoima and Arleta, friendships were forever even if it meant laying down your life.

That was why everyone who knew Missy Avila was completely baffled by her disappearance. After all, she had last been seen with one of her friends.

5

BY THE EARLY 1970s Missy had grown from a toddler to a little girl, and each day she grew prettier. In fact, Missy's parents would beam with pride when people noticed their beautiful daughter.

These were busy times for Irene, who sometimes felt overwhelmed by the task of raising three small children. There were groceries and shoes and school clothes to buy, homework to be done, and an endless amount of housework and laundry. Still, despite the effort, Irene often dropped to her knees at the end of the night and said a silent prayer, thanking God for her children and the happiness they brought her.

In 1973 Irene could hardly believe that Ernie junior was nearly ten and Mark seven. Her boys were growing up. Missy, too, had slipped through the preschool years and was proud to be five years old and ready for kindergarten. She wasn't worried about the older kids who sometimes picked on kindergartners, because Ernie junior and Mark had developed a reputation for protecting her. In fact, there wasn't a child in the neighborhood who would mess with her.

Just as her uncle Ron had predicted, Missy was a beauty with every sign of becoming a heartbreaker. Her dark brown hair was thick and her green eyes danced whenever she was excited, as on the day she started kindergarten. Missy was so thrilled about her first day of school that she woke up before dawn and was dressed in her new school clothes before Irene's alarm clock rang.

Midway through the school year Missy's teacher pulled Irene aside and gave her a progress report.

"Mrs. Avila, Missy is very bright," the woman said. "She is reading and writing at a higher level than the other children in the class. But there is one problem."

Irene listened as the teacher continued.

"Missy seems to be very popular with the other children. She, well, the boys love chasing her and showing off for her and the girls all want to be her friend."

Irene looked puzzled. "Is there something wrong with that? I don't understand."

The teacher cleared her throat. "No. It's just that the other children need to spend more time on their schoolwork. Missy is going to have to try to spend less time socializing and more time listening. That way the other children will do the same thing."

Irene nodded and smiled to herself. Sometimes Missy was the center of attention and didn't even know it. She decided to have a talk with the child that evening.

When she did, Missy was very understanding.

"Yes, Mommy. I can be quieter in school and then maybe the other kids won't make the teacher mad all the time," she said.

"That's a good girl, Missy." Irene hugged her daughter and sent her to bed. "Every mother should have it so easy," she mumbled as she went out to the living room to watch television.

Several weeks later Irene began noticing a familiar

wave of nausea. She had missed her last period but blamed it on the stress of running the household. Now she began to wonder, and the next day her doctor confirmed her suspicions—she was pregnant.

Although this child wasn't planned, Irene was more sentimental than usual throughout the pregnancy. She told herself this would certainly be her final child. It was another difficult pregnancy, but despite the problems Christopher Avila was born several months later, soon after Missy's sixth birthday.

"Well, we have another boy," Irene said, grinning up at Ernie.

"I feel sorry for any boys that give Missy a hard time with three brothers looking out for her," Ernie said, taking his wife's hand as they stared at their newborn son.

Chris grew quickly, always striving to keep up with his siblings despite the age gap between them. By then Ernie junior and Mark included their sister in their games. She was nearly eight and destined to become a tomboy. Most of her girlfriends lived too far away for her to play with after school, so when a for-sale sign went up in front of the house around the corner, Irene allowed herself to dream. Maybe the family who moved in would have a little girl Missy's age and the two would become friends.

A month passed, and Irene had all but forgotten the house around the corner, when Missy brought a new friend home from school. Missy led her up the walkway to the porch. The new girl was chubby and much taller than Missy, but watched her with adoring eyes.

The new girl didn't seem the type to make friends easily, but Missy liked to seek out children no one wanted to play with. Even at that young age she knew that some children attracted friends naturally and others didn't, through no fault of their own. Missy didn't like life to be unfair.

Some of the other kids had been making fun of the girl that morning when she walked into the classroom for the first time. So Missy made a point of talking to her. By the time school let out, Missy and the new girl had discovered they lived six houses apart from one another and walked home hand in hand.

"Mommy, I brought home a new friend," Missy announced. "Her name is Karen and she moved in down the street."

Irene wiped her hands on her jeans and smiled at the new girl. She wasn't very pretty, but she seemed to adore Missy. Irene had a feeling this friendship was the start of something good.

"What's your last name, Karen?" Irene asked the child.

Karen looked around the living room at the family pictures that decorated the walls.

"Karen Severson," the girl said. "Can I have something to eat?"

Irene laughed and nodded. "Sure. I'll get you girls some milk and cookies and you can play in Missy's room."

The series of events that brought Karen Francis Severson into the life of Missy Avila was twisted with ironies that in hindsight take on a great deal of importance. Karen was born in Oregon on October 17, 1967, to a mother who couldn't raise her. When she was three days old, she wound up in the home of Paula and Loyal Severson of Arleta, California. Like many adopted babies Karen in a matter of days went from being unwanted to being the pride and joy of her new parents. The Seversons had waited months for their precious baby girl and they had vowed early on to give her everything she wanted.

Eight years passed before they had saved enough money to buy a house, and they looked long and hard before settling on the cute, spacious family home on Nagle Street in Arleta. Nagle Street ran into Ottoman Street, which is where Missy Avila had spent her eight years under the protective wings of her doting brothers.

Karen Severson was only four months older than Missy Avila, but she seemed years wiser. While Missy had been learning to read and write, it seemed Karen Severson had been learning how to lie and have her own way at any cost. By age eight Karen Severson knew how to use her parents' unconditional love to her advantage. Apparently, if Karen wanted something, and if she had just the right look, just the right tilt to her head, Karen got it. And if Karen had to lie to get her own way, well, then, she would do that. For Karen it was a game more enjoyable than any childhood game she had learned in kindergarten or first grade. Best of all, she could play it on certain other little girls without their knowing about it. If Karen wanted to be friends with a girl who was already friends with someone else, she might walk over to the girl and say something like this about the girl's friend:

"Did you know that girl you hang around with hates you? She told me so during recess. She told everyone you were just a big baby."

When the girl grew angry or sad about her friend's betrayal, Karen would offer her own friendship as solace. Before long Karen made friends with the girl and the other child was completely ignored. Of course, not every child would fall for this kind of manipulation. The girl would have to be gullible enough to believe Karen's story and trustful enough to side with Karen and become her friend.

In Karen's opinion Missy was such a girl. This became obvious in hindsight, but when Karen and Missy were eight years old and had only met earlier that day, no one suspected that Karen wasn't telling the absolute truth.

Karen was busy playing this game of deception and manipulation when Irene returned with the milk and cookies. There Karen sat, face to face with Missy, talking about how much larger and better her family was than Missy's. "And then I have two cousins who live nearby and I have another set of parents and three brothers, just like you."

That was strange. "Two sets of parents?" Irene looked confused. "Why is that, Karen?"

Karen looked seriously at Irene and explained. "My parents are divorced. So most of the time I live here with this set of parents and I have them all to myself, but other times I live with my other set of parents. I have three brothers and lots of cousins and aunts and uncles. Just like Missy."

Irene tried to keep from smiling as she nodded in understanding. "I see. Do you like belonging to a big family?"

"Oh, yes! My brothers and I have a lot of fun together. They're even nicer than Missy's brothers."

Irene shook her head and laughed. In her opinion girls were so much funnier than her boys had been. Girls seemed to compare everything from clothes to family members; they tried so hard to make a good impression. The boys and their friends had never worried about social distinctions. Irene walked out of the room and left the two girls to play by themselves.

After that Karen and Missy became best friends, holding hands as they walked home from school each day. Slowly, with Missy's help, Karen grew confident. Still, many people thought them an odd pair, Missy so petite and pretty and Karen so thick waisted and plain.

Two weeks later Irene found time to walk over to Karen's house and meet her mother, Paula. Irene commented on what fun the two girls seemed to be having and asked Paula when Karen would be leaving to spend time with her other parents.

Paula's face went blank. "Other set of parents? What do you mean? We're Karen's only parents."

Puzzled, Irene told Paula Karen's story about having three brothers and another set of parents.

Paula laughed. "I'm sorry about that. I'm afraid Karen has quite an imagination sometimes. You see, Karen was adopted and we don't have any other children. She's never really enjoyed being an only child, so sometimes she invents brothers and sisters."

Irene understood. Karen realized how much Missy was adored by her brothers; she created three of her own so she wouldn't feel left out.

Later, Irene thought about Karen's story and how convincing it had been. The poor child was probably jealous of Missy. Still, the lie bothered Irene and she considered talking to Karen about it the next day. But a week passed before Irene thought of it again, and at that point she felt that a chat with Karen would only hurt her feelings. There was no way Irene could have known about the game Karen liked to play, the game of manipulation and deception. Irene thought it was just a harmless little lie.

6

SINCE 1959 ROBERT SANDERS and Jim Rutledge had made a ritual out of hiking in the Angeles National Forest. It started when both men were in their late twenties and Sanders was leader of a Sunland Boy Scout troop. Sunland, lodged in an area between Pasadena and the San Fernando Valley, lay adjacent to the Angeles National Forest.

The men discovered Camp Colby in 1962 after experimenting with other hiking trails and camping spots. Camp Colby was beautiful and serene, a piece of land once owned by the Colby family and now located off Big Tujunga Road. A stream ran through the area, and a dirt path took hikers up beyond the water to an open area under the trees where the Scouts had permission to camp.

Several times each year Sanders and Rutledge took carloads of young Scouts up to the spot. The boys would run up and down the shore of the stream, and the group would stay up late at night telling ghost stories. Neither man considered this outing dangerous, because the stream was only twenty yards wide and never any deeper than a foot or two even in the rainy season.

When the two men retired from Scout activities

twenty years later, Sanders approached Rutledge about continuing their hikes at Camp Colby. His long-time friend agreed, and the two began spending one weekend every other month hiking and camping in the mountains. Something about the fresh air and the sound of the stream in the background made the men forget about the increasing congestion in Sunland. They used the time away to talk about their families, and whenever they returned from a weekend in the Angeles National Forest they looked and felt considerably younger.

After breakfast on October 4, 1985, Sanders and Rutledge had started packing for what was to be their sixth trip that year.

Sanders slipped a sweater over his shoulders as he thought about how much he and Rutledge had been through since they first started their hikes.

It was just after 10:00 A.M. when Sanders finished loading his backpack. He picked up the telephone, dialed Rutledge's number, and told him to be ready by 11:00 A.M.

By 12:15 P.M. Sanders and Rutledge were winding through Big Tujunga Canyon and nearing the dirt-road turnoff for Camp Colby. For some reason the twenty-mile winding trip up the mountain seemed to have taken longer this time, and Sanders commented that he was glad the weather had been so dry. No rain for a month and none in sight. The stream might be a little shallow, but at least they could count on a quiet weekend of camping without having to worry about a storm.

A car was approaching them, and Sanders pulled his station wagon over until it was inches from the mountainside. Not much passing room, he thought. Camp

Colby was so far out of the way, it was amazing anyone else even knew about it. Sanders shook his head as the car raced by, narrowly missing his door.

"Darn kids," he muttered.

About three years ago teenagers from the San Fernando Valley had started coming to Camp Colby. They called it Wicky-up and they loved it because they could smoke dope, drink beer, and do the things parents and police typically forbid. The evidence of their presence was all around. Graffiti on fence posts, carvings in trees, and beer cans stashed in the brush along the stream. Sanders had mentioned this invasion to Rutledge on several occasions and the men had agreed the kids were ruining the place.

They pulled into the dirt parking lot; Sanders was pleased to see there was no other car in the area. The kids might be around at night, but for now the two men could hike in peace and enjoy the perfect serenity.

Sanders opened his car door, climbed out, and stretched. He and Rutledge were in excellent shape; their bodies might have belonged to much younger men.

"Great afternoon to hike upstream," he said, lifting his backpack from the car. Rutledge unloaded his gear and nodded. It was part of their ritual to save talk for later in the evening, after the tent was pitched and the two men were tired from their hike. For now, they would walk in silence, enjoying the scenery.

Sanders led the way, walking past a metal barricade that kept cars from the hiking trail. About ten yards down the path the trail narrowed and the brush grew denser on either side. This was the easy part, the part of the hike they took each time. A mile up the trail it branched into less traveled pathways. The men kept walking, eyes straight ahead. A gentle breeze blew through the trees, and all around them leaves were fluttering gracefully to the ground. The trail descended and veered in closer to the stream until finally the brush cleared and the two men could see the water. A few steps ahead lay a series of large rocks that formed something of a footbridge across the stream. Sanders and Rutledge knew these rocks just as well as they knew the trail. Years before someone, probably one of the Boy Scouts, had lined them up across the stream.

Sanders noticed how shallow the water had become. It couldn't be more than six to eight inches deep. He remembered when it used to be much deeper, back in the 1970s during the big rainfall years.

Still, it was too deep to wade through, and with the experience that comes from knowing an area well, the men began making their way across the rocks to the other side of the stream.

Only, this time something was different.

Rutledge saw it first: The log was missing. Usually there was a large log lying against the rocks to make them more stable. It had been there as long as either man could remember. Rutledge stopped on the other side of the stream and scratched his head. He glanced back, and then he saw it.

The log had been moved about five feet away from the rocks and was no longer parallel with them. It seemed to cover something, and Rutledge strained his eyes to see.

Suddenly he felt his blood run cold.

Keeping his eyes on the log he grabbed Sanders's arm, but moments passed before Rutledge could make himself speak. "Dick, it's a body. Do you see it? Over there under the log. Oh, my God, it's a body."

Sanders looked back at the log and took a few steps toward the stream. His eyes weren't what they used to be, but he could see some blue jeans and a tan-colored shirt.

"No, Jack, those are just some clothes caught up on the log. You know how kids are out here. Probably got drunk, stripped down to their underwear, and forgot their clothes."

Rutledge shook his head, and a chill ran down Sanders's spine as he studied the scene more carefully. His friend was serious.

Slowly, Sanders followed Rutledge back across the rocks. They were halfway across when Sanders noticed long dark hair floating in the water near the log. Rutledge was right. As they got closer he saw everything. The girl was facedown in the shallow stream, her arm stiff and bent behind her back at an unnatural angle. They stopped several feet short of her body, but it was easy to see how she'd died. The log lay across her back and neck, forcing her face down into the streambed. She may have been dead when the log was placed there, but if she had been alive, it wasn't for long. Rutledge sized up the log—it was nearly four feet long and must have weighed a hundred pounds. This was no accident. She wore a tan sweatshirt and blue jeans and her feet were crossed at the ankle. A school of minnows swam just over the girl's back, biting at her flesh, and there were flies swarming near where the log pinned her under the water.

Sanders fought an urge to vomit. She looked so young, she might even have been a child. Sanders turned away and when he spoke, Rutledge could barely hear him. "Let's get out of here."

The two men ran back to the car and sped down the dirt road to the Camp Colby headquarters.

Inside, John McConnell had been sorting permits and working on other paperwork when the doorbell rang.

"Yes?" he said as he opened the door.

Instantly he knew something was wrong. The two men had to be in their fifties and McConnell had seen them hiking the grounds on several occasions. This time they looked frightened and sick. One of the men began to speak.

"There's a body in the stream," he said, stammering to catch his breath. "We were up there hiking. Near the footbridge there's a body in the stream with a log over it. It looks like a young girl."

McConnell felt faint.

He wondered how long the body had been there. The thought occurred to him that a murderer could be lurking on the mountain.

McConnell sprang into action. "I'll call the Forest Service and get someone down there right away. You mind going back up and waiting till someone arrives?"

The men agreed and McConnell dashed to the phone.

Several miles down Big Tujunga Road, Forest Ranger Robert Libershal was perusing his daily charts when the phone rang.

"Robert, we've got a problem," the dispatcher said. "A couple hikers just found a body in the stream by Colby Ranch. I need you to go up and check it out. Don't leave the scene until the police arrive. They're on their way."

Libershal looked at his watch. One-fifteen P.M. He quickly hung up the phone, grabbed his keys, and headed up the hill in the station's truck. As he took the winding turns with practiced skill, Libershal shook his head in disbelief. Someone had found a body. Near Camp Colby. Here, in the San Gabriel Mountains. What was the world coming to? Libershal knew that kids had started hanging out and partying in the area, but he could handle the teenagers. Now they were dealing with a killer, and Libershal wondered if he would ever feel safe working the night shift again.

Five minutes later Libershal spotted two men waiting at the foot of the trail. Must be the hikers, he thought. Poor guys. Libershal hopped out of the truck and introduced himself, then asked to be led to the clearing.

When they arrived, Libershal immediately spotted the body. He could see part of the girl's face, bloated from lying in the water. Libershal wondered what kind of madman would drown a young girl and then place a log that size over her back—just to be sure she was dead. He knew the log from his routine checks of the area. It would have taken at least two people to pick it up and place it over her. It dwarfed the girl underneath.

A sickening thought occurred to Libershal as he took in the scene. This girl wasn't killed by one person. Based on the position of her arm and the way her feet were crossed, one person must have held her arm behind her back to control her while the other pinned down her feet. Libershal noted that the girl had probably been raped, although she still wore her clothes.

He forced these thoughts from his mind, turning his

back to the scene. Sanders and Rutledge did the same, and the men stood in silence waiting for the police. Later Libershal would remember it as the longest twenty minutes of his life.

7

BEFORE MISSY AVILA met Karen Severson, both
girls had longed for a sister. Someone with whom to
share summer afternoons and secrets and picnics under the shaded trees along Ottoman Street in Arleta.
For all of Karen Severson's manipulative ways, she was
a lonely child in a new neighborhood whose parents
were as thrilled as Irene Avila when the two girls
found each other.

Six years had passed since Missy first brought Karen
home, and the two had long since become best friends.
They thought of each other as sisters, though over the
years a bond had developed that real sisters sometimes
never share.

In 1981 Karen and Missy began attending Byrd Junior High School, which provided a fertile field of op-
portunities for Karen to envy her best friend. At first
Karen was bitter about Missy's academic success—her
high grades and constant praise from teachers. Inevitably—and Missy never knew this—Missy's looks
drove Karen crazy with jealousy.

Missy had blossomed since her childhood days. At
age thirteen her young body had developed curves
that caused men to stop and stare at her. Despite the

attention she received, Missy was unaware of her effect on people.

Karen Severson feigned indifference to Missy's looks. It wasn't until too late that people understood the depth of Karen's jealousy. In those days people had no reason to doubt Karen when she boasted about protecting her best friend from the teasing advances of boys in their class.

"I have to look out for Missy," Karen told Irene one day when the two girls were at the Avila house doing homework. "She doesn't need those boys chasing after her."

The boys certainly weren't chasing Karen. While Missy had become more beautiful over the years, the Severson girl had grown heavy and almost homely.

Karen's parents knew the girl had a weight problem, but she was often hungry. So when she asked for food she got it. After all, she was an only child, lonelier than other children. If she wanted a few extra chocolate chip cookies, well, then, she should get them.

On the surface Karen never seemed to mind her weight problem or Missy's popularity. Then, in just one year, people began noticing changes in Karen. At first they were minor—Karen began wearing more makeup and occasionally she would get angry at Missy for dressing or acting a certain way around the boys.

After school one day Karen approached a group of girls who sometimes hung around Missy.

"You guys must really get around," Karen told the girls. "I mean, I can't believe you all slept with the same guy at that party last week. Aren't you worried about diseases?"

The biggest girl in the group walked over to Karen and stood inches from her face. In fact, they had all been to a party the week before that had gotten a little out of hand.

"What are you talking about, Karen? Who says?"

Karen shook her head. "Can't tell you. Sorry."

The girl stepped closer still, and this time she looked as if she was ready to hit Karen. "Tell me who told you. Tell me now!"

Karen stepped backward and put her hands up in mock defense. "Okay, okay. I'll tell you. But don't say anything about it to her. She'd kill me if she knew I'd said anything." Karen paused a minute for effect. "It was Missy Avila."

The next day Missy found a nasty note on her locker. After that, those girls never again made an effort to talk to Missy. As far as they were concerned, she didn't exist. Of course, that suited Karen Severson just fine, and because Karen had been right about her initial assessment of Missy's naïveté, Missy never had any idea why the girls stopped talking to her.

"Karen, did I do something wrong to them or what?" she asked Karen one day. "Those girls used to be my friends and now they don't even talk to me. I can't figure out what I did."

Karen looked at Missy and shook her head. "I don't know. I've noticed it, too, but they must be having problems or something." Karen took Missy's shoulders in her hands and stared into her eyes. "But don't worry about them. You have me. I'm your best friend and I always will be. You don't need those other girls."

Missy and Karen began spending even more time together. By then Karen had told Missy a secret.

A boy had finally started calling on Karen. His name was Michael. Overnight, Karen's life had started revolving around him. Missy didn't approve of the relationship, but it was something of a coup for Karen, who was finally getting the attention usually reserved for prettier girls. Girls like Missy Avila.

But happy as Karen was about her relationship with Michael, Missy worried Karen would get pregnant. Finally she did, and the girls agreed to tell their parents.

"Mom, it's not easy to tell you this," Missy began, during a nightly talk. "Karen is six weeks pregnant. She told me she wants to have the baby."

There were tears in Missy's eyes when she looked up at her mother, and Irene's heart went out to her. Until now she had been spared hardship in her life.

"Is she going to keep it or give it up for adoption?" Irene asked softly, taking her daughter's hand. "She has that option, you know."

"I know. I think she knows, too, but she says she wants to keep the baby and raise it." Missy sighed and wiped her tears with the back of her hand. "We're going to be so different now, Mom. She's not old enough to be a mother and what about high school? What about dating guys? We have so much ahead of us."

Irene nodded, leaning across the bed to hug Missy. "I know, sweetheart," she said. "But if this is Karen's decision, you need to stand by her and be the same kind of friend you've always been."

Missy sobbed in Irene's arms, and the two talked about the rough road that lay ahead for Karen Severson. She would become a mother at age fifteen, when her friends were just starting to date and dream about the prom.

Irene prayed that Missy would be more sensible now that she, too, had started dating. She wondered why Karen had slept with Michael, why she had given in at such a young age.

Irene believed that her daughter wasn't having sex, because Missy would have told her. But Missy's friends, and boyfriends, knew that Missy was very close to losing her virginity at age fourteen—even though the thought of going all the way scared her. Missy saw no reason to worry her mother about her budding sexuality. So that evening, rather than suspecting Missy, Irene was thankful the girl had confided in her about Karen.

"It's too late for Karen, but now you see what can happen if you get serious with a boy, don't you?" Irene brushed Missy's hair away from her face and looked into her eyes.

"I know. I've been telling Karen that for a long time, but she wouldn't listen to me. Guys make better friends, anyway. Then you don't have to break up all the time."

Irene resisted the urge to laugh. She believed that Missy would remain a virgin long after her friends, but in truth, each day Missy's fear of going all the way was dissipating. Her reluctance didn't bother the boys. They saw a lot of potential in pretty Missy Avila, and if she wanted to wait awhile, they would too.

One of Missy's best friends that year was a boy named Jimmy Mitchell. He had been over to the Avila house a few times, and it was obvious to Irene that he had a full-blown crush on her. Although the two sometimes held hands and made out behind the bushes at the park, Missy was determined not to go too much farther.

"You're a smart girl, Missy," Irene said as she and

Missy finished their conversation that night. "Karen is lucky to have you as a friend."

While Irene and Missy were saying their good-nights, the Seversons were crying and discussing Karen's condition. They knew they would have to be responsible for the child. After all, it wasn't fair to make Karen take on that kind of adult challenge at such a young age.

In the weeks that followed, Karen grew heavier and Missy seemed to mature overnight. Suddenly, Irene found her daughter discussing disposable diapers and baby care as easily as she and Karen used to talk about their homework. Missy had a sensitivity about Karen's situation that went beyond her fourteen years.

As Karen's pregnancy progressed, her parents tried to warn her not to overeat because it would be difficult to lose the weight after she had the baby. Karen only ate more. Finally, in her fifth month, she dropped out of school.

Missy was crushed. Until then she had hoped their daily lives wouldn't change much. But even though Missy began spending more time with her classmate, Laura Doyle, she remained true to Karen. Each day after class she would visit her, recounting school stories.

"I keep hoping that she'll come back after she has the baby," Missy explained to her mother one day.

On January 31 Karen gave birth to a dark-haired baby girl and named her Andrea. The infant was fussier than most babies and often Karen would thrust her daughter at her mother, storm out of the house, and run to see Missy.

"I can't handle it," Irene overheard Karen confide

in Missy one day. "She takes all my time and I don't get anything in return."

Karen was also frustrated because Michael had deserted her. He was only a teenager himself and he wanted nothing to do with raising a baby. One day Karen came to visit Missy when Jimmy was over. The two were laughing and listening to records. Irene watched as Karen stood at the doorway, taking in the scene.

"If you're such a good friend, why don't you get rid of him and come over and help me with Andrea?" Karen shouted. Missy looked shocked, but she stood up, approaching her friend. Karen moved away.

"Forget it. You always did have everything going for you. You're just too perfect, Missy. I can't stand it. Sometimes I think I hate you." Karen slammed the door and ran down the street toward her house.

Missy stood paralyzed in the middle of the living room as tears started rolling down her cheeks. She looked at her mother and shook her head. "What did I do wrong, Mom? Why does she hate me?"

Jimmy moved aside, embarrassed by the incident, as Irene walked over to Missy and hugged her. "It's okay, honey. You didn't do anything. This is a hard time for Karen and she's just jealous of you. Try to understand."

Irene, though, was confused. She knew Karen had been jealous of Missy, probably for a long time. But she never realized how much it had affected her until now.

It was a long time before Irene could forget the look in Karen's eyes that day.

8

AT APPROXIMATELY 3:00 P.M. Deputy Sheriff Catherine Scott was searching intently through documents on her desk. It was October 4, 1985, and it had been a frustrating day. No clues, no leads, and several of her cases were getting old.

On days like these Catherine wondered why she investigated homicides in a county like Los Angeles. There were so many easier counties in which to work. She could spend most of her time planning lunches with local activists or heading the fund-raiser committee for the 10-K run. Los Angeles was the kind of county that reeked of homicide.

Every day a murder was committed. Sometimes it was gang related, sometimes it was for money. But at heart was the same truth. Someone was dead and she needed to find out why. There was something in the adventure of discovering those answers that kept Catherine coming back each morning.

Some days she wondered if she was becoming callous. Dead bodies stuffed in trash cans, dead bodies riddled with bullets in parked cars. The body was always the first piece of the puzzle. After she'd learned as much as she could about it, another investigator would head to the scene of the crime and collect evidence, taking pictures and saving items that might be covered by fingerprints. Anything that might help a district attorney make a case for the prosecution.

Catherine remembered her first months working homicide in 1983. There were nights she couldn't sleep because of the investigations, nights when the dead bodies stayed in her mind long after quitting time. Somewhere along the way the murders had begun to blend, making her job more routine, the investigations a means of carrying out her assignments. She couldn't remember the last time she had lost sleep because of a case.

Catherine looked up just as her phone rang. It was 2:44 P.M., Friday afternoon, and she hoped it wasn't anything important. She was looking forward to getting home and relaxing before the weekend.

"Homicide, Scott."

"Scott, I need you and Jenkins over at Camp Colby up in the Angeles National Forest as soon as possible." Catherine knew immediately that a body was involved. She automatically picked up a pencil and began scribbling notes.

"Jenkins is in court, he won't be able to make it," she said. "I'll bring the lieutenant."

"Fine. A couple hikers found a body in the stream that runs through Camp Colby. The forest ranger is at the scene and the hikers are waiting until someone from our department gets out there. The coroner's office is on their way and I want you to get pictures. The ranger's office said it was a young girl. Found her pinned under a log. I guess it's pretty ugly."

Catherine sighed. "I'm on my way." So much for relaxation. Catherine grabbed her jacket and an evidence kit and headed for the patrol car. She thought about what the dispatcher had said. Young girl. Pinned under a log in a stream. Catherine shook her head in disgust, knowing it would be a long evening.

The wind had begun to whistle through the barren trees and a chill had fallen over Camp Colby by the time sheriff's investigators arrived at the scene. Ranger Robert Libershal had spent what seemed like an eternity making small talk with the hikers and guarding the body. He couldn't seem to shake the uneasy feeling that had come over him, causing him to look over his shoulder every few minutes. The hikers were good people, willing to stay around until the officers arrived. But there wasn't much to say to one another and the men had spent most of their time lost in thought.

At 3:30 P.M. Libershal was the first to hear the crunching sound of people walking down the trail. Within seconds Detective Catherine Scott and Lieutenant Ed Emerson appeared.

"Thanks for waiting, Mr. Libershal," one of the detectives said.

Libershal nodded sternly and pointed behind him toward the stream. "The body is right over there." Two people from the coroner's office joined them, and for a few moments no one said a word.

Catherine knew what to do next.

She took the camera from the evidence kit and began snapping pictures. Different angles, different perspectives. Each showed the log and how it dwarfed the girl. Whoever killed her had used the log to make sure she wouldn't rise out of the water. Technically, it didn't matter whether she'd died before or after the log was placed over her body. As far as the law was concerned, the log showed intent to kill.

Meanwhile, Emerson interviewed the hikers, took their names and phone numbers, and thanked them for waiting. He told them they were welcome to continue hiking in the area, but Robert Sanders and Jim Rutledge had no such plans. They returned to the parking lot and started back down the mountain road. Silently, each man wondered how long it would take to forget the nightmare at Camp Colby.

Down at the shoreline Catherine had finished taking pictures of the body as it lay under the log. Because of the lack of rain the stream was almost stagnant. Catherine picked up a leaf on the shore and dropped it into the water. It quivered for a few seconds and then, soaked with water, began to sink. There wasn't even enough movement in the water to carry a leaf downstream.

She took a deep breath and walked with Emerson to the shore. They bent to roll their pant legs. The water was very cold, having come from miles back in the mountain range where the temperature never rose above forty degrees. At this juncture in the stream the water was probably about sixty-two degrees, cold enough to preserve a body for some time.

Emerson began to wade into the shallow water and noticed that the streambed was covered with tiny pebbles, rather than the soft sand farther down the mountainside. He looked back to see if Catherine was following him, but she stood hypnotized on the shore.

This was not just another murder, and for the first time in months Catherine felt a sob well up in her throat. The girl was so tiny. So helpless under the heavy, water-soaked log. Catherine Scott silently wondered why someone would do this to such a small girl. The way the body lay facedown in the stream was almost haunting. From the shore the detectives could only see two jean-covered legs, crossed at the feet, and one arm. The girl wore a tan sweatshirt and her arm was bent at the elbow, twisted behind her back. Catherine wondered how long she had been here.

"You coming?" Emerson asked. Catherine nodded and joined him several feet into the stream. They were losing sunlight quickly and a chilly wind had started to blow through the canyon. Catherine walked to the opposite side of the log and watched as the coroner's investigator helped Emerson lift the log from the girl's back.

"That's one heavy log," he said. "We don't have a vehicle here large enough to take it, so we better make sure we have lots of pictures. It must weigh over a hundred pounds."

Slowly they set the log to the side of the body and took more pictures. It was clear that rigor mortis had set in long ago, because her body was no longer soft and flexible but stiff and unbending. The indentation from the log remained across the girl's back, giving her an unnaturally arched look. Catherine snapped more photos.

"Let's turn her over," she said, trying to keep her feelings for this girl at bay. She looked like her own daughter might have—if she'd had any children.

The fact that Catherine Curtis Scott had chosen a career in law enforcement at a time when it was unheard of for a woman to do so was one reason she had never had children. The other reasons were more complicated.

In 1966 Catherine Curtis was a conservative twenty-one-year-old who had grown tired of the junior-college scene and was seeking something more adventurous than secretarial work. She was five feet ten, with striking features, sandy-blond hair, and a natural all-American beauty, and she had been told by more than one well-meaning friend to pursue a modeling or acting career. But Catherine had been born with a brilliant mind and an insatiable desire to use it.

During the mid-sixties Catherine began dating a tall dark-haired man by the name of Richard Scott. Richard had a lot of things going for him. He was handsome, polite, and had a high-paying job as an electrician. Most important, he was one of Catherine's few suitors who stuck around after the first kiss. The good-girls-don't of the fifties had become the experimental girls of the sixties, and guys were beginning to expect more than a kiss in return for a month of free dinners and movies. Catherine didn't care that times had changed. To her, good girls still didn't. Catherine's father, a respected sheriff's deputy with a reputation that made hardened criminals quiver, had often warned her that only sluts and whores did it before they were married. Pretty, statuesque Catherine Curtis knew she wasn't a slut or a whore, and she knew how disappointed Daddy would be if she ever let her passions get the better of her. As for Richard, he was determined to marry a virgin or be single the rest of his life, and Catherine's chaste kisses suited him just fine.

On a sunny Saturday in May 1967 Catherine's proud father walked her down the aisle and gave her away to Richard Scott. The wedding was memorable: The bride's dress was a fashionable satin gown with lace appliqué, flowers cascaded across the altar in pastel ribbons, and the organist filled the church with the kind of sounds that brought tears to the eyes of many guests. But there wasn't a soul in the church who knew the real terror coursing through Catherine's veins as she waltzed gracefully into the arms of her betrothed.

Acting on her father's suggestion Catherine had applied to the sheriff's department. Back then, women didn't work in patrol cars, and they didn't solve crimes; they only dispatched those who did. But there was something so irresistibly exciting about working in a sheriff's station that Catherine went through the application process with an energy her father hadn't known she had.

A week before the wedding Catherine got a call from an officer with the sheriff's personnel department offering her a job starting at a respectable $640 a month.

Ecstatic and anxious to tell Richard the good news, Catherine dialed his number and told him everything. Nearly thirty seconds of utter silence followed; in the minutes after that Catherine Curtis got her first true look at the man she was pledged to marry. In no uncertain terms Richard told Catherine she could accept the job only if she worked in the women's prison, where she would not be working with men. When Catherine hung up the phone her eyes were wide and there were goose bumps on her arms.

These were Catherine Curtis's thoughts that Saturday as she was becoming Catherine Scott in front of more than one hundred people. But it was too late to back down. After all, good girls didn't make waves, and they certainly didn't leave a handsome gentleman like Richard at the altar.

A month later Catherine Scott was only beginning to realize what it meant to marry a man like Richard. She was not allowed much of a social life outside Richard's presence. Catherine believed that Richard must love her very much if he needed to keep such a close eye on her. In fact, she was luckier than most women, and if she didn't remind herself of this every day, well, then, Richard did.

Gradually, Catherine was becoming two people. During the days she was the competent Catherine Scott who had a no-nonsense knack for handling criminals and a promising future in law enforcement. At six o'clock she became Richard's wife, a humbly quiet, submissive woman with no opinions or friends or ideas of her own.

Meanwhile, changes were taking place in the sheriff's department. In 1973 Los Angeles Sheriff Peter J. Pitches saw the feminist writing on the wall and graciously offered women an opportunity to work the patrol cars. At Catherine's station in Altadena there were twelve positions made available for uniformed women officers. When Catherine heard about the opportunity, she immediately submitted an application. That night she asked Richard, even begged him, to let her be a real uniformed deputy out on the streets. For a minute she almost thought he might say yes. Instead, he told Catherine never to bring up the topic again. Like an obedient child Catherine nodded and the next day withdrew her application. Within a week Catherine's dream of being a uniformed officer was dead. In half that time so was her love for Richard Scott.

It was 1975 when Catherine got another opportunity to work a patrol car. By this time she resented Richard so much that she didn't care what he thought. She had accepted the job and undergone training before she even told him about it. Although their marriage wouldn't officially end for several years, she placed the marital tombstone on 1975. From that point on Richard realized he had lost control of his bride, and within a few years he was as willing to divorce as Catherine.

Catherine loved working the patrol cars. She had a male partner and with his help she learned to make arrests, follow suspects, and take crime reports. It was a whole new world and she felt more alive than she had in years. Still, something was missing, and even though it was unheard of for a woman, Catherine knew she wanted the top of the law-enforcement ladder—she wanted to be a detective.

Every day for the next three years Catherine Scott went out of her way to see the station's chief lieutenant.

"You know what this department needs, don't you?" she'd ask him.

"I know, I know," he'd say, rarely bothering to look up from his desk. "This department needs a female detective. Am I right, Scott?"

"That's right, sir. I'm ready when you are."

In 1978 public attention focused on the insensitivity with which rape victims were being treated. Daily headlines shouted about the unfairness of a crime committed by men, investigated by men, and then tried by men. In Los Angeles, Sheriff Pitches again broke the ice by announcing that his department would be the first to allow women officers a transfer to the detective bureau.

The next morning when Catherine walked into the lieutenant's office, he was expecting her.

"Sit down, Scott," he said, looking straight at her. "We've got a proposition for you."

So it was that Catherine Scott became the first female detective in Los Angeles County. There were restrictions, of course. She couldn't investigate murders and she would have to work the night shift for the first six months. Otherwise she was finally doing what before she had only dreamed of—solving crimes.

At home Richard had no interest in Catherine's ambitions. This was unfortunate, because Catherine was working on things no one should have to keep bottled inside.

As a result of the public pressure Catherine's superiors put her in charge of investigating rapes and other sexual-abuse crimes. She began handling the cases involving children, and quickly learned how these girls and boys were society's worst rape victims in more ways than one.

"I listen to a four-year-old girl describe oral copulation and where her daddy makes her sit while she's doing it and I have to make an arrest," Catherine told a friend one day. "Then we take Daddy away and the little girl winds up in juvenile hall, which is really only a prison in disguise. That's how we take care of our abused children? It isn't right."

Catherine began going out of her way to make things better for the children with whom she worked. She brought them toys, spent time listening to them and coloring with them. In fact, before long they became the children she and Richard never had.

The reasons Catherine and Richard Scott never had any children were obvious. Catherine did not want to raise a child with Richard. Also, she was afraid of anything that might take away from her career as a sheriff's investigator, which she had worked so hard to achieve. So Catherine poured all the love she had inside her into the county's sexually abused children. Each child she dealt with was hers, nearly a thousand of them.

It wasn't until 1981 that Catherine and Richard Scott amicably went their own ways. The end came because Richard had long since given up changing Catherine's career interests and Catherine had grown distant and lonely living with a man she couldn't talk to. As Catherine would later tell people, "We had a quick and easy, ninety-five-dollar walk-through divorce, and for the first time in years we were both free."

About that time the sheriff's department officially recognized the brilliance in Catherine Scott's ability to solve crimes. They made history again that year by promoting Catherine to homicide investigation—the big time. Corpses and murder weapons, maniacal suspects, everything a detective could ever want. Catherine only missed her children, because the ones she dealt with in homicide were past the point of worrying about daddy going to jail. They were past the point of worrying about anything.

Sometime during the years of homicide investigation Catherine Scott's appearance began to change from what it had been in the mid-sixties or even the mid-seventies. She was still pretty, still tall and graceful, but she had gained a few pounds and there was something hard around her eyes, something hard in her voice, that told people she had been through a lot of pain and survived. She was smoking filtered Winstons and dyeing her hair a color that wasn't quite flattering, and she had learned some of the mannerisms of her male colleagues. She hadn't lost her femininity, but when Catherine brought in a guy with bloodstains on his hands and a wild look in his eyes, he somehow shrank in her presence. Still, for all her hard exterior, there was something soft and loving that lived inside Catherine Scott.

So when she was called to the Angeles National Forest Colby Ranch area October 3, 1985, to make a report on a young dead girl, Catherine Scott was silent for most of the forty-minute ride. And when she saw her, pinned under an enormous tree trunk in the shallow creek, Catherine Scott had to swallow back a sob. It had been a long time since she'd investigated the murder of a young girl. Her memories of children she had worked with came flooding back in an instant.

At that moment Catherine came close to feeling the way a parent feels when her child has been murdered. Later that night, somewhere in the city, some mother would be devastated, a piece of her forever gone. Catherine didn't want to think about that yet.

The coroner's investigator had no trouble rolling the girl over and propping her up. She was light, even though water had filled her chest cavity. Her eyes were partially open and still intact. If her face hadn't been underwater, the eyes probably would have rotted by now. Catherine made a note of the scratches and bruises around the girl's face and eyes. It looked as if she'd been beaten up pretty badly before she was drowned. The coroner touched the cold, gray skin of the girl's face and arms. It slid grotesquely from her bones and tissue.

"We have skin slippage," he said. "Make a note of it. She's probably been dead a couple days."

Emerson lifted the girl's legs and together they carried her body toward the shore. Catherine followed as the two set the girl down on the soft dirt. There were still more pictures to take.

It was then that Catherine noticed the hair.

Clumps of dark brown hair lay on a boulder just a few feet from the shore. Catherine walked closer and saw more hair on the ground near the rock. Making the connection, Catherine glanced at the girl's body. Same hair color.

"Look at this," she said, motioning Emerson to the spot. "It looks like someone cut her hair before they drowned her."

Emerson nodded. "Better take some for analysis."

Catherine took several evidence bags and gingerly began collecting sections of the cut hair. While she worked, a sudden chill ran through her. At first she had figured it was a sexually related murder, but now she wondered. What kind of person would seat his victim on a boulder, cut her hair, drown her, and then cover her body with a log? Catherine had an eerie feeling that this was not a routine case.

After Catherine and Emerson had inspected the surrounding area and taken enough pictures, they let the coroner's investigator proceed. They would perform a preliminary autopsy on site and then later, in the examining room, verify those details.

Brenard Bodley had been an investigator for the Los Angeles County coroner's office since 1965. He'd seen more bodies than he could remember, but as he took pictures of this dead girl he knew he would not forget her.

He would always remember her face and how it seemed frozen in fear, despite the slipping skin, bruises, and abrasions. And the log. He had measured it at forty inches long and approximately twelve inches in diameter. Whoever had killed this girl, one thing was clear—she'd never had a chance. Her killers had completely overpowered her. He made a note that possibly the girl had still been alive and semiconscious when her killers placed the log over her back. It was too heavy for someone so small to move aside. Bodley thought of what it must have been like to drown in such shallow water, how frustrating. How hard she must have tried to get free of her attackers.

Quietly, Bodley set about doing his routine before the body could be loaded up and taken to the morgue. He checked for stiffness, to verify that rigor mortis had indeed set in long ago, and he noted trauma to the girl's face and arms. Her face had bruise marks near the nose, mouth, and forehead—probably the result of having her face smashed into the streambed, although they might also indicate a beating received prior to her death.

Next, he examined the marks on her arms. *Defense bruises,* he scribbled on his notepad. Small finger-sized bruises. Coroner officials called them defense bruises because they usually came from one of two kinds of trauma: She had either been grabbed tightly against her will or had used her forearm to ward off blows delivered to her face. No, she'd never had a chance.

Next Bodley checked for jewelry and found a gold anklet covered by the girl's jean pant leg. He also found two earrings, one in the girl's ear and the other tangled in her hair. It hadn't been much of a fight. Bodley finished his preliminary examination and motioned for the stretcher. Once the girl's body had been removed, hours before the official autopsy, the detectives had to collect clues still at the scene. Before heading back down the mountain Libershal gave the detectives a denim purse, still wet from having lain in the stream. Catherine took it and made a quick check through the contents. Red lip balm. Purple compact. Perfume. Yellow comb. Small orange wallet. Finally Catherine found what she was looking for. Inside a leather wallet was the girl's high-school identification.

Michele Y. Avila. Four feet eleven. Ninety-seven pounds. Brown hair. Brown eyes. Birth date: February 8, 1968.

Catherine closed her eyes, quickly calculating. She was seventeen years old, just a few months shy of her eighteenth birthday. She had looked so much younger because of her size. Catherine used the patrol-car radio and ran a missing person's check on the girl.

"That's affirmative. Michele 'Missy' Avila was listed missing on October 2, 1985, in Arleta by her mother, Irene Avila. Last seen wearing blue jeans and a tan-colored sweatshirt."

"We have her," Catherine said softly. "You can take her off the missing person's list, but don't release any information on her until the next of kin has been notified."

Catherine thought again of Michele's mother.

Somewhere right now she would be terrified, wondering why her daughter hadn't called, wondering where she could be. Soon she would know. What every mother fears deep in her heart would become a reality today for this girl's mother. Even worse, there were no leads, no arrests, no motives, nothing to soften the blow.

Catherine waited for Emerson to join her so the two could head back down the mountain to the address on the girl's driver's license. But there was still something Catherine felt she had to do.

Quickly, she walked back to the shoreline where the girl's body had been found. By then her chopped-off hair had already been collected for analysis, but some still lay near the rock on the shore of the stream. Quietly, Catherine walked to it, bent down, and picked up a small, shiny dark lock of Missy's hair. She placed it on a piece of paper, folded it into a tiny square, and tucked it inside her pants pocket.

She would never forget this girl, never give up on solving her murder. For the next three years, wherever she went and whatever she did, Catherine Scott carried that lock of Missy's hair with her.

Later, in the examining room, Dr. Eva Heuser performed a complete autopsy on the body of Missy Avila. She found that there were several bruises—on the girl's chin, chest area, arms, hands, and face—that must have been inflicted prior to her death. A person needed blood pressure in order to experience a bruise. Heuser also noted that the abrasions and bruises on the girl's face represented partial decomposition of skin tissue where her face had been smashed into the gravelly bottom of the streambed as she was held underwater.

Heuser noted the official cause of death as homicidal drowning. Of course, a person can live a long time underwater, as long as thirty minutes. That was probably why her killers had placed a log over her back—to make sure she was dead.

In addition, Heuser tested Missy's body for drug and alcohol content and found none, other than a .03 percent alcohol reading. This, however, was probably the result of ethanol, an alcohol-based fluid secreted by the body during decomposition. In Missy's stomach Heuser found a gray fluid and some digested food—

probably the sandwich and milk Missy had eaten hours before her death. The stage of digestion combined with the level of rigor mortis told Heuser the girl's time of death had probably been at least two days earlier.

Heuser also discovered that Missy had been having her menstrual period at the time of her death—as was evidenced by the fact that she had a tampon inserted in her vagina—but Heuser still ran routine tests to determine if the girl had been sexually assaulted. The tests were negative.

9

ANDREA WAS NEARLY eleven months old when Karen Severson decided to go back to school. It had been a long year, filled with sleepless nights, dirty diapers, formula, and everything Karen had never pictured about having a baby. Paula and Loyal Severson had picked up the slack—Karen had fallen back on them when she couldn't stand to spend one more minute with her daughter.

That winter Karen and Missy had been discussing the idea of Karen returning to school. Missy was all for it, because school hadn't been the same since Karen dropped out. Missy had other friends, of course. There were Christy Crawford, Laura Doyle, and a few others with whom she spent time. But after eighth grade Christy left for Long Beach, and Laura Doyle was always too involved with her boyfriends to spend much time with Missy.

Because of Karen's absence Missy had floundered through the ninth grade. She spent very little time with the boys who still pursued her, spending more time at home than usual.

When tenth grade started, Missy was a budding sophomore at Poly Technic High School. Her popularity at Byrd Junior High followed her to high school, even though Missy didn't much care. Her best friend wasn't around and even though she still got good grades, school wasn't the same without Karen Severson.

So when Karen announced her decision to return to school, Missy was thrilled. It would be just like old times, walking back and forth to school, talking about who was dating whom and making plans for the weekend.

Then Karen announced the rest of her plan. She wouldn't return to Poly Technic High School. Instead, she would enroll in Poly's continuation program—Mission High School. Continuation school was for students wanting to graduate early; typically, students who attended were dropouts, drug users or kids who couldn't make it at the real high school. Teachers at Mission High often allowed students to take the course work at their own pace and when people drove past the school, they often saw students lounging around on benches, talking and smoking cigarettes. It didn't seem much like school to Missy and she told Karen as much.

"But all our friends are at Poly," Missy pleaded with Karen. "Your grades were good enough to get you back in and everyone would understand why you were gone for a year."

Karen didn't listen to Missy. She had made up her mind and planned to enroll at the continuation school that January in time for the second school semester. She would never tell Missy, but she would have had her reasons for wanting to switch. She had gained fifty pounds when she was pregnant with Andrea. Fifty pounds she couldn't afford to gain. Although she was ready to return to school, she would not have wanted to walk around Poly High looking like she did.

Missy had noticed Karen's weight gain, and she knew how badly Karen felt whenever they walked Andrea up and down their street. Guys in the neighborhood would drive by and when they saw Missy they whistled and howled in approval. Inevitably one of them would add a comment or two about Karen. Something like "Who's your double shadow?" Or even more direct—"Hey, Tubbo, ever heard of dieting?" The attitude people had toward Karen's weight made Missy more determined than ever to remain true to their friendship.

Because of all the name calling and the pressures of being a teenage mother, Missy was concerned about Karen and how continuation school might change her. Missy had heard that kids at the school were tough, and she didn't like the thought of Karen hanging around them. Missy tried not to think about all the terrible things those kids might do to Karen.

Karen's choice of schools, however, paled in comparison to events happening in Missy's own household. For the past month or two Missy had noticed her parents spending less and less time together. At first she tried to ignore it, hoping it was just a passing phase, but there were several times when she came home from school and found her mother crying.

By now, Ernie junior was married and had a life of his own, and so Irene gathered Mark, Chris, and Missy together one day and carefully told them what was happening.

"Your father and I are separating for a while," she said, holding back tears so they would believe her next words. "It is for the best. For both of us." She took a deep breath and continued. "There are some things that I don't want to discuss, reasons for this that you don't need to know. But you do need to know that your father has taken an apartment across town and he will no longer be staying here with us."

Mark was not surprised. He had blamed his father for upsetting their mother. Knowing he would have to be supportive of her now, he walked over and put an arm around her shoulders.

Chris, not yet ten years old, began to cry softly. He couldn't understand why Daddy wouldn't be sleeping at home anymore. As Irene watched him, she knew he would be okay. He and Mark were very close and he idolized his older brother. In time the boys would get over this trauma.

It was Missy who took the news harder than the others. She hung her head as Irene spoke and when she looked up, Irene noticed that something in her daughter's eyes had died. The sparkle was gone. Missy stood up quickly and ran to her room. Ten minutes later when Irene approached her, Missy said she didn't want to talk.

Missy had always been close to her mother, but there was something very special about the relationship she shared with her father. When she was a little girl, Ernie senior would come home from work, pull Missy onto his lap, and tell her a story. He remarked constantly about her pretty hair and long dark eyelashes, and every few days he would bring her a piece of candy or a small toy.

"Missy, you're Daddy's little princess," he would say as he tossed her up in the air. Missy would giggle the way little girls do when they're with their daddy. He was different with Missy's brothers. Although he loved his children equally, he was stern with the boys, but usually let Irene discipline Missy. In his eyes Missy could do no wrong.

Ever since Missy had turned fourteen, Ernie senior had spent less and less time at home in the evenings. Missy never said anything about his absence to her mother, but she knew something was wrong. Now her mother confirmed her fears, and the separation angered and confused her. Why would her father leave the family he loved?

During the next few days Missy's angry silence was punctuated only by the screaming fits she and her mother had. At one point Missy even tried to run away. She went to Christy Crawford's house and cried for hours talking about her dad and how much she missed the way he had treated her when she was little.

Then, two weeks after Irene's announcement, Missy made one of her own. She was going to drop out of Poly High and enroll with Karen in the continuation program at Mission High School. A year earlier it would have been impossible for Missy to make such a move because continuation programs don't take students with high grade-point averages. But ever since Karen Severson dropped out of school, Missy had barely been able to maintain a C. When the principal reviewed her situation, especially her attendance record, which had gone from regular to occasional, he gave his approval for the change.

"Don't worry about it, Mom," Missy said, sounding defiant.

Irene shook her head angrily. "I'm not worried. I just think that dropping out of high school for that other program is the wrong choice. Listen, Missy, if you want to throw your education away like that it's a decision you'll have to live with, but I want you to know how I feel about it."

Mother and daughter had frequently disagreed since Irene and Ernie's separation. Later Irene realized this was only the beginning of a period of rebellion and defiance on Missy's part. Missy seemed to blame both her parents for the separation and tended to ignore anything either of them had to say. In the middle of her sophomore year Missy went with Karen to the continuation school and registered for classes.

The changes happened overnight.

Missy no longer was interested in school spirit, letter jackets, and straight A's. Instead she began listening to heavy-metal rock music and bought a black biker jacket like those worn by many of the other kids at continuation school. Soon she was spending more and more time with Karen and less time than ever on her studies. Occasionally Irene would ask Missy about homework and her studies. Missy always brushed her off, saying such concerns weren't important and that she was keeping up.

When grades were released midway through the semester, it was obvious Missy was spending her school days on something other than schoolwork. She was barely passing her classes, and not one of them carried the academic challenge of her previous courses at Poly High.

Despite Missy's lack of interest in school her friendship with Karen had flourished. She and Karen spent nearly all their time together playing with Andrea or hanging out at the park.

Sometimes, Missy would call her mother asking if she could stay at Karen's house for dinner. Once, when

Irene thought she was talking to Missy, she was suddenly aware of Missy giggling in the background.

"Oh, that wasn't me on the phone, it was Karen," Missy said when Irene mentioned the call. She broke into a grin. "She can imitate me pretty good, don't you think?"

Karen must have practiced for hours to sound so like Missy, but Irene never thought to ask the obvious questions: Why would Karen put so much effort into imitating Missy? In the days before her divorce was final, Irene had enough on her mind without analyzing the behavior of Missy's best friend.

Later that semester Missy left her notebook on the kitchen table after school. The writing on its cover was revealing.

> *Deep Purple. Led Zeppelin. Twisted Sister. Scorpions. Harley-Davidson #1. Mission High School Crazy Girls. Party Hardy. Missy & Karen Friends Till the End.*

Irene sighed as she opened the notebook, wondering when Missy had become so interested in Harley-Davidson motorcycles and partying. Inside the notebook Irene found a poem Missy had written describing herself. Looking around to be sure no one was watching, Irene read it:

> *Missy.*
> *Energetic, small, young.*
> *Impatient.*
> *Friend of Karen.*
> *Lover of*
> *Happiness, mother, and music,*

Who feels lonely, desperate, and hurt.
Who needs love, comfort, and caring.
Who gives friendship, advice . . .
And second chances.
Who fears
Big roller coasters, windy days.
And the ocean.

Tears streamed down Irene's face as she stared at the poem. At that moment she finally understood how very confused Missy was over her parents' separation. Ernie had moved out ten weeks earlier, and during that time Irene had felt more strain in her relationship with Missy than ever before. The poem helped Irene understand what the girl was going through. Missy thought of herself as lonely and needing love; as someone who gave advice and second chances. Naturally, Irene was among the list of things Missy loved. And when it came to Missy Avila's fears, the ocean was last on the list because it scared her more than anything else.

As a little girl Missy had loved the ocean, but that was before she got caught in a strong undertow while swimming with her friends at the beach one day. After that she had nightmares that she would drown, struggling and gasping for breath until finally she would be swept under a powerful wave and never seen again.

Irene put the poem back neatly into the notebook and decided to talk with Missy later that night. It was after ten o'clock when Missy got home, and she had a funny look on her face. As she spoke, Irene was almost certain that her daughter was high.

"Missy, is there something you want to tell me?" Irene asked, taking her hand.

Missy looked down, not sure what to say. When she looked up, Irene could see that Missy was going to tell her something very private. "Mom, a few of us got together and tried some pot. We didn't smoke a lot, but I just wanted to see what it was like."

The truth, according to Missy's friends, was that Missy had been smoking pot off and on for nearly two months. Laura Doyle had tried it first and then Karen. Since they seemed to like it, Missy also gave it a try. Christy Crawford, who also started smoking marijuana later that year, remembers that Missy always looked at the drug as a way to escape the problems her parents were having. But as Missy sat there that night, on the edge of her mother's bed, explaining why her eyes looked a little funny, she couldn't possibly admit to two months of smoking pot, especially two months of smoking pot because of her parents' problems.

If Irene had suspected there was more to Missy's story, she didn't say anything that night. Irene felt that Missy was making a valiant attempt to be open and honest, and so she decided not to lecture her too harshly. Besides, drugs were a reality in the lives of most East Valley teenagers.

"Well, Missy, I think it's okay to try it so long as you don't get used to it. Drugs don't help you in the real world, you know. They can only bring you down."

Missy agreed with her mother and the two talked for almost an hour before the teenager slipped off to her own bedroom and went to sleep. Irene stayed awake long after Missy left, wondering what her husband was doing. If she had known, it would have made her night that much harder.

Ernie Avila, Sr., was busy reliving the days of his youth and enjoying every minute. He knew nothing of the trials Irene was going through with Missy or how much Irene needed a husband to comfort and help her. Changing diapers and bandages paled in comparison to the kind of help their children—especially Missy—needed now.

A few days later Missy was listening to records in her bedroom when she called to Irene.

"Listen to this song, isn't it great?" Missy turned up the volume and "Lady Starlight" by the Scorpions filled the room. It was Missy's favorite song. Irene listened as Missy sang along.

" 'I see the stars. They're miles and miles away, like our love.' " Missy reached over, turned down the volume, and looked up at her mother.

"Mom, if I die, I want that song played at my funeral," she said seriously.

Irene laughed. "Missy! Don't talk like that. Kids your age aren't supposed to be thinking about death."

"I know, Mom. But I just really like this song and I think it would be neat to have it played at my funeral. Whenever I die."

Missy had just turned sixteen, and no one would ever understand what caused her to make such a request. Once, when Irene told Karen Severson about Missy's strange request, Karen shrugged it off. It was March, and Karen was having severe trouble at Mission High. Her grades had plummeted, and she was spending much of her time drinking and getting high. Sometimes she even partied with tiny Andrea in the room. Her behavior was beginning to worry even Missy, who still spent most of her afternoons with Karen.

Missy wasn't always aware of Karen's activities at school. One day, when Missy stayed home from school with a sore throat and fever, Karen put into action a plan she'd been devising for weeks. There had been many other plans through the years, but things were different now.

Karen was no longer satisfied with tricking other girls into leaving Missy alone, thereby keeping Missy's friendship all to herself. This time Karen wanted them to hate Missy. She wanted them to act on their hatred in a way that Karen was unable to do, because by then Karen's jealousy of Missy had grown even larger than she was. Later people would have no trouble marking 1984 as the year Karen's longtime jealousy of Missy began eating away at the place in her heart that still loved her. Each day that year and the next Karen's jealousy grew more dangerous, until finally Karen could no longer remember a time when she had cared for Missy at all.

No one ever guessed the true feelings Karen was harboring in the dark corners of her soul. To Missy's other friends Karen's actions seemed like nothing more than teenage insecurity. So what if Karen caused a few problems between Missy and other girls? Wasn't that like any other group of teenagers, each vying for the sole attention of a more popular classmate? If anyone had been asked to describe Karen Severson she would have said a variety of things, but without exception she would have said, "Karen Severson is Missy Avila's best friend." That was exactly what Karen wanted them to think. It wasn't all an act, either. Karen enjoyed the attention that came along with being Missy's best friend, even the attention she got by sticking up for Missy on occasion.

Ultimately, Karen must have realized that if she was

going to make Missy pay for being beautiful and popular, she was going to have to be sly about it.

One day, while Missy was home sick, Karen walked up to a group of four tough girls at Mission High and set a plan into motion.

They glanced disapprovingly toward Karen as she walked up. "What do you want, Severson?" a girl named Tina asked. Tina was going through rocky times with her boyfriend, Shawn, at the time.

"Just wondering why you weren't at that party last night, you know, the one over near Joe's house," Karen said politely, waiting for their reaction.

"What party? There was no party last night." The fish were biting.

"Yeah there was," Karen said, sincerity written across her face. "I thought the only reason you weren't there was because of Shawn and Missy."

Tina walked closer to Karen. "What do you mean, Shawn and Missy?"

"Come on, Tina. You know Missy's sleeping with Shawn these days."

Tina had never seen Missy Avila anywhere near her boyfriend, but now that Karen mentioned it, Shawn had been acting strangely. Suddenly everything made sense. Karen watched as rage mastered every inch of Tina's face. Then, with what appeared to be an anguished look of concern, Karen begged Tina to keep quiet about Missy and Shawn's affair.

"Missy would be so mad if she knew I told you," Karen said. "I really thought you knew, I didn't think it was any big deal."

The next day Missy was on her way home from school—her throat still sore—when Tina jumped from behind a bush and blocked her path. Within seconds, three other girls stood at her side, each glaring angrily. Tina was nearly six feet tall and had the build of a linebacker. In the seconds before she began slapping Missy's face, Missy searched her mind for a reason why Tina would be angry with her.

"You whore, Missy!" Tina screamed. "If I ever hear about you sleeping with Shawn again you'll wish you were never born!"

Missy was shocked, and even though they weren't listening, she tried to exonerate herself. She told them she had never uttered so much as a single word to Shawn.

Tina quickly tired of slapping Missy because she was completely defenseless, and by then the four of them had bruised her face pretty badly. So on Tina's command the others turned to run down a nearby alley. "You can thank your good friend Karen Severson for this one!" Tina said as she ran.

When Missy came home sobbing with a welt on her arm and bruises across her cheeks, Irene rushed to her side. Missy collapsed in her arms.

"What is it, what happened?" Irene asked, and she forced Missy to look up.

"I—I was leaving school," Missy said, trying to control her sobs. "And these four girls jumped out from behind this bush. They started hitting me and screaming at me and one of them said she heard I was sleeping with her boyfriend."

"Who were these girls?" Irene was furious. She couldn't imagine why four of them would pick on someone so small. "Honey, why in the world would they think that?"

"I don't know. They go to continuation school with me and Karen." Missy wiped her eyes. "I thought they were my friends." As Missy stopped crying, she suddenly looked angry.

"You won't believe what one of them said, Mom." Missy shook her head, her green eyes burning. "She told me that Karen set the whole thing up! Can you believe that?"

Irene looked shocked. "Karen Severson?"

Missy nodded. "First they beat me up for something I didn't do, then they blame it all on my best friend. What kind of people would do that?"

"They said Karen Severson told them?" Irene repeated.

"Yes! I don't know why they thought I would believe something so stupid. Karen knows I haven't even talked to the guy, let alone slept with him. Anyway, if anyone cares about me at that school, it's Karen. I just can't understand why those girls would blame it on her."

As Irene listened, an uneasy feeling came over her; but in the end she decided Missy must be right. After all, Karen had no reason to tell lies about Missy.

The story was all around school. Karen waited until four o'clock that afternoon before calling Missy.

"Missy, are you okay?" Karen sounded breathless, as if she'd just learned what had happened.

"I guess so. My mom gave me some ice for my cheek, but the bruises are still there. Did you hear what happened?"

"Yeah. Tina and her friends beat you up because they thought you and Shawn had something going?" Karen sounded hesitant, like someone who isn't sure of the facts. "I mean, that's crazy. You don't even know the guy, do you?"

"No. But did you hear the rest?"

"There was more?" Karen was incredulous. "What else happened?"

"They told me you told them about me and Shawn."

Karen sounded surprised. "Me! You've got to be kidding!"

For the next hour Karen and Missy talked about how mean Tina and her friends had been to make up such a lie. In the end, Karen assured Missy they were simply jealous of Karen and Missy's friendship.

10

DURING MISSY'S JUNIOR year at Mission continuation school, she discovered two things in earnest—boys and beer. It was inevitable that one day Missy would notice the boys who had chased her since kindergarten. That fall Missy and Karen were both sixteen, and they spent nearly all their time talking about boys or dating them.

Missy's hair had grown to her waist, and it hung like a thick dark curtain, gently framing her face. Her eyes had recaptured some of their sparkle and she didn't talk as much about her parents' separation. Irene understood why. She had discovered boys, and more than that she had discovered sex. In fact, she'd been barely sixteen when she and a special boy at Mission High skipped school and spent the afternoon in bed at his house.

She told Irene about it later that week when she came home after a date with the boy. By then the late-night talks between mother and daughter had become routine, and Irene was still convinced that Missy was telling her everything.

By the fall of 1984 Arleta, Pacoima, and other East Valley communities had become even tougher. The East Valley kids were tougher, too, and often Irene found herself concerned about the rough-looking boys Missy brought home.

That semester Missy went out with several boys, but she was particularly close to Victor Amaya. Vic had dark hair and dark brown eyes and he was two years older than Missy.

Christy Crawford would always remember the first time the kids at Stonehurst Park saw Vic and his brother. He was so cute that everyone wanted to get to know him, and Vic wanted to get to know Missy. It was obvious to Christy that Vic adored Missy, but even though the two became very close—physically and emotionally—Missy never labeled him her boyfriend. She and Vic had agreed that if they made a formal commitment to each other they would lose their friendship.

So while others came and went in their lives, Missy and Vic remained close. They slept together sometimes but felt that was only part of their friendship. Vic respected Missy more than any other girl he knew.

Years later, when Vic testified in Missy's murder trial, one of the defense attorneys grilled him about his relationship with Missy, calling her a sex partner and trying to make their relationship sound cheap and sordid. But Vic never saw it that way. Their closeness was something special that Missy and Vic never found with anyone else.

Their friends sometimes wondered whether Vic and Missy might one day get married. They had the kind of relationship that might possibly last a lifetime. Irene liked him and felt safe when Missy was out with him.

That semester Irene noticed that the friendship between Karen and Missy had cooled. She asked Missy about it, but Missy shrugged.

"Everything's fine, I guess," Missy said. "It's just that we're both busy. And we're growing up, Mom. Anyway, we still see each other a lot at school and at the park."

Stonehurst Park.

Five minutes from the Avila home, the park had become much rougher in recent years. When Irene and Ernie were dating, it had been a fun place to talk under the trees. Small children used the play area and gardeners kept the place maintained so that it always looked clean and inviting.

During the early 1980s gangs had begun hanging out in dark corners where gardeners hadn't worked for years. Most children were afraid to use the play area, especially after dusk.

The park was the perfect place to hang out for Missy and her friends at Mission High. It was large enough that they could drink beer without being hassled by the police and there were plenty of spots in which to make out. They could even get high there without anyone knowing. In those days continuation school let out at noon, so the group spent five or six hours every day passing the afternoons.

The past few months had been hard for Karen because she couldn't seem to get a boyfriend. Missy knew of several boys whom Karen had a crush on, but none of them was interested in her. Still, Missy never gave up hope that one day Karen would lose the weight she had gained during her pregnancy and find the right boy.

At the beginning of the spring semester Karen began dating Jimmy Mitchell, Missy's friend from junior high. Everyone was surprised to learn about Karen and Jimmy because, though he was discreet, Jimmy had never gotten over Missy. Besides, Karen and Jimmy seemed like such a physically mismatched couple. Jimmy was barely five feet three and had a slight build. Karen stood at least two inches taller and was nearly two hundred pounds.

Missy didn't care that Karen and Jimmy seemed like an odd combination; she was happy that Karen had finally found a boyfriend. Irene wondered whether Karen was bothered that Jimmy had liked Missy when they were younger.

"Oh, Mom," Missy said, rolling her eyes slightly. "Jimmy Mitchell? He and I were just good friends. Karen knows that."

Karen and Jimmy had been dating two weeks when Missy came home one day in tears.

"Mom, something's happening to Karen. She doesn't seem to trust me around Jimmy. She keeps telling me to stay away from him, but she should know better, Mom." Missy dropped her head into her hands and Irene smiled gently. Teenage girls were so jealous of one another.

"Missy, you've seen Karen like this before. She's just jealous. She knows that Jimmy used to like you, even if you never had the same feelings for him."

Missy sighed and slowly lifted her head. "You're right. I guess I'll have to do a better job of showing Karen that she means more to me than any guy."

Missy went out of her way to make Karen feel less threatened by her presence, which did nothing to lessen Karen's envy. The two continued to disagree until finally she began spending less and less time with her. By then Karen was completely losing control of her jealousy. Boys still flocked around Missy and Karen was running out of ways to stop them. Soon, however, she'd started dating Jimmy Mitchell. For the first time in years Karen Severson was finally free of Missy's shadow, free to have some attention of her own.

With Karen busy dating Jimmy, and Christy Crawford away at school in Long Beach, Missy began seeing a lot of Laura Doyle. Laura Doyle and Missy had never been best friends, but they ran with the same crowd and lived in the same neighborhood.

There was no strange path or twist of fate that placed Laura Doyle in the same middle-class neighborhood as Missy Avila. Laura had lived there all her life, just like Missy, but their childhood circles had never crossed because Laura lived on the other side of Branford Park, which to a child is like living at the other end of the country.

Laura Ann Doyle was born on the first day of May in 1967. Her parents brought her home from the hospital to the same Arleta home on Reliance Street that she would live in for the next twenty years. However, Laura Doyle had no happy household and doting brothers to mark her childhood. Instead she had been led along a trail of alcohol and abusiveness that, while not of an intensity requiring professional intervention, had caused her to be a withdrawn child who was most comfortable blending into the scenery. Laura Doyle seemed like a born follower. When Laura's mother proposed modeling school during her teenage years, Laura shrugged and went along. Her parents were constantly arguing with each other, so agreement would have seemed the easiest course of action.

At first, she avoided alcohol, and instead at age fifteen she began smoking pot with her friends at

Stonehurst Park. However, one year later she began sneaking beers and then finally drinking blatantly.

In the spring of 1985 Missy and Laura had begun spending long afternoons at Stonehurst Park playing Frisbee, drinking beer, and sometimes smoking a little pot.

It was during this time that Laura Doyle began calling Irene Avila "Mom." In practice, Irene was Laura's mom. Her own parents knew nothing of Laura's activities, they were so immersed in their own problems. When the truth about Missy's murder finally came out in the newspapers, everyone was quick to say that the signs had all been there. Missy shouldn't have been hanging out at Stonehurst Park, shouldn't have been drinking, smoking, and trying cocaine. But those problems didn't seem life threatening, and what could a parent do? Irene figured that kids will be kids and in Arleta, kids were a little tougher than in other places. At least she and Missy had a closer relationship than most mothers and daughters.

Laura and Missy were at the park one afternoon when Vic showed up with a few friends. Missy was busy talking to one of them when she noticed Laura and Vic holding hands.

Later when they were alone in Laura's car, Missy asked Laura about Vic. "So, you and Vic are hitting it off pretty good, huh?" Missy grinned and she noticed Laura's cheeks growing red.

"I guess so. He's pretty nice." Laura turned to look at Missy. "You guys used to go together didn't you?"

Missy shook her head. "No, Vic and I have always been great friends, but we decided a long time ago never to get involved. I'd rather be his friend."

Missy was glad Vic had found Laura. She had been

spending less time with him lately because a good-looking Irish boy from Poly High had been calling on her. Handsome Bobby Miller had his share of girls chasing after him, but the only girl he wanted was Missy Avila.

When school let out in June, Laura Doyle and Vic became a serious item and the two spent nearly all their time together. Missy was dating Bobby, but sometimes Vic would call her late at night to complain about his relationship with Laura Doyle.

"She's too possessive!" he told her late one night.

"Don't worry about it, Vic," Missy assured him, whispering so nobody would wake up. "She'll settle down eventually. She doesn't have any reason not to trust you."

But Vic knew that if they'd been older and the timing were right, he would be spending less time with Laura and more with Missy.

Laura was just someone to date. Missy was the kind of girl who had something special about her, the kind of girl Vic knew he could marry. Sure, she was feisty sometimes and she had a lot of guys chasing her. But he loved her. He never felt anything close to love for Laura. Vic didn't mention these feelings to Missy now. It wasn't the right time.

Had Missy known, she would have been shocked at the reasons for Laura's insecurity. Laura hated Missy for being the center of Victor Amaya's attention. Laura wanted Vic to stay with her forever, but there was no denying the look in his eyes when he spoke to Missy, and Laura was incensed that Missy seemed to enjoy it, seemingly savored the thought that Victor really wanted her, not Laura.

That summer Karen rented an apartment in Panorama City, where she and Jimmy lived together. Missy rarely talked to Jimmy anymore because she didn't want to jeopardize his relationship with Karen. But there was tension in the girls' friendship, and one day Missy talked it over with Karen.

Karen was empathetic, hugging Missy and assuring her that she would never let a boyfriend come between them. She told Missy that she trusted her and that she knew Jimmy was totally faithful to her. The conversation lifted Missy's spirits, and although she continued spending less time with Karen than before, she knew their friendship was strong.

Later that summer, with Karen and Laura busy with their boyfriends, Missy spent her days with Christy Crawford. Christy had returned to Arleta as soon as school let out, and she and Missy had been inseparable. Christy was so much nicer than the girls from continuation school, and everyone remarked at how happy Missy seemed. The tensions in her other friendships didn't matter when she was with Christy. Missy was also seeing a lot of Bobby Miller, but not seriously. They spent time together and whenever he took her out she felt like a princess, but there were other boys that summer too. Missy didn't feel ready to settle into any kind of commitment.

As Christy would say later, "That summer we were enjoying the end of our childhood. We knew we had to grow up soon, that being an adult was right around the corner. But that summer we were still kids."

Christy was there when she and Missy first tried a few lines of cocaine. The drug became part of the credo that summer that time would never run out, that the girls had forever to grow up and face reality.

Eventually, like all seemingly endless periods of ad-

olescence, summer ended and Christy returned to
Long Beach. She had been gone for two days when
Karen called one afternoon and asked Missy to come
over to her apartment for the day. Missy had only
visited Karen there a few times because Jimmy made
her feel uncomfortable.

Missy thought it over while Karen waited on the
other end of the line. She still remembered the Fourth
of July when they were all at Stonehurst Park and
Jimmy had thrown a handful of fireworks at her face.
Missy had brushed them away before they could catch
her hair on fire, but Karen had laughed at her. Missy
remembered how badly it had hurt. Not the fireworks.
But seeing Karen laugh at her. It was the first time
Missy had felt betrayed by Karen Severson. Missy
would never have believed Karen had put Jimmy up
to it. After all, Karen had apologized for Jimmy the
next day. Missy nodded, instantly forgiving them both,
but still she was hurt by the memory of Karen's laughter.

Missy considered that incident when Karen called,
but she sounded lonely and Missy didn't have anything
else to do. She decided it was time to make up and she
agreed to meet Karen at the apartment at 2:30 that
afternoon.

At first everything went smoothly.

The three sat around the cramped living room
watching two-year-old Andrea play with her toys.
Then, an hour into the visit, Karen's bedroom phone
rang and she left the room. Missy stood up and
stretched, bending over to play with Andrea. Suddenly she felt someone grab her from behind. Before
she had time to catch her balance, Missy fell backward

onto Jimmy's lap. Jimmy laughed as Missy struggled to get back on her feet.

"Missy, you know how I feel, don't you?" Jimmy whispered in her ear, running his hand along her side. "You know I never stopped loving you. Karen doesn't mean anything to me."

Missy's first reaction was to raise her hand and slap Jimmy across the face, but before she could move Karen walked back into the room.

For a few timeless seconds Karen stood frozen in the doorway, her eyes glued on Jimmy and Missy. When she finally spoke, Missy almost didn't recognize her.

"Missy, you slut!" Karen shrieked. "Get off Jimmy's lap right now before I kick your ass."

Quickly Missy scrambled to her feet, but before she could explain, Karen grabbed her arm and pushed her toward the door.

"Get out of my house. I don't ever want to see you back here again," she screamed. "Isn't it enough that you have half the guys at school in bed with you? Jimmy is mine!"

By the time Missy had grabbed her keys and left the apartment, both Karen and Missy were crying. Karen wasn't finished yet.

She turned and glared at Jimmy while Andrea sat huddled in the corner, afraid to move. "I'm leaving. I'm taking Andrea and we're going to the store. But when I get back I want you out of here. I've had it. I knew I couldn't trust you." Karen moved closer to Jimmy and slapped him hard, leaving a red welt on his cheek. "Just take your things and get the hell out of my life."

Karen stormed across the room, grabbed Andrea and her purse, and left Jimmy sitting in the chair, stunned.

Her last shred of control over her jealous feelings was snuffed out. Missy had done it again. Just when Karen had found a boyfriend, Missy had to go and ruin it.

"That's it, Missy. I've had it," Karen hissed as she put Andrea's seat belt on and climbed into the front seat. "I really thought you'd learned your lesson."

Before this scene erupted, Karen had been disgusted by the number of guys who ogled Missy Avila, but as long as she had Jimmy's attention she didn't really care. Jimmy had made Karen feel good about herself for the first time since she'd become friends with Missy. Sometimes Jimmy even made Karen forget her looks and her weight problem.

But as Karen screeched out of the parking lot she knew that everything had changed. Karen glanced in her rearview mirror and watched the apartment building get smaller.

The wheels in Karen's mind began turning until finally she could see the answer to her problem. It was obvious. As the plan took shape, Karen knew it would have to be better than any plan in the past. This time she would stop Missy's interference once and for all. She couldn't wait to set the plan in motion.

Back at the apartment Jimmy was still reeling from Karen's outburst. For nearly twenty minutes he sat in the living room, trying to make sense of it. Slowly, he made his way to the bedroom and began tossing his things into a bag. It was over.

He felt sorry for Missy, because he knew Karen

would make her pay for the way he'd flirted with her. But as he picked up his bag of clothing and locked the door behind him, he cared for only one thing: He was free.

11

ONE WEEK AFTER the incident at Karen's apartment, Missy was home cleaning her room when the phone rang. She ran to the kitchen and answered it on the second ring.

"Hello?" Missy sat down at the kitchen table, brushing her hair back from her face. Several seconds passed before the caller spoke.

"Missy. It's Karen." Missy felt her heart beat faster. This had been the longest time the girls had gone without talking to each other, and Missy had worried that their friendship would never be the same.

"Hi." Missy's voice was hesitant.

Karen began to speak, and Missy could tell from the beginning that everything was okay. "Missy, I'm so sorry. I didn't mean the things I said to you and, well, I kicked Jimmy out of my apartment." Karen paused and began doodling on a sheet of paper near her phone. "I don't want him to come between us. You know I could never be your enemy. You're my best friend in the whole world. Can you forgive me?"

Missy smiled and felt a burden lift from her heart. Karen hadn't meant her nasty words after all, and now they could be best friends again.

Irene walked in as Missy answered.

"It's no big deal, Karen. I wasn't really upset. I know how you felt about Jimmy, but I think you'll be happier now that he's gone." There was silence on Missy's end as Karen responded. Then Missy continued. "I know. Want to get together and do something later on?"

"Sure. I'll come over after I get Andrea something to eat. See you in a while."

Later that day, Karen came to the Avila house. Irene was told that the girls were going to meet some friends at Stonehurst Park.

What Irene didn't learn until later was that they were really going to Wicky-up, a place East Valley teenagers often went to snort a little cocaine in peace without the risk of cops interrupting their fun. Some of the boys Missy knew at Mission High had become small-scale cocaine distributors. Most of the time Missy and her friends got the drug at such a discount that it wasn't any more expensive than a night at the movies. Missy felt at peace there and sometimes she would talk about living in such an area, near a stream and with mountains around, when she got married and settled down.

When Missy came home that night, she flopped onto her mother's bed.

"Karen and I aren't fighting anymore," she announced. They talked for a few minutes, then Missy sprang up from the bed. "Well, good night, Mom. I need my beauty sleep, you know." If Missy was a little too lively for such a late hour, this detail, like so many other warning signs that often mark the road to tragedy, went unnoticed.

It had been a wonderful afternoon for Missy. The group had hiked around Wicky-up and then Karen had found the big walnut tree near the stream. Sometime last semester Karen and Missy had been up there and Karen had used her pocketknife to carve the words *Karen and Missy, friends forever* right above where Jimmy had carved *Jimmy and Karen 1985*.

That afternoon, while they were sharing a few beers, she had pointed to the words and told Missy that she still meant them. Friends forever. When Missy finally fell asleep, her mind was filled with thoughts of Karen and the fun times they had shared over the years.

School started in September, and less than a week later Laura and Vic broke up. Missy felt sorry for both of them, but she knew Vic had been unhappy for some time.

Nearly a week after the breakup Laura still hadn't returned to school, and Missy wondered if she was planning on dropping out for good. Missy went over to Vic's house that evening to see how he was doing.

For more than an hour Missy and Vic stood outside his house talking. Vic told her that he had broken up with Laura because she hadn't trusted him. Once she had even bribed a friend of hers to call Vic and flirt with him. It was a test to see if Vic would be faithful and it had infuriated him.

"The worst part of all was she kept accusing me of being in love with you." Vic looked down at Missy. "I told her we were just friends, but she never liked it." Vic paused. "I didn't want to tell you before because I thought it would hurt your feelings."

Vic watched as Missy's eyes filled with tears.

"I don't get it, Vic. Why does this keep happening to me? They're two of my best friends, but secretly they worry that I'm going to steal their boyfriends. Is it me, Vic? Do I do something wrong?"

Vic pulled Missy close to him and hugged her tight, gently rocking her until she stopped crying. Slowly she looked up and smiled. Vic was always so nice to her. He bent down and kissed her on the cheek and she hugged him again. This time when he leaned toward her, there was something more in his kiss, something they hadn't shared since before Laura Doyle had entered the picture.

Suddenly a car horn broke the silence of the evening and Vic looked up. Parked twenty feet away in front of his house was Laura. He wondered how long she had been there, how much she had seen.

"Vic, go talk to her," Missy whispered, quickly pulling away from him. "I don't want her to think there was anything between us."

Vic sauntered toward Laura's car. She was really beginning to irritate him. First she hadn't been able to leave him alone while they were dating, and now, even after they'd broken up, she was still coming around. *Nice timing, Laura,* he thought.

Laura rolled down her car window as Vic walked up.

"What's that bitch doing here?" she snarled, and Vic could feel his anger rising.

"What's it to you? You don't own me anymore. I can be friends with whoever I want. Or did you forget?"

Laura was silent for several seconds. When she spoke, Vic was thankful Missy couldn't hear her.

"I'm going to kill that bitch," she said, her words measured and deliberate. Laura turned the key in her engine and squealed down the street.

Vic was disgusted with her. What an awful thing to

say about a friend. Laura's words rang out again and again in his mind. "I'm going to kill that bitch."

In the years to come Vic would blame himself for not having taken Laura's threat more seriously. But people say a lot of things they don't mean, and there was no reason to think Laura was serious. She was jealous—everybody felt so at one time or another. Vic walked back to Missy.

"What's wrong? She wasn't mad at me, was she?" Missy looked anxious as she spoke, and Vic knew he couldn't tell her the truth. Missy was too sensitive, her friends mattered too much to her.

"No. She was mad at me. I told her I didn't want her hanging around because it was all over between us, and she peeled off."

Missy looked uncertain.

"Hey, Missy. Don't worry. She wasn't mad at you, I promise."

The next week Missy was still uneasy, but she forgot about the incident when she heard the news.

Karen Severson was pregnant again, this time by Jimmy. Everyone at school knew, and Missy wondered if that was why Karen had been absent the last few days. Missy had been so busy worrying about the silent treatment she was receiving from Laura that she hadn't talked to Karen since last week.

Missy raced home after school, burst in the door, and found Irene in the kitchen.

"Mom, you won't believe this, but Karen is pregnant. It's Jimmy's baby. Oh, Mom, what will she do now? She can't even handle one child, let alone two. And she and Jimmy haven't talked to each other in weeks."

Irene sat down to talk to Missy, but the news was no

surprise. That afternoon Karen had been by with another of their friends, Cindy Silverio. Cindy hadn't done much talking, but Karen had been full of accusations.

"Listen, Irene. I want you to keep Missy away from Jimmy. I know she's been seeing him on the side, and now I found out I'm pregnant." Karen had always referred to Irene by her first name, but now she sounded very disrespectful. "This is how it is, Irene. I'm going to have Jimmy's baby and we're going to get married and spend the rest of our lives together."

Irene hadn't known what to make of Karen's speech, so through most of it she remained silent.

"Irene, I want you to know that Missy is sleeping around with too many guys. She sleeps with Jimmy, she sleeps with Victor, and she slept with this guy named John. I really think she ought to have herself checked for some disease."

At that point Irene interrupted her.

"Listen, Karen. I don't know anything about what you're saying, but I will tell you this. If you have something to say to Missy, say it to her face. Don't come to me while Missy is at school and can't defend herself."

"Now, Irene, it's not that I'm mad at Missy, it's just that I want you to tell her this for her own good. She needs to know that she's hurting a lot of people by sleeping around like that. One of these days someone's going to get so mad at her that they're not going to take it. I'm just trying to look out for Missy."

The girls had finally driven away, and for the next two hours Irene wondered how Karen had come to mistrust Missy so. After all, Missy wasn't sleeping with those boys, at least not now.

Later, Irene would regret sparing Missy the details

of Karen's visit that afternoon. At the time she felt that revealing the truth about her best friend's feelings would have devastated Missy. But the information might have saved her life.

Karen and Missy grew more distant in the final weeks of September, after Karen announced that she was pregnant, but it was obvious Karen never told Missy the things she had told Irene that afternoon. Otherwise, Missy never would have been so happy when she left with Laura for Stonehurst Park on October 1.

By then, Missy had forgotten the incident in front of Vic's house. No one would have thought Laura Doyle angry at Missy. Christy Crawford had gone with Missy to Laura's house only a few days earlier and the three had sat around for hours talking about boys, parents, and the summer. Later Christy would remember that Laura seemed nicer to Missy than ever before, listening carefully to her and telling her how nice she looked in her new jeans. Certainly Missy didn't think Laura was upset with her. When Irene asked her about it once, remembering that only weeks earlier Laura hadn't been speaking to her, Missy looked surprised.

"Of course not, Mom! Laura just needs some time to get over Vic."

Any doubts Irene had about Missy's answer were erased when Laura dashed into the house that October day.

The girls laughed and giggled as they got into Laura's car. Both looked exactly how teenage girls should look, happy and lighthearted, without a care in the world.

12

THE PLAN WAS SET.

Everything was perfect.

The timing, the location. Even the weather had co-operated.

At first people would be shocked. But Missy would never tell them what had really happened. In time they would forget.

It was a brilliant plan. Brilliant and necessary.

She had lied and cheated and enjoyed every minute. Now she would pay.

It was too bad this problem couldn't have been solved in an easier fashion, years ago when she started taking all the attention. It was bad enough to be adopted, an only child with no brothers and sisters, but with Missy around, life had become unbearable. Too bad it had come to this.

But it was too late now. Too late to change the facts and mend the ties that had been broken.

Never again would she get in the way. Never would she cast those twinkling eyes toward someone who belonged to another.

Any minute now the plan would be set in motion. Just like every other plan she'd ever orchestrated, it would run smoothly. But this one was even more perfect than the others had been.

Suddenly the clock struck three. It was time.

"Come on, let's get out of here," she yelled down the hallway. "We're meeting them at three-fifteen."

Excitement filled the air like electricity.

13

A KNOT FORMED in Catherine Scott's stomach as she and Emerson drove down the winding hill from Camp Colby. She was a seasoned veteran, a homicide detective who was used to handling these cases, and she was used to being the bearer of bad news.

But this case was different.

She couldn't get the girl's face out of her mind. The girl had been seventeen, almost eighteen, according to her school identification. Her whole life had been lying ahead of her and now she would never experience it.

Emerson had been equally disgusted by the murder scene. The girl's body pinned helplessly under the log. The cut hair. It looked like a deliberate execution.

Catherine spoke out loud as she drove. "Why would someone want to kill her? You saw her. She couldn't have weighed more than ninety-five pounds. What hideous reason would someone have for killing her? And why would they cut her hair?"

The detective drew in a deep breath, and when she continued, her voice wasn't much more than a whisper. "I can't imagine the fear, the terror, that girl must have gone through before they killed her. She must have known what they were doing when they cut her hair. And she was completely defenseless."

They pulled into the station and Catherine waited in the car while Emerson went inside. In a few minutes Dan Jenkins joined her. Dan wasn't Catherine's usual partner, but his own was on vacation and hers was out with back surgery. So this was the second murder they had worked together and they were getting used to each other's style. Catherine filled him in on the details of the murder scene while they drove to the Avila house.

It was growing dark as Catherine turned onto Ottoman Street. She began scanning the curb numbers for the address on Michele Avila's school ID. Then she saw it—a simple, single-story family house. Nice lawn. Nice bushes. Palm trees out front. Nice place to grow up.

There was a car in the driveway, and Catherine noticed the house lights were on. The family was home. Except Michele, of course. Michele would never be home again. Catherine wondered if this was the house where the girl had grown up.

Without saying a word the detectives got out of their car and headed up the walkway toward the house.

Inside, Ernie junior, Mark, and Chris sat at the kitchen table talking in hushed tones. Their mother had finally fallen asleep an hour earlier, and the boys wanted her to get some rest. The past three days had been a hellish nightmare for all of them.

They had called friends, teachers, and neighbors. They had called boys Missy hadn't seen in years and they had called the police, which had become an obsession for Irene. The day before, her doctor had prescribed sedatives. Finally, when she couldn't bring herself to make another phone call, Mark had taken over.

By now Mark was sure of one thing: Something had happened to his sister. She hadn't disappeared on her own. He knew Missy better than the others, and he was certain she would have called by now.

He wondered when the nightmare would end. He hoped with all his heart that when it did, Missy would be alive. The doorbell rang as the boys were discussing their next move.

From where she lay on the sofa, Irene heard the sound. Suddenly she realized what it was. A doorbell! Missy was home. She had finally come home. Who else would be here at this late hour?

At the same split second Mark realized two things.

First, the caller was not bringing good news. When the doorbell rang, he had looked outside and seen the unmarked patrol car. But Mark also realized that his mother was still half asleep and in her confusion believed Missy was at the door. He could tell by the excitement in her eyes, her anticipation as she reached for the door.

He stood back and waited.

At first Irene didn't understand what it meant to have two officers standing on her porch.

"You're here about my daughter, right? Did you find her? Is she okay? When can I see her?"

Catherine Scott stepped inside the house and asked Irene to sit down. One of them motioned for the boys to join them in the living room, and they quickly filed in and found places to sit.

Irene was impatient, and she grabbed Catherine's

arm. "What is it? Where is she? I need to know where she is. Something's happened to my baby!"

Detective Scott raised her hand and Irene allowed her to speak. "I'm Catherine Scott, detective with the sheriff's department. I presume you are Mrs. Avila, Michele's mother?"

Irene nodded.

"Are these other relatives?" Catherine pointed toward the three boys.

"Yes, they're my sons. What can you tell us about Missy?"

Catherine leaned forward. "Mrs. Avila, I'm afraid I have some bad news for you."

Bad news. The words slammed around in Irene's head and black dots began to appear. They filled her vision, dancing about and making it difficult to see.

Irene grabbed the arm of the sofa and steadied herself. She shook her head and tried to clear her mind so she could listen to the detective. She closed her eyes hard, and when she opened them she nodded.

Catherine swallowed before continuing.

"Missy is dead, Mrs. Avila. I'm sorry. She was drowned in a forest stream. A couple of hikers found her body earlier this afternoon. We don't know who did it yet, but . . ."

Irene didn't hear the rest. Her head was spinning. Missy was gone. She was dead and she would never come home again. What had the detective said? She had drowned. Missy had drowned. Missy, who was afraid of the ocean, had died in a forest stream. Irene felt herself losing consciousness. She wanted to talk to them and tell them it was all a mistake, but no sounds were coming from her mouth and no one was listening to her. Suddenly she didn't understand why everyone was standing around staring at her. Then, in an instant, the black dots filled her vision. It was over.

As she fell to the couch, Irene told herself that everything the tall woman in their living room was saying was part of a terrible dream.

Catherine moved quickly to the phone and called the paramedics. The dispatcher took the report from Catherine and in the background he could hear screams. Anguished screams, soul-wrenching screams. They were male voices. He could hear one of them sobbing and suddenly he understood why they needed paramedics.

Someone had died.

14

IRENE TOOK A slow shower. She had to look nice today, had to make Missy proud.

It was time to say good-bye.

She knew what she would wear: the black dress Missy had admired. It had been expensive when she and Missy had picked it out three years ago.

"Get it, Mom!" Missy had encouraged. "Come on. You deserve it. Only the best for my mother."

Irene had no choice but to wear the dress today. Only the best.

It was time for Missy's funeral.

In some corner of Irene's mind life still functioned as usual. She still remembered how to shower and dress herself and do her hair. She had even remembered to eat breakfast.

She was running on automatic.

Anyone could see it by looking into her eyes. Ever since receiving the news about Missy, Irene seemed gone. She was a machine, going through the motions.

And now to her daughter's funeral.

Irene turned off the shower and stepped out of the tub. She wrapped a towel around herself and moved slowly into her bedroom. She felt the fog envelop her mind and, standing there dripping wet, tried to re-

member what she was doing, where she was going.
Everything was blurry and she wondered if she was
going to faint again.

Then she saw Missy's picture, hanging over the bed.
And suddenly she remembered. Missy's funeral was
about to begin. It was time to say good-bye. Irene
could no longer move. She was frozen, paralyzed by
the pain.

Tears came like a flood, bursting the gates that had
contained them. Sobbing, Irene let herself fall slowly
onto the bed. It was all over.

Missy was gone. Her little girl, precious Missy, gone
forever. Sobs were choking her now, and mechanically she stood and slipped into her bathrobe. Then all
at once her knees gave out and she fell to the floor. She
couldn't move. All she could do, all she would ever do
for the rest of her life, was ache for Missy. Irene
screamed and her weeping grew stronger.

From out in the living room the guests could hear it
now. Irene's sobs filled the house, and one by one her
sons began to cry too. The truth was sinking in. Missy
was dead. Someone had killed Missy.

The visitors and relatives stood around the Avila
living room, looking uncomfortable. There was nothing anyone could do for Irene now, nothing anyone
could say that would bring Missy back.

There was someone else in the Avila living room
that day. An evil person whose evil none of Missy's
grieving family members could see. But she was there,
large as life, and she knew everything that had happened to Missy that afternoon in the mountains. Yet
even that knowledge wasn't enough, because now she
wanted to be part of the aftermath, as if she thrived on

seeing them all suffer. Maybe it gave her a sickening reassurance that finally the shadow was gone.

And as they sat around—Missy's brothers and relatives and the evil one in their midst—someone began walking back toward Irene's bedroom. Mark looked up, and when he saw who it was he smiled.

Karen Severson.

Mark thought that if anyone could comfort Irene, it was Karen. After all, she had been Missy's best friend since they were eight years old. They had spent so much time together, it was impossible to look at Karen without seeing Missy. Missy playing dolls with Karen, Missy walking hand in hand with Karen, Missy jumping rope with Karen, Missy at the park with Karen.

Karen reached Irene's bedroom and knocked. There was no answer, but Karen could still hear Irene crying. She opened the door and went inside.

Irene had crawled back onto her bed. She looked up as Karen approached. For a moment Irene wanted to ask Karen where Missy was. Then she remembered. Missy was dead.

"Irene, I'm so sorry about Missy." Karen sat down and put an arm around her best friend's mother. "It's so unfair that something like this would happen to her."

Irene nodded and reached for a tissue as Karen looked around the room.

"I know how much it hurts," Karen continued. "I feel the same way. Whoever killed Missy killed a part of me too. She was my sister, my best friend."

Karen paused, and the mask transformed into tears.

"And I promise you, Irene, I will do whatever I can to help catch the animal who did this terrible thing to Missy."

Irene smiled through her tears, her eyes nearly swollen shut. "Thank you, Karen."

Irene's heart went out to Karen, who was sobbing now as she dropped her head into her hands. It felt nice to have Karen here, now that Missy was gone.

When Karen spoke again, her voice was soft and she wasn't crying anymore. "I want you to know that I will always be here for you."

Karen looked up at Missy's picture on the wall. "Now that Missy is gone, I will be your daughter. You will always have me, Irene. I might not be Missy, but I will never, ever leave. I mean it."

Karen reached out and took Irene's hand. "Now come on, get yourself ready. We're all in this together. I know today isn't going to be easy, but I'll be there for you. You can count on me."

Karen hugged Irene and then left the room.

Inside her room Irene stood up and stretched. She felt a little better. Karen was right, everyone wished this day had never come, but she had to get ready, had to be there to say good-bye to Missy.

Fifteen minutes later Irene was dressed, and aside from her swollen eyes she looked beautiful in the black dress. Irene looked up again at Missy's picture.

"What do you think, sweetheart?" she asked aloud. She felt the tears begin again as she turned to leave the room.

They were almost out the door when Irene suddenly remembered the song.

"Lady Starlight."

A chill ran down Irene's spine as she thought back to that day more than a year ago when Missy had played the song for Irene.

"Mom, if I die, I want that song played at my funeral."

Irene remembered her words so clearly now.

She turned and ran down the hall to Missy's room. The tape was right near her bed. Irene held it tightly for a minute, lifting it to her face. It was just a piece of plastic, but somehow it smelled like Missy. Irene tucked it into her purse and joined the others out in the car.

The service was held at the Catholic church in Arleta and was attended by more than a hundred students from Poly High and Mission continuation school.

Irene surveyed the group through dark glasses. Missy would have been pleased. The friends she had loved so much, even those she wasn't close to, had all shown up. Christy and Laura Doyle and of course, Karen. They had come to say good-bye to one of their best. Irene noticed that many of the girls and some of the boys were crying softly. Others sat alone, staring at the white closed casket near the front of the church.

Missy's brothers were pallbearers, and Irene looked them over now as she waited for the service to begin. They were so handsome, especially Mark. Shiny dark hair, perfectly etched features, and clear tan skin. Missy had always looked more like Mark than any of her other brothers.

Suddenly, music filled the church and Irene recognized the song. She had given Missy's tape to one of the boys, who had given it to the priest. This was it.

Irene closed her eyes and stared down at her lap.

Oh, Missy. . . . My precious, precious daughter. . . . Why did you have to go when I need you so badly? . . . Did you struggle? Did it hurt? . . .

Sweetheart, I'm so sorry, so sorry I wasn't there to help you.

The music played on. "You're up in the stars now, but we'll meet again."

Irene prayed it was true.

Someday, little girl, someday. When this life is finished and the pain is gone forever. Good-bye, Missy. A day won't go by when I don't ache for you, when I don't remember the little girl who slept in my arms and lay in a hospital bed poisoned by cleanser. Oh, God, why didn't you take her from me then? It would have been easier than this. No. It would have been worse. At least I had seventeen years with you, Missy. Seventeen years. Someday we'll meet again. I promise you, Missy. Someday.

Irene was lost in her own world through most of the brief service. It was over in thirty minutes, and when Irene looked up, people were starting to move. But the fog was settling over her again. Irene saw her boys carrying the coffin. People were talking to her, telling her to get up and go to the car, but she couldn't move, couldn't talk. Her eyes were focused on the coffin.

Wait. Where are you taking her? Doesn't anybody hear me? Stop! That's my daughter in there and you can't take her, you can't have her. . . . Why can't I speak?

Suddenly she found her voice and Irene screamed her daughter's name.

A few people turned and looked, but most realized what was happening. This was a mother come to say good-bye to her only daughter. She was entitled to an outburst, allowed to break down. Irene went limp as two people helped her to her feet. The casket was gone, now. It was over.

Slowly, Irene and the others made their way to the waiting limousines. They were off to the cemetery, off to bury Missy.

The doors closed and suddenly Irene felt her skin begin to tingle. Within seconds dots appeared again before her eyes and she couldn't hear what people were saying.

I'm going to faint. I'm going to faint and I'm not going to be there when they bury Missy. Wait! They can't bury Missy. She won't be able to see the sunshine and it might get cold down there. Someone needs to know. This is all wrong. Missy doesn't belong in the ground. . . . She belongs here, in my arms. Beside me. Missy . . .

"She passed out," someone shouted to the driver. He quickly turned the car out of the procession toward the nearest hospital.

Hours later Irene awoke in a hospital bed. At first she was confused, unsure of where she was. Then the realization hit her. Missy was dead. There had been a funeral and then they were going to bury her. That was all she remembered. She looked at the clock on the wall. Five P.M.

Her only daughter was gone forever.

15

THE CAR FLEW down the mountainside, nearly careening over the canyon edge as it approached the main highway.

It was almost dark now, and the driver was delirious, ranting and shouting about what they had done. The passenger held on. Afraid to speak. Afraid to move.

It was over.

She was dead and now it was just a matter of getting off the mountain and away from the scene.

The car picked up speed and then suddenly the driver hit the brakes.

"Wait, maybe she's not dead!" The driver turned suddenly and stared at the passenger. "We should go back."

But the passenger said no.

"Not now. It's too dark, too late. We have to get out of here."

They were back on the road and the car went faster.

It occurred to the passenger that they might crash. They might never make it down the hill and then everyone would know what had happened. They would find the wet shoes in the trunk and they would figure everything out.

The passenger shuddered.

What had they done to her?

The driver started talking again, but the words didn't make sense.

Then came the laughter. The driver was laughing and the passenger looked out the window.

This has been crazy. I never should have agreed to go. Something could have been done, someone could have stopped them. I could have stopped them. And now, what if no one ever finds out who did it? I know who did it. I can't live with the knowledge, can't take it.

The driver started laughing again, and sometimes when the driver turned toward the passenger it was easy to see the hatred.

The car screeched around a turn and the passenger grabbed on to the armrest.

Just let us get down this mountain. Let me forget I ever took part in this. I could have saved her, could have made them stop. Could have done something. But now she's dead.

The passenger wondered if the incident could ever be forgotten.

"What's wrong with you, why are you so quiet?" The driver laughed louder this time. "She's dead. We did it. Oh, my God, we really did it."

The passenger didn't want to hear the laughter anymore. It wasn't funny. It wasn't time to laugh. Someone was dead. They had left her up there. And the passenger was certain they had killed her.

"You'd better never say anything about this," the driver said. "Say a word and we all go to jail. Got it?"

"I won't say anything. Never."

"Better not. I mean it."

The warning was unnecessary. The passenger knew

what would happen if anything was said. Look what had happened to the victim—they'd drowned her. These weren't people to mess around with.

The car was going faster now, and everything seemed to be rushing by in a blur.

Why did I go? I could have stayed home, could have told them to do this without me. I think I'm going to be sick. I'm so sorry. I could have helped her.

A chill ran down the passenger's spine.

They were almost to the bottom of the mountain now, and the driver was staring straight ahead, in a trance. A happy trance.

Suddenly the driver slammed on the brakes and pulled off to the side of the road.

The passenger heard the sound before the driver spoke.

Laughter. Evil, hateful laughter.

"She's dead."

Laughter.

"We killed her and she's dead."

More laughter.

"Finally she's dead. And we killed her."

As the driver slammed the gas pedal down and skidded back onto the road, the laughter grew louder.

16

DETECTIVES CATHERINE SCOTT and Dan Jenkins were assigned the task of solving the murder of Michele "Missy" Avila. It was Monday, October 7, 1985. Both detectives were worried.

In some ways it was an open-and-shut case. They had a body, they had details of the murder, and they had a witness—Laura Doyle.

Catherine sifted through some papers and pulled out the sheet containing Laura Doyle's interview. Catherine read it again. By now she had almost memorized it.

Laura had picked up Missy Avila at three o'clock the afternoon of October 1, 1985. The two had driven to Stonehurst Park, near where Missy had grown up. There, Missy saw three boys she knew. They were standing by a blue Chevrolet Camaro. Missy told Laura to pull over so she could talk to them, but Laura needed gasoline for her car. So she dropped Missy off to talk with the boys. Fifteen minutes later she returned from the gas station to the same location and everyone was gone. Laura figured Missy must have left with the boys, so she went home. At six o'clock that evening Laura called Irene Avila asking to speak to Missy, but Missy wasn't there.

That was all. Laura Doyle was the last person known to have seen Missy Avila alive. But there were the boys in the Camaro, and Catherine knew that when they apprehended the killers, Laura would be an important witness.

There was one problem, and Catherine knew it could make Missy's murder one of those that never get solved—a frequent occurrence in Los Angeles County, when the key witness failed to recall important details. A majority of murders were solved because someone remembered a detail, and Laura Doyle's details were vague.

The detectives had the make and color of the car, but they didn't have a plate number. They had no idea how old the car was and no real identifying traits about any of the three boys. They had grilled Laura Doyle over and over again, but she simply couldn't remember.

She didn't know which of the three boys was the driver, couldn't tell the difference between a 1985 Camaro and a 1975 Camaro, and she couldn't remember what color hair the boys had, let alone any special identifying traits.

Laura had been frustrated during the interview. She was upset with herself for not having paid more attention, but she hadn't thought she would have to remember such details. She had been planning to buy gasoline for her car and come right back.

Catherine sighed.

Missy's funeral had taken place earlier and Catherine received information that Irene Avila hadn't made it to the cemetery. Instead she had been taken to a hospital and treated for severe shock. Catherine could understand why.

The lab had developed the pictures taken at the crime scene, and Catherine looked through them now as she thought about the direction the investigation would take.

Such awful pictures. They showed the girl's arm, bent stiffly behind her back, and they showed her long dark hair floating in the stream. Her face and the rest of her upper body were covered by the log.

Catherine was certain the pictures would be effective in court. There weren't twelve common jurors anywhere who would have trouble seeing this was a murder. There were other pictures too—the ones taken when Missy's body had been pulled from the stream. Catherine hoped they wouldn't need them in court. No one should have to see pictures like those. Especially Missy's family and friends.

Catherine thought over the evidence. It looked like a simple prosecution. First-degree murder if the district attorney could prove Missy's killers had taken her to the stream with the intention of killing her.

Then the boys who had done this would be sent to prison for a very long time.

Catherine hoped they were older than eighteen. She couldn't stand the thought of these killers serving time in juvenile hall for such a hideous crime.

She took a deep breath. First things first.

The boys were still at large. The next step was finding them and making the arrest.

Catherine leaned back in her chair just as Detective Jenkins walked up. Jenkins was a very talented detective with a reputation for solving cases. He was one of the division's best, and Catherine was thankful to be working with him on the Avila murder.

"You have the list?" Catherine smiled and motioned for Dan to sit down.

He pulled up a chair and took three sheets of paper out of a folder. "This is it. Every Camaro registered in the state of California. There are hundreds of them."

Catherine figured as much. But they would whittle that list down quickly. After all, if Missy knew the driver he was probably from the area. They would start with the Camaro owners who lived in the San Fernando Valley.

There was still the matter of interviewing Missy's brothers and close friends. Maybe one of them knew the boys or recognized the description of the car. Then they could find them and lock them up in jail. The job could be that easy.

In any murder investigation there is a small detail, an aspect of the crime, that the detectives won't dare breathe a word about to anyone. It is the only way an investigator can weed out the real witnesses from the eccentric folks who read about a story in the newspaper and show up at the station with a fabrication and the desire to be a hero. The investigation into Missy's murder was no exception. Catherine Scott and Dan Jenkins had a hook, a surefire way to know if the person sitting across the table really knew what had happened.

It hadn't been difficult to agree on which detail to use, the only detail that told of the hatred Missy's killers felt toward her. It was the hair-cutting, of course. The detectives considered it ritualistic and torturous that before they murdered Missy her killers had cut her long, beautiful hair. For the next three years during the investigation the detectives mentioned it to no one—even when Irene Avila called the station one day

and asked Catherine straight out if it had been cut
before she was killed. Mark had seen his sister's body
at the morgue before the funeral and had told his
mother that Missy's hair appeared to have been cut
before she was killed. Catherine cleared her throat
and, telling a half truth, informed Irene how the coroner had probably cut off some of Missy's hair for analysis. A routine procedure.

But the whole truth, that Missy had been teased and
tortured, that her killers had cut off chunks of her hair
before her death, well, that was something she did not
tell Irene. The information was her bait, and it had to
be kept from everyone until that magic day when
someone would bring it up. The day every detective
dreams of.

Originally the detectives had kept two bits of information quiet. The hair-cutting and the information
about the log. They figured that whoever killed Missy
had placed the log on her back to keep her down.
After all, time is of the essence during a murder, and
whoever was responsible wanted to leave the crime
scene quickly. But the killers also wanted to make sure
Missy wasn't just pretending to be dead or maybe
semiconscious. So they had placed a log on her back,
just to be sure she wouldn't ever come up from that
mountain stream. From the beginning Catherine
knew one thing was certain about Missy's murder, that
once the log was placed over her back, she wasn't
getting up. Unfortunately, someone from the coroner's office leaked the information about the log to
someone in the Avila family and before too long it was
in the newspapers. So the detectives had to be extremely careful to keep the hair detail secret.

Catherine had a hunch about the hair-cutting,

something that never quite fit into the picture Laura Doyle had given them of Missy's disappearance. Catherine thought the hair-cutting meant a woman was somehow involved in Missy's murder. When men wanted to humiliate their female victims, they did something sexual. Men raped women or forced women to do things they didn't want to do before killing them. Of course, if a victim struggled, then the man might yank her hair, and at the crime scene an investigator might find a few strands that had been ripped out during the attack. But a man wouldn't harm a woman by cutting her hair, not in Catherine's experience, anyway. Nevertheless it was only a hunch, and in Missy's murder investigation there were plenty of hunches to go on.

The detectives also figured there had to be at least two people involved, because of the log. It easily weighed a hundred pounds, and it would have taken two people to lift it up and put it over Missy's body. But there could have been more than two people involved. Because of the hair-cutting Catherine thought that Missy might have been killed by a small group of people—probably the guys in the Camaro and one of their girlfriends.

Still, none of those guesses provided real clues about who had killed Missy Avila. And there was that business of needing a motive, which at this point was one aspect of the girl's death that was sorely missing.

Most likely, the girl had stolen something from the wrong people—maybe dope or a cocaine rock. Of course, in Catherine's mind there was never a good motive for murdering someone, but in Los Angeles people killed each other for all sorts of ridiculous reasons. This girl might even have been killed by a jealous

boyfriend; but then why would a girl have partici-
pated in the murder? Maybe it was done by a psycho-
path, someone who knew detective work well enough
to disguise his crime by the hair-cutting. There were a
hundred possibilities.

Whatever grudge her killers harbored, they hadn't
forced the girl into anything sexual before killing her.
Her autopsy had proven that much. She had been
tortured, chunks of her hair had been cut off, and she
had been forced into the stream against her will. She
had been held down in the water and when she
stopped struggling—whether she was unconscious or
already dead—she had been buried under a massive
log.

But she hadn't been raped.

Of course, it was possible the boys in the Camaro
hadn't killed her. They might have taken her somewhere and dropped her off or taken her to meet other
people who were responsible. But if that was the case,
why hadn't the boys come forward?

The newspapers had all run stories about the girl's
murder. By now all her friends knew what had happened. If Missy had known the boys, as Laura said,
then by now they would certainly know of her murder. If they hadn't killed her, they at least knew where
she had last been seen alive; but so far they hadn't
come forward.

The detectives were nearly certain that solving the
murder was as simple as finding the three boys in the
blue Camaro.

"I've gone through the list and highlighted the ones
registered in the Valley," Dan said.

Catherine smiled. "You're one step ahead of me."

"I have a few phone calls to make, and then let's

meet for about an hour and see what our next move is."

Catherine nodded. She had some work to finish up before she could tackle the Avila murder.

She still felt as strongly about this case as she had the day the girl's body was found. More than once since then she had opened the tiny piece of paper that held Missy's lock of hair and thought about the girl and her mother. What if she were in Irene Avila's place, totally dependent on the local sheriffs to solve the murder of her only daughter? She felt a great responsibility. And Catherine knew Dan felt as committed as she did. This was one mystery they wanted to solve. Soon.

The next three days passed quickly.

There were phone calls and vehicle checks and plenty of interviews. Finally, Catherine was back at her desk after talking to several people who had known Missy for most of her life.

Catherine looked over the list of those already interviewed. Laura Doyle, of course. Missy's brothers— Mark, Chris, and Ernie junior. And of course, Missy's mother.

As she thought about her next move, the phone on Catherine Scott's desk rang.

"Detective Scott."

"Hi, Catherine. This is Irene. I have something for you that might be interesting." Irene Avila sounded nervous and excited, and Catherine straightened up in her chair.

"Go ahead, what've you got?"

"Well, Karen Severson, you know, Missy's best friend, Karen, well she called me a few minutes ago and told me something kind of weird. She said her daughter, Andrea, had a dream last night that Missy came to her and told her that Christy Crawford killed her."

Catherine bunched up her eyebrows and shook her head. "Wait a minute. How old is Karen's daughter, Andrea?"

"She's almost three."

"And who's this Christy Crawford?"

"Christy and Missy have been friends for a long time, but I don't know, maybe they had a fight that week. I think it's worth checking on, don't you?"

Catherine chuckled under her breath. "Tell you what, Irene, I'll make a call and get Karen in here and let her tell me about it."

Later that day Karen Severson drove down to the Van Nuys police station, where the detectives were conducting interviews regarding Missy Avila's murder. As Karen began speaking she broke into tears. Later, Catherine would remember that she seemed to turn them on. Catherine had encountered strange things like this dream. That Karen's two-year-old daughter should have had a dream in which Missy told her who did the killing was an example of grief manifested. From what Irene had said, Christy Crawford and Karen Severson were never the best of friends, because Karen wanted Missy's friendship to herself. So maybe in her grief Karen had actually convinced herself that Christy killed Missy. Catherine made a note to talk to Christy Crawford. She offered Karen a box of tissues and thanked her for coming down to the station.

17

ONE WEEK AFTER Missy's murder an investigation of another kind began. It was less sophisticated than the one being staged by the Los Angeles County Sheriff's Department, but it was more intense, more emotional.

This was the investigation by Missy's friends and family. By then the sheriffs were putting in overtime to solve the case, but that didn't matter to these people. They had known Missy, loved her, and simply couldn't rest until they had followed up their own personal hunches.

Despite the efforts of Missy's family and friends and the hours being put in by two of the county's toughest homicide detectives, there wasn't anyone who had any idea how very close they were to the truth. They knew nothing of the degree of madness with which they were dealing on a daily basis. Who would have known? By this time most people with any knowledge of a murder would have slithered into the background, lying low until one day people no longer remembered it. But the venomous soul who knew more about Missy's death than anyone was still thirsty for more.

By placing herself in the center of the Avila family's

investigation, Karen Severson was completely in control. She knew what had happened to Missy and the others didn't. That being the case, she could always steer them in every direction but the one that would solve the murder. She was writing the entire story, in which she could play any part she wished. For now, she was the grieving friend, helping the others find clues.

The others—Irene and Missy's brothers—were so paralyzed with grief that they often sat around the Avila living room unsure of what to do next. During those times Karen would step in and make decisions for them. This wasn't unusual. After all, when there is a death in the family, well-meaning, clear-thinking friends often help out with basic needs, from making dinner to making decisions. It was easy for Karen Severson to think clearly in the days after Missy's death, because when grief is false, it does not interfere with living.

So Karen Severson became the Avilas' leader. She made decisions, dug up phony clues, directed them on mystical chases, and at the end of each day offered her shoulder to cry on.

Of course, Karen had always controlled people, but she had never been so bold. In fact, when Missy had been around, Karen almost always took a backseat, allowing her smaller friend to make the decisions about where they would go and what they would do. But even back then Karen was a different person when Missy wasn't around. It was that different person —controlling, dominating—who took charge after Missy's death.

So it never surprised the Avilas that Karen was leading the group, pushing them on to find more clues about who might have killed Missy. In those days of blind grief Karen had a way about her that was almost hypnotic, making everyone around her feel compelled to respond.

The week after Missy Avila was brutally murdered, Karen Severson moved in with the Avila family. It made sense to everyone at the Avila home. After all, since Missy's murder Karen and Andrea had spent most of their time with the Avilas, and one day Karen asked Irene if she could spend the night. That night had turned into the next, until finally Karen and Andrea were part of the family. A family driven to find Missy's killers.

If Karen was enjoying keeping the details of Missy's murder a secret, she would have been thrilled at moving in with Missy's family. It would have been like watching a cat writhe in pain after being hit by a car, giving a high like none other.

After Karen and Andrea moved in, their days became a ritual. Wake up, eat breakfast in silence, and get dressed. Looking back, Mark remembers thinking it a bit odd that Karen would sit in Missy's chair, sleep in Missy's bed, eat Missy's favorite foods, and occasionally wear one of Missy's oversized sweatshirts. In ways none of the family was noticing, Karen seemed to be trying to take Missy's place.

One night during that first week Karen walked into Missy's room and quietly opened her closet. She was able to smell the lingering fragrance of Missy's perfume and hair spray.

She sorted through the clothes in Missy's closet until she found what she was looking for: Missy's white sweatshirt. It had always been too big for Missy, and now Karen wanted it for herself. She slipped it over her head and tiptoed to the mirror. Even in the dark Karen could see enough of her reflection to be sure of one thing: The sweatshirt made her look just like Missy Avila.

Moving slowly, Karen made her way toward Missy's bed, pulled back the covers, and climbed under them just as she had done for the past several nights. Only this time Karen couldn't sleep. She tossed and turned, but she seemed to hear something. Finally she lay flat on her back and opened her eyes.

"Missy!" It was a quiet gasp, and Karen's eyes grew wide as she stared into the eyes of her dead friend, now floating over the bed. "Go away, Missy! Leave me alone."

As quickly as she had appeared, Missy's image vanished and Karen began shaking.

"I'm sorry, Missy, I'm sorry." Karen began to cry softly as she got up from the bed and smoothed the covers. "Please leave me alone."

Karen ran out to the living room, joining Andrea under the blankets on the floor. It was the last time she slept in Missy's bed.

During the next few weeks, nearly every evening, the family would gather in the living room and Karen would force them to think of leads. People upset with Missy. People with blue Camaros. Angry boys who had been turned down by Missy.

Each day the group became larger. At first it was just Karen, Missy's brothers, and Mark's fianceé, Shavaun. Sometimes Irene joined them. Soon Victor Amaya—Laura's ex-boyfriend—started coming, and Brian Taylor and Katy Vincent, who were good friends of Victor's and knew how much he'd loved Missy. Even though Brian and Katy hadn't been close to Missy, they were angry about her murder and were more than happy to help track down the perpetrators. Everyone but Karen had a noble reason for wanting to be involved.

No one thought it strange that Karen had taken up residence at the Avilas. Neither did anyone think it strange when Laura Doyle stopped coming around the house. They knew that she was busy working at the Vons Supermarket as a bakery clerk.

Two weeks after the murder this group—led by Karen Severson and excluding Laura Doyle—gathered in the Avila living room and made a plan.

Irene knew the kids were there. Karen had told her about the meeting earlier that day, but Irene was too tired to do anything more than lie in the back bedroom. She had spent many days since Missy's death in her room, waiting for sleep, waiting for the pain to go away. Sometimes Irene tried to reason with herself. Other people lost children. They hurt and cried, but at some point life went on. Irene didn't think she would ever reach that point. But the kids helped—Missy's brothers and Missy's friends. They were sincere, loving, so eager to help. Especially Karen Severson.

Ever since she had started staying with the Avilas, Irene had felt comforted by her presence. It was almost like having a part of Missy back. Irene saw how intensely Karen wanted to find Missy's murderers— she was willing to spend all her free time working on the case.

That particular night Irene was awake in her bedroom, tired but not sleepy. She didn't want to be out with the kids in the living room, so she sat up and reread some of the sympathy cards she'd received from Missy's friends. Each one talked about how dear

Missy had been and how badly she would be missed. There was one that especially moved Irene.

It was the card from Laura Doyle.

I know there's nothing anyone can say or do to make you feel better, Laura wrote. *But I'm going to try. I'm sorry she's gone. But she's not really gone, she's right here with all of us. Irene, if there's anything you need, please give me a call. I'm right here for you. You were Missy's mom and you were like mine too. I'm sorry it happened to Missy and not someone else who deserved it.*

All my love, Laura.

Tucked inside the card was a twenty-dollar bill. Laura had told Irene the money wasn't much, but maybe it could help in some small way. Everyone felt sorry for Laura Doyle, and maybe that was part of the reason no one expected her to come around after Missy's murder. After all, Laura was the last person seen with Missy. She was the one who had dropped Missy off to talk with the boys. She was the one who hadn't noticed a license-plate number.

Irene slipped back to sleep as Karen was talking to the others in the living room.

"I'm serious," Karen was saying. "Let's just go up there and see if they missed something. You never know. Maybe we'll find a clue. Something small, something they overlooked. It might make the difference."

Karen was in control, and the others were already nodding in agreement. Nobody thought to suggest that it was too late to drive up a winding mountain road to the spot where Missy had been killed; nobody thought to mention that it was too dark to find any clues. It also never occurred to them that the detectives had already made a thorough search of the area.

At that time Karen Severson had their attention.

"I say we go!" Karen continued. "This is the perfect time because no one else will be up there."

The group agreed and decided to take little Andrea with them. In the moments before they left, after several of them had already gone out to the cars, Karen disappeared into Missy's bedroom for a few minutes. At about the same time, the phone rang in Christy Crawford's house.

"Hello?"

"Is this Christy?"

"Yes, this is she. Who is this?" Christy sounded tired, like she'd been drinking. She had been devastated by Missy's death and she was still trying to accept the fact that her friend was gone forever. She waited for the caller to speak, but for a few seconds she could only hear muffled breathing.

"This is Missy," the caller finally said. Christy gasped.

"Everyone knows you did it, Christy. You can stop hiding. The police will be checking with you soon. And so will I."

Christy slammed down the receiver before the caller finished speaking. As she cried herself to sleep that night—after drinking more than seven beers—she couldn't imagine what horrible person would pretend to be Missy. The next morning, as her hangover began to wear off, Christy Crawford convinced herself it had all been a dream.

As Karen ran out to join the others, she was quietly laughing to herself. In the other room Irene, though she vaguely thought the kids shouldn't go out so late at night, made no move to stop them.

Five minutes later Karen, Andrea, Vic, Brian,

Shavaun, and Katy had gotten into two cars and were following each other through Arleta to Big Tujunga Road.

The members of the group were silent as they drove up the mountain road, each wondering what they might find. Mark had even brought his new gun, which he had purchased a few days after the funeral. After all, Missy's killers were still at large and Mark wanted to protect his mother and brothers should they show up at the Avila home.

Karen led the way and drove the dark mountain highway with skill. It was nearly 10:00 P.M. when they turned onto a dirt road and made their way across an old bridge that crossed the Big Tujunga Stream. As they drove, Mark noticed that Karen kept looking at him in the rearview mirror.

Karen paused for a moment on the bridge before driving on. "This is it," she said, waving a hand toward the stream. "This is where they killed her."

Everyone knew Missy had been killed in this stream. It was all over the newspapers. But many of the details had been kept out of the press. Certainly no one knew the exact spot where Missy's body had been found.

Karen drove off the bridge and parked her car in the center of a dirt parking lot. Katy Vincent followed closely behind. Quietly, they got out of the cars and huddled together.

Karen whispered the directions.

"Let's go down that path and head over to the stream. If there's anything to find, it will probably be along the shore."

The group split in two, Mark and a few others following the path and Karen, Andrea, and Katy taking a shortcut down to the stream.

They were nearing the water and Katy was beginning to feel sick. They shouldn't be here. It was too dark, and what if someone was lurking in the bushes? She became conscious of every snapped twig, every rustle of leaves. The wind was picking up, whistling through the trees. She reached for Andrea's hand and walked on.

Two feet from the water Andrea suddenly burst forward. "Missy, Missy!" she exclaimed. "Missy in water, she in water!"

Katy felt a chill run down her spine as she held the child back.

"No, Andrea. Missy is gone. She isn't here."

Andrea shook her head. "Missy in water, Missy go in water."

It took several minutes to quiet the child, and Karen walked on ahead. Katy held tight to Andrea's hand and began walking quickly to catch up with Karen.

To this day no one knows why little Andrea thought Missy was in the water, but it was odd enough that Katy mentioned it in court years later. The detectives do know that while Missy was being killed, the child was not up at the site, which means that when she was all alone with the child, Karen Severson must have told her the details of Missy's murder.

"Karen, where are you?" Katy whispered through the darkness. Then she heard their voices. Karen had met up with the others; they were just ahead, near an opening along the shore.

Katy could hear Karen talking as she walked up.

"I say we get out of here," she said. "It's too dark and

I've got the creeps. Let's come back in the morning when we can see what's here."

Everyone agreed, and one by one they began walking back up the trail toward the parking lot. Karen was the last to leave, and when Katy looked back to see if she was coming, she saw Karen stop and face the stream.

Several seconds passed and when Karen turned back around, she saw Katy watching her.

"I don't like it," Karen said as she caught up with Katy. "I've got such a bad feeling being here. It's like I know Missy died somewhere around here."

Katy nodded and picked up her pace. The others were already at the cars, and Katy Vincent was scared to death. She had a horrible feeling that whoever had killed Missy was standing just a few feet away, lurking in the bushes or hiding behind a tree, watching everything they did.

The next day the group went back to the stream in search of clues. This time Andrea was even more certain that Missy was in the water.

"Missy! Missy!" Andrea danced up and down, pointing to the water. "Missy in water, Mommy. Missy in water."

A wave of fear swept over Katy as Karen took her daughter's hand and looked into her eyes.

"No, Andrea," Karen laughed. "Silly girl. Missy is all gone, she isn't in the water anymore. No more Missy."

Then Karen and Andrea walked briskly along the shoreline. Katy didn't move. It was weird, spooky, how the child seemed to know where Missy had been killed. Katy tried not to think about it as she caught up with the group. By then Karen and Andrea were walking very slowly, looking along the shoreline in the shallow water and on the sand.

They were coming to a sandy clearing, and Karen slowed her pace. She looked toward the area and her eyes rested on a large boulder at the edge of the clearing. From there she looked out to the middle of the stream where a footpath of rocks crossed water that looked about seven or eight inches deep.

"Do you feel it?" Karen asked, turning to the others. "It's Missy. I know it. I can feel her here. She's trying to communicate with me."

Karen walked a few more steps and then moved next to the boulder. Suddenly she threw her arms around the rock and cried out. "Missy! Why did they kill you!"

The others watched her, their eyes wide, and Katy thought about running back to the cars. The situation was too frightening, too strange.

Karen turned to them, and when she spoke her voice was barely a whisper. "It happened here. Right here. Missy just told me. Our Missy was right here on this rock and then they took her out to the stream and drowned her."

Karen looked at the others, absorbing their fear and shock. *You're all so stupid,* she must have thought to herself, *just as stupid as Missy.*

Mark was the first to break the silence.

"Come on, let's look around and see what we can find," he said. Immediately the others began looking on the ground and near the shore.

It took Mark less than a minute to spot the tree.

Just a couple yards from the boulder the tree had dozens of names carved into it. Mark walked steadily toward it but he could see the words from several feet away. *Jimmy and Karen, 1985.* And then above that, *Karen and Missy, friends forever.*

Everyone saw it now. The words were yellowed from age, probably there for nearly a year. But then they could see new carvings. Fresh green slash marks had been carved across Jimmy's name and above it there were slash marks through *Karen and Missy, friends forever.*

Mark looked puzzled as he turned toward Karen. When he spoke, there was confusion in his voice.

"Karen?" Mark took a few steps toward her. "You've been up here before? Why didn't you tell us?"

Karen's face grew red as she looked first at the tree and then at Mark.

"Don't be crazy, Mark. Of course I've never been up here. Missy might have been here a long time ago. I think some of the people she hung around with last year used to party here. They called it Wicky-up."

Karen shook her head as she marched up the embankment toward the tree. "This is the first time I've ever been here. I never knew about this tree."

Karen looked at the carvings and the fresh slash marks etched into the tree. Her face filled with anger.

"Obviously, Jimmy has been up here," Karen said, the hatred in her voice mounting. "He must have carved our names in the tree a long time ago."

Karen looked at the stream again and suddenly she gasped. They were ready for the punch line.

"That's it! Jimmy must have been up here and crossed these names out." Excitedly, she turned to the others. "If Jimmy was up here to do that, he must have been the one who killed Missy. He must have!"

Karen was very excited now, and the others began to consider the possibility. Of course. Jimmy Mitchell had been in love with Missy since they were in junior high, and Missy never really gave him the time of day.

"Jimmy always hated Missy, always." Karen moved slowly over to the boulder and leaned on it. "He hated her because she was so pretty and because she never really liked him."

Karen buried her head in her hands for a few seconds, and when she looked up it was the first time Mark had seen such hatred in her eyes. "It was Jimmy. I just know it. Jimmy tricked her into coming up here and then he killed her." Karen paused and shook her head. "I can't believe it, but I just know he killed her."

Karen slammed her fist onto the boulder. "And now I'm going to see that he gets what's coming to him. He's going to pay for killing my best friend. I bet he killed her because he knew she was my best friend and he was mad at me."

The others had gathered closer, listening to Karen, believing her. They wanted her theory to be true. Then they would have the answer; they could stop looking. Jimmy Mitchell must have killed Missy. Why else would he have crossed out his name next to Karen's and then slashed out Karen and Missy's names?

Karen stared out at the stream and slowly turned her head toward the others. She was in a rage-filled trance when she finally spoke.

"Jimmy must die."

The group was silent during the ride home, shocked by the discovery that Jimmy Mitchell had killed Missy. Halfway home Karen popped a cassette tape into the car radio. Mark recognized the song immediately and felt tears well up in his eyes. "Lady Starlight" by the

Scorpions. Missy's favorite song. The song they had played at her funeral. Mark and Shavaun cried softly in the backseat while up front Karen sang along with the words.

18

IT WAS LIKE a nightmare, only all the details were real, and there was no sleep to go with it. There hadn't been sleep for days.

Her words kept flashing through the participant's mind. It was part of the nightmare.

"The worst thing you guys could do is leave me up here all alone. . . . The worst thing you guys could do is leave me up here all alone."

She had been terrified. She thought they were going to leave her up there by herself, but they didn't. They did worse. They killed her.

She had been afraid of being alone and now she was dead.

It's my fault, I went along, I should have warned her.

The picture grew larger and she wondered when the dreams would ever stop. There she was now, larger than life. Pleading. Begging. Screaming for help. But there was no one around, no one for miles.

She could see the girl's eyes now, frightened, desperately frightened.

"Help me! What's happening? Why are you guys so mad at me?"

And then she had started crying. The girl was crying

now and the dreamer couldn't blot out the image. The nightmare was insistent.

They were there, by the edge of the stream, and suddenly she had seen enough. Running back, far away, she heard a scream. It was her. She was screaming for help and then there was a gasping sound. Someone was holding her underwater and she was going to die. She ran faster, faster, to get away from the screaming.

I should have stayed. Should have helped her. They killed her. Are the nightmares haunting them too? Maybe I'm going crazy.

It was 3:00 A.M. Morning was an eternity away and the pictures were getting larger. There she was, crying and crying.

"Please help me. Why are you doing this, what did I do wrong? The worst thing you guys could do is leave me up here all alone. . . . The worst thing you guys could do is leave me up here all alone."

She began to cry.

I'm sorry. I'm so sorry. There is nothing I can do now. It's over. She's dead and it's over. Forget it or you're going to go crazy. You'll lose your mind and if you say anything they'll kill you too. You have to forget it.

But the nightmare continued. Her words were clear now, like she was standing nearby. Right by the bed.

"Please, please help me. The worst thing you guys could do is leave me up here all alone. . . . The worst thing you guys could do is leave me up here all alone. . . . Please, somebody help me."

19

JIMMY MITCHELL WAS at work when he got the call.

It was late October, and the mechanics were in the middle of the busy season. Something about the upcoming holidays and predictably cold, wet weather made people think about their cars.

Jimmy had been hired by the shop nearly a year before and now was one of the senior brake and front-end technicians on staff. It was a good job, and not one Jimmy took lightly. He hoped the phone call was important. The boss didn't look too kindly on his employees getting personal calls during working hours.

Jimmy picked up the phone and pressed the flashing red button. "Hello, Jimmy here."

For a moment there was silence on the other end. "Jimmy, hi. It's Karen."

It had been a week since Karen's last phone call, and Jimmy had hoped she would never call again. He remembered her accusatory words that day, and now he debated whether to hang up.

But Karen started talking before he could make up his mind.

"Jimmy, I'm sorry. You know how much I love you. I didn't mean the things I said, but it's really hard with

Missy gone. I want to find out who did it, and it just seemed like you were the one."

Jimmy said nothing. He thought back to their conversation the week before. That day he had been home working on his car when she had called.

"Jimmy we know what happened," she shouted, and Jimmy thought he heard someone listening in on an extension. "I'm at Missy's house and we're all here. We know you killed her. You killed Missy, didn't you?"

Jimmy had been shocked. Him? Kill Missy?

Jimmy figured Karen must be out of her mind. She knew how much he had cared for Missy. The only reason he had ever been mean to Missy was to make Karen less jealous. He didn't like having her mad at him all the time, so he had acted as though he didn't like Missy. But Karen knew how he really felt, which was partly why they had broken up.

"That isn't true, Karen!" Jimmy had shouted back. "You know I'd never want to hurt Missy. Why would you accuse me of killing her? You're the one who didn't like her."

Karen screamed louder. "You're a liar! You hated Missy. You've always hated Missy, haven't you? You killed her, and now we're going to get you. We're going to tell the police that you did it."

Jimmy had tried to respond, but Karen was relentless.

"Jimmy, better watch behind you. You never know what might happen to you now that we know."

Then she had hung up.

He thought of this phone call as she waited for an answer, now, at the other end of the line.

"How can I believe that you're sorry after all you

said?" Jimmy demanded. "What reason do you have for calling me now?"

Karen drew a deep breath. "Well," she began, "Christy Crawford is having a party tonight in Missy's honor. We're all going to be there, and Missy would have wanted you there. I want you to see that no one has hard feelings about you anymore."

Jimmy thought it over. It had been a hellish week because of the rumors. He had had his car windows broken and his brand-new tires slashed. Everyone in Arleta thought he had killed Missy, and all because Karen had accused him. It would be nice to put the rumors behind him and clear his name once and for all. Besides, if he didn't go, everyone would think it was because he had something to hide.

"Okay. I'll go." As soon as Jimmy said the words, he had a feeling he was making a mistake.

"Good. I'll pick you up at your brother's house at eight o'clock." Karen sounded cheerful, which made Jimmy feel better about the plan.

At eight o'clock that evening Karen Severson pulled up in front of Jimmy Mitchell's house. Two seconds later Vic Amaya pulled up behind her and waved. Jimmy stood still for a moment. Why had Vic followed Karen over? Jimmy ignored his fears and waved back as he trotted over and got into Karen's car.

They pulled up in front of Christy's house at 8:15 and Karen turned off the engine. "Thanks for coming, Jimmy," she said. "I wondered if you would. But I really am sorry."

Jimmy was so involved in listening to Karen that he didn't notice Vic dart into the house and come out again with several guys.

"Come on, Jimmy. Let's go inside. They're all waiting for us." They stepped out of the car and just as Jimmy turned toward the house a beer bottle smashed against his head.

It took him a moment to realize that he had been set up. He could see them now, Vic and a dozen others walking toward him.

He turned to look at Karen, but she had stepped away, taking refuge by a parked van.

She smiled as his eyes met hers. "You were a fool for coming, Jimmy. A fool."

The group was advancing and Jimmy felt suddenly lightheaded. He was only five feet three, no match for any of the guys coming his way. Suddenly Jimmy wondered if he would live through whatever was about to happen.

"Welcome to the party, Jimmy." It was Bobby, the one who had been dating Missy when she was killed. "I'm surprised you came. But that's just like most killers, I guess. No remorse for what you did."

By now Bobby and Vic were standing in front of Jimmy and the others had circled around. Bobby grabbed Jimmy by the shoulders and held him tightly.

"You can forget trying to get away. Missy probably tried to get away too. But you killed her, didn't you?"

Jimmy started to shake his head, but just then Victor kicked him in the ribs, his steel-toed boot making contact with Jimmy's side. There was a cracking sound and Jimmy doubled over.

I'm going to die, Jimmy thought. He felt pain searing through his insides.

Jimmy struggled to stay on his feet as Vic delivered one kick after another. First his ribs, then his sides. He could hear them in the background. Karen was leading the chant.

"Do it for Missy! Do it for Missy!" Jimmy looked up and saw Karen laughing. She screamed again, and this time she looked right at him. She had set him up, brought him here with her lies, and now she wanted to see him die.

"Kill him! Do it for Missy! Do it for Missy!"

Vic kicked him again and again.

At that moment Jimmy Mitchell knew he was going to die. He could no longer breathe and his lungs had stopped working right. Slowly, he was losing consciousness.

"Stop!" Jimmy screamed desperately as white splotches appeared before his eyes and the other voices grew fainter. He fell to the ground and lay motionless.

Fifteen minutes after they left him for dead, Jimmy finally regained consciousness and was able to make his way to the corner pay phone and call home for a ride. A visit to the hospital confirmed he had one broken and several bruised ribs and a concussion.

The doctor wanted him to fill out a police report, but Jimmy refused, terrified that they would seek revenge if he did so.

That night, despite the pain, Jimmy was most bothered by the last words he remembered hearing before he passed out. He couldn't see the person, but he recognized her voice as she shouted. "He's dead! We did it! We killed him!" It was a victorious happy cry.

As he lay in bed, trying to fall asleep, Jimmy was certain the statements came from Karen Severson.

20

SHE HAD KNOWN the secret about who killed Missy Avila for six weeks, and still, no one had the slightest idea that her words and deeds weren't based on complete sincerity. She was still spending nearly every night sleeping in Missy's house—although no longer in her bed. She was still sitting in Missy's chair when she ate her meals and still playing the role of Missy's best, brokenhearted friend.

A newspaper reporter had visited them the week before to write a small story about the family's frustrations over what was an unsolved murder in the community. During the interview Karen sat next to Irene, dabbing at her eyes. The reporter asked Karen how she felt about Missy's murder—not knowing that she knew every detail about it.

"I loved Missy," Karen said. "I will not rest until I catch the animal that did this to my best friend."

One day, the week after the article appeared on an inside page of the local newspaper, Irene wandered into the kitchen and found Karen and Andrea eating lunch. It occurred to Irene how very large Karen had become since Missy's murder. She had ballooned to at least two hundred and twenty pounds.

Karen motioned for Irene to sit down. She seemed

excited and Irene wondered what she had found out this time.

"Irene, I just know it's Jimmy who killed Missy, and I've decided to do something about it."

Irene sat back in her chair and crossed her arms as Karen continued.

"We have to kill him, Irene. I want him dead and I want his body thrown into the flames." She slammed her fist down on the kitchen table and Irene jumped. She had never seen Karen so angry, and for a brief moment she was worried that Karen was serious, just as she had been weeks earlier when she brought about Jimmy's beating.

"Karen, we haven't proven anything about Jimmy. It's really up to the police to catch him if he's guilty."

Irene stood up and turned her back. Karen was silent as she saw Irene begin to shake and heard her try to contain the sobs.

"The police are our only hope," she said, and Karen could barely understand her. "We can't take the law into our own hands like that."

Karen walked over to Irene and hugged her. "I know. I'm sorry. I didn't mean to upset you."

Karen pulled away from Irene and grabbed Andrea's hand. "We're going back to my parents' house for a while. I want to get some clothes for Andrea."

"Okay." Irene wiped her eyes and sat down at the table. "We'll see you for dinner."

Karen grabbed Andrea's hand and the two walked out the front door toward the Severson home. "I know, Andrea." Karen was excited and she turned the little girl toward her. "Let's go into my bedroom and we'll play dress-up."

Andrea nodded, giggling, as they hurried into the

house like a couple of mischievous children. This was her favorite game.

"Okay. Now, first we have to make you look like a grown-up girl. You sit here on the bed and I'll get the makeup."

The child giggled with delight. She and her mommy had played this game lots of times in the last few weeks and Andrea knew what was coming. A minute later Karen walked into the room with a box of mascara, eye shadow, lipstick, and hair ribbons.

Andrea sat straight up while her mother set to work. First she applied foundation, a light beige liquid that made the child's complexion look like a teenager's.

Karen stepped back and admired her daughter.

"Perfect," she said. She reached for the brush.

Carefully, she stroked the child's dark hair until it shone.

"Tilt your head back, Andrea." Andrea pointed her chin up, and her hair fell almost halfway down her back.

Karen took a rose-colored blush out of the box. She filled the applicator with powder and spread the color over her daughter's tiny cheeks.

"Okay. Hold still. We're almost done." Karen reached into the box and pulled out a light pink eye-shadow and dusted it over Andrea's eyelids. The girl giggled again. It always tickled when Mommy did her eyes.

Karen stood back and looked at the girl. "Just one more thing."

Rummaging through the box, Karen found pale pink lipstick. She applied it to Andrea's lips while the child sat perfectly still. The little girl loved their special dress-up game.

"Now. Stand up and turn around." Karen moved back as Andrea twirled in a circle. She looked ridiculous, a toddler made up like a young woman.

"There." Karen smiled and hugged the child. "You look just like Auntie Missy."

21

THE GUILT HAD grown into a cancerous fear that spread with each passing day.

Now, six weeks after the murder, the fear was beginning to intrude. She couldn't stay out after dark and hated being anywhere alone. The fear was at its worst in the shower.

The mornings were unbearable.

Her alarm would sound and then it was time to prepare for the day. First there was breakfast, then time to choose an outfit.

Inevitably, there was the matter of showering, which created a fear that strangled her, a fear greater than death itself.

This morning was no different, but it was 8:30 A.M. and she could not wait much longer.

When the terror first started, days after the murder, she'd asked her roommate to stay in the bathroom with her so that she could shower. Even now that was the only way she could turn on the water.

Missy had been alone in the water, right before they killed her. And when the water began to spray in the shower, it was easy to feel the way she must have felt—suffocating, struggling for a breath, alone in the water.

The water sprayed gently through the shower head. She drew a deep breath.

This is insane. It's a shower. A simple shower.

The knowledge didn't help. Showers had become more frightening than that day on the mountain.

Get in. You have to get in. Just stay calm. It's a simple shower and nothing is going to happen.

Her heart began pounding then, banging on the chest walls, faster and faster and faster. It was difficult to breathe. She wanted to run, but he was watching, waiting until the shower was over. What would he think?

She began to cry.

Will this fear ever go away? Will I ever be normal again? Oh, why does it stay with me? Why can't it ever leave my mind? I'm sorry, so sorry.

She stepped into the tub, and then it became audible—the voice that always spoke through the shower head.

"The worst thing you guys could do is leave me up here all alone. . . . The worst thing you guys could do is leave me up here all alone."

I have to run, have to get out of here. I'm going to die. I can't breathe and my heart is beating too fast. If I don't get out of here I'm going to pass out and crack my head on the tub and bleed to death. I need to breathe. Oh, the walls. The walls are closing in and I'm not going to be able to get out.

Enough.

She turned off the water and hurried into a towel.

He was waiting there, as usual. He understood the fear and was willing to sit in the bathroom until the shower was over.

"I'm sorry, Steven." She began to cry. "I know you must think I'm weird or something."

Steven shook his head.

"I understand." But he wondered when the obsession would end, when life would return to normal and showers would just be a way to get clean. He knew what had happened to the girl. They were cold-blooded killers and they had eliminated a girl half their size. The thought made him sick to his stomach. He was certain he had given her the best possible advice: Don't tell anyone.

They had killed her and they would kill again.

He stared out the bedroom window. They needed to get far, far away from Arleta, someplace where they could forget that October day and get on with their lives.

22

AUTUMN WAS IN the air; overnight the trees in Arleta had become bare. The warm Santa Ana winds had stopped blowing just before Thanksgiving weekend. Seasons were barely noticeable in southern California, but by late November summer was clearly gone. A chill hung in the air and people had taken to wearing sweaters after sundown.

On an evening like this, three days before Thanksgiving, Karen Severson organized another group meeting at the Avila house. By now Christy Crawford was receiving phone calls every day or so with messages from Missy. And Karen was talking to Missy each night, often dressing her own daughter to look like her. Karen was becoming more and more dangerous. In fact, Catherine Scott would say later that anyone who spent any time with Karen Severson in those months after Missy's murder could have been putting his or her own life in jeopardy.

That afternoon, true to Catherine Scott's later assessment of her mental condition, Karen Severson was about to orchestrate a murder. The victim would once again be Jimmy Mitchell.

Karen paced the Avila living room nervously as she waited for Vic Amaya and Brian Taylor to arrive. She was frustrated because Jimmy was supposed to have died that night in the street. Vic had kicked him and kicked him until he lay so still that Karen was certain he was dead.

But he had lived.

Karen turned as someone knocked at the door. A moment later Brian and Vic walked in. They were all there, and they needed to make a plan.

"You all know why we're here." Karen spoke with a calmness that hid her excitement. "This time Jimmy has to die."

Brian and Vic nodded. They had agreed with Karen that if the investigators caught him, he'd make up some excuse and they'd let him off.

That Missy's friends were willing to kill for her sake said something about the kind of teenagers who lived in the East Valley. Their socioeconomic status being significantly lower than that of teens in other parts of the Valley—and gang mentality being a way of life— revenge killing was commonplace. Although the majority of Missy's friends wouldn't kill for any reason, several of the tougher kids from continuation school were violent.

Adults in Arleta had another opinion of the excessive teenage violence in their community—they were angered and disgusted. By the late 1980s they were not, however, surprised by it. They believed no amount of police patrol could change the East Valley's gang mentality.

Vic and Brian could justify killing for revenge even if they weren't affiliated with a gang. Missy's brothers and family, however, were astonished to find a murder being planned in their living room.

Mark put an arm around Shavaun and looked down

at the living-room floor. He was as convinced as everyone else that Jimmy was guilty. Karen had decided
Jimmy needed to die, and even though Mark was nervous about the murder, at least he wasn't going to pull
the trigger.

Karen looked at Brian and Vic. "You have the
guns?"

They nodded and Vic spoke up. "They're in the
truck. Loaded."

"Good. Now, we'll wait until tomorrow after he gets
off work. It will be dark and you can park outside his
apartment. I'll tell you when he gets home and where
he parks."

Karen looked at Vic and Brian and paused. "You
aren't going to back down, are you?"

Vic and Brian shook their heads.

Vic wanted this more than anyone, except Karen, of
course. No one understood how empty Vic Amaya had
felt since Missy died. She had been so sweet and Vic
was certain—even if Missy hadn't been—that one day
they would have gotten married. Now she was gone
and Vic dreamed about her every night. Each time it
was the same dream—him crying because Missy was
dead, and then the doorbell ringing and Missy standing there, hugging and kissing him and telling him it
was okay. Then he would wake up and the misery
would begin again.

Vic had been searching for someone on whom to
vent his anger, and when Karen Severson realized
Jimmy must have done it, Vic needed no convincing.
Now Jimmy Mitchell was the focus of all the hatred
and anger Vic Amaya wanted so badly to express. He
had never enjoyed beating someone to a pulp as much
as he had that night at Christy's party. He hadn't ex-

pected Jimmy to live through it, but Jimmy was tough and now they needed to finish him off. With Brian willing to help they were sure to get him this time.

Karen was still watching him, and when Vic answered her, there was no hesitation in his voice. "We aren't backing down. He's dead."

Karen smiled. She hadn't been so sure about Brian, but she knew she could count on Vic.

"There's one more thing." Karen waited until everyone in the room was watching her. "Tomorrow we'll go to my house and get some pool acid. After you kill him, take his body and pour the acid on it until he's burned and no one can recognize him. Then use your knife and cut off his little finger."

Shavaun and Mark gasped, and Karen laughed at them.

"What's wrong? Nothing says I can't get a memento out of this." Karen looked pleased. "He killed Missy and I want proof that he's dead."

Mark didn't like the tone of Karen's voice, but years would pass before he would realize her reason for saying such a terrible thing. That night, it seemed only that Karen hated Jimmy for killing her best friend. Certainly Mark could understand that kind of hatred, even if it was a bit sickening.

Karen continued talking to Brian and Vic, telling them exactly when Jimmy left work and when he arrived home. She drew them a map and described what he and his car looked like, because Brian had never seen him before. Finally, the plan was set and everyone went home.

In the back bedroom Irene slept soundly. She still needed the medication at night and she had been unaware of the details of the plan. Karen had worked it that way on purpose. Irene wouldn't approve of their killing Jimmy any more than she had approved of their beating him up.

The next afternoon Irene was busy in the kitchen when Katy Vincent came to the house to meet Karen. The two girls began talking and then together got up and walked quickly down the steps toward the Severson house.

They said very little, and Katy wondered if Vic and Brian really would use the pool acid on Jimmy and bring back his little finger for Karen. In some ways she couldn't believe they would really kill Jimmy. She knew this happened sometimes, but she had never been this close to a murder. She wanted to be on the sidelines of this plan because she found the idea of revenge rather exciting. But it still seemed unreal. She kept expecting Karen to step back and tell her it was all just a joke.

Since the plan was Karen's idea, she would have to take the rap if the police came around. That being the case, Katy didn't mind being part of the group seeking revenge for Missy Avila. In some ways Katy Vincent, who hadn't really been that close to Missy, felt bigger than life itself hunting down a killer. It was exciting and dangerous and forbidden.

It occurred to Katy, as she walked alongside Karen Severson that afternoon, that they could be mistaken. What if Jimmy really hadn't killed Missy? Katy glanced at Karen and noticed she was grinning and humming to herself. She looked like someone getting ready to start a vacation, not plan a murder. At that moment Katy Vincent had a very strong urge to turn around and run away from Karen's crazy plans. In the end she decided she was letting her imagination get the better of her and she kept walking.

They spent just five minutes at the Severson house. Karen walked through the back gate toward the pool and grabbed a greenish-blue plastic container before quietly shutting the gate behind her. Katy recognized the container. It was pool acid.

When they returned to the Avila home, they set the container near the side of the house. Vic and Brian would pick it up later before they left to kill Jimmy. Karen was pleased. She felt almost as excited as she had when she'd learned Missy was killed. Karen laughed out loud. Her plan was working out beautifully, and soon Jimmy would be gone.

It was nearly eight o'clock that evening when Vic and Brian arrived at the Avila home. This time Irene was still awake, sitting in the living room with Karen and the others. "What are they doing here?" Irene asked, looking around the room at the blank faces.

Karen was the first to speak. "Irene, they're going to get Jimmy. Tonight. Before another day goes by."

"You mean they're going to kill him?" Irene's eyes grew wide in disbelief, and she began to shake her head. "You can't let them kill Jimmy. This is something the police have to handle. Revenge can't bring Missy back, and all of you could get in trouble for taking the law into your own hands!"

Karen stood up and let the boys into the room. She muttered something to them, and they quickly turned and left.

Then she turned to Irene. "Don't worry, Irene. After tonight it will be all taken care of."

Irene sighed. With Karen in charge she felt helpless to change their plans.

Fifteen minutes later Vic and Brian had staked out their spot, just a few yards from Jimmy's apartment. If it worked out, he should be arriving in ten minutes and they would take care of him. Vic cocked the gun and sat back to wait.

Five minutes passed, then ten. With each passing car Vic felt a knot form in his stomach. He was seconds away from becoming a murderer, and he didn't like the thought of it. Missy was the only person in the world he would kill for.

Twenty minutes had passed now, and Vic was beginning to think they had missed him. "Let's give him another ten minutes, and if he doesn't come we'll do it tomorrow night instead."

Brian nodded. He had hoped they could get it over with tonight, but he was willing to come back tomorrow. He hadn't known Missy as well as Vic had, but he knew what she looked like. It burned Brian to the core to think of some weasel like this Jimmy Mitchell holding her pretty face down in a stream until she drowned.

It was nearly 9:00 P.M. and Vic shook his head. "Look, man. He's not coming. Either we missed him or he's out doing something else, but we can't just sit here forever. Let's get out of here."

They drove back to the Avila house to let Karen know the mission had failed.

Irene felt her breath catch as she saw Brian and Vic pull into the driveway and get out of the car. She watched as Karen ran toward the door. She looked like a child at Christmas, waiting to see what Santa Claus had brought.

"Well? Is he dead? Did you do it?"

Vic and Brian shook their heads as Karen opened the screen door and let them inside.

"He never showed up."

"Damn!" Karen slammed her fist against the wall, leaving a network of cracks in the plaster. She turned toward Brian and Vic, her eyes burning with hatred. "Can't you guys do anything right?" She paced the room and threw herself down on the nearest chair.

From where she sat, Irene breathed a sigh of relief. But Karen was furious.

"What are we going to do now? We can't let him continue on like this after what he did to Missy. Something has to be done."

Vic nodded intently. "Don't worry. We're going to go back and do it tomorrow night. This time we'll get there earlier."

Karen nodded, satisfied. She didn't like to wait, but after tomorrow night Jimmy would be dead.

The next night Vic and Brian returned to Jimmy's apartment and waited. It was just after eight o'clock when Vic saw Jimmy's car drive up and park. Jimmy turned off his headlights and stepped out of the car. Vic cocked the gun and took aim.

"Wait!" Brian knocked Vic's hand and forced him to lower the gun.

Vic looked first at Brian and then at Jimmy as he walked up the sidewalk to the apartment. Vic couldn't understand why Brian had stopped him. He had ruined a perfect opportunity and now he was completely confused. "What are you doing, man? That was our chance! What's your problem?"

Brian shook his head and kept his gaze on Jimmy. "Something's wrong, Vic." Brian waited until

Jimmy stepped inside his apartment. When he spoke there was fear in his voice.

"As soon as I saw him I got this weird feeling." Brian paused. "It was like something told me he didn't do it. I just don't think he could have killed her."

Vic dropped his gun. He didn't want to admit it, but he had felt the same way. His mind had been clouded by revenge.

"Let's get out of here." Brian turned the key in the ignition and motioned for Vic to start driving.

Vic looked at his hands. They were shaking so badly, he could barely hold the steering wheel. If it hadn't been for Brian, Jimmy would be dead. And he would be a murderer. He took a deep breath and pulled the car away.

Across town that night, while Vic and Brian were changing their minds about killing Jimmy, someone snuck quietly about the front of Christy Crawford's house.

The next morning Christy's grandmother came running into their house screaming Christy's name. The girl jumped up from bed, grabbed her robe, and followed her grandmother outside. It was her car. Someone had smashed out the back window and across the front windshield scrawled a message in soap that made Christy's knees shake and her face grow deathly pale. It was one word: MURDERER!

23

TWO DAYS LATER, on Thanksgiving day, everyone in the Avila household—excluding Karen Severson—was frustrated that the sheriff's detectives were not making any progress in their investigation.

Earlier in the week Catherine Scott had called and explained that they were still working on several leads. Dan Jenkins had called once or twice too. They hadn't ruled out the Camaro owners in the area, and they had other people to interview. But there were no suspects and no pending arrests.

The smell of turkey filtered through the Avila house, and Irene worked quietly in the kitchen, trying not to think about Missy. By then Karen and Andrea had been living with them for nearly a month.

Most of the people involved had been relieved to learn that Vic and Brian decided not to kill Jimmy, but Karen had been livid. She wasn't used to people countering her wishes.

But the next day Karen seemed to forget. If people were starting to doubt Jimmy's role in Missy's murder, then Karen would have to think of someone else on whom to focus their attention. There was no shortage of names flickering through her mind.

Thanksgiving Day Karen told Irene she wasn't sure

Missy had been killed by Jimmy after all. Because Irene and the others were willing to grab at any possible leads, they agreed with Karen and helped her think of other people who might be responsible. In front of the Avilas she never again acted as though she hated Jimmy Mitchell.

Of course, they all wondered how that made Karen feel about the abortion. A week earlier Karen had been so angry at Jimmy that she had gone to an abortion clinic. She had been injected with a saline solution that had slowly killed her nearly five-month-old unborn child. When Karen had returned home she seemed happy and cheerful, announcing that the child had been a boy.

"Yes, I killed Jimmy's baby boy because he killed my best friend," Karen had said with a smile. "I can't tell you how happy I am to have his child out of my body."

Everyone knew Karen was upset about Missy, but her joy over the abortion was disgusting. After all, the child was innocent. And now that Karen had changed her mind about Jimmy's role in Missy's murder, she still showed no remorse about the abortion.

It was nearly five o'clock when Irene called the group to dinner and began setting the steaming dishes on the table. Karen was the first to arrive, and she walked over and hugged Irene.

"Happy Thanksgiving, Irene." Irene tried not to cry. "I just want to thank you for loving me like your own daughter. I know it's hard with Missy gone. We all miss her so much. But you've made it a little easier for me. I feel like you are the family I never had."

Irene hugged her tight. "Missy was lucky to have you for a friend, Karen. And now I'm lucky to have you as mine."

Later on during dinner Karen Severson interrupted the group chatter and made an announcement.

"I know this isn't the time to talk about it, but I want you all to know that we can't give up on finding Missy's killer. Maybe it wasn't Jimmy." Karen paused and looked at Missy's family. They were still hanging on her every word. They still had no idea that she knew what had happened to Missy. And she seemed to have no intention of ever letting them find out. Karen cleared her throat and continued. "But it was someone out there, someone cold and mean who is hiding the trail very well. I think if we all work together, we will find the people who killed Missy."

Everyone agreed and later that evening, when the dishes were done and the leftovers wrapped in the refrigerator, Karen brought the subject up again.

"You know what I've been thinking?" Karen waited until the room was silent before she continued. "Maybe Laura Doyle knows more than she's telling us. Maybe she knows who the boys were that picked up Missy but she's afraid to say."

Mark and the others nodded, considering the idea.

"And I've been thinking about some other boys Missy knew," she said. "There were lots of guys who weren't very nice people. Maybe it was one of them."

For thirty minutes Karen tossed out more than a dozen names and encouraged the family to think hard about each one.

On the other side of Stonehurst Park, Laura Doyle was having a very quiet Thanksgiving holiday, most likely lost in a blurry haze of beer. During this period she was sullen and withdrawn and often drunk. Of course, had life been different in the Doyle home, someone might have wondered why she was so depressed. But her behavior may have seemed quite normal to Laura's parents, because by then celebrating the holidays in an alcohol-induced haze was something of a tradition.

24

IT WAS THE worst Thanksgiving ever.

The food had a putrid smell, reminding her of a rotting carcass.

They were gathered around the dinner table and people were talking and smiling as though this holiday were like any other.

She tuned them out and let her mind drift away, back to the mountain stream, back to the girl's last words.

"The worst thing you guys could do is leave me here all alone. . . . The worst thing you guys could do is leave me here all alone."

She felt someone poke her ribs and turned to see Steven.

"Didn't you hear me? I've been talking to you." She shook her head, avoiding the curious stares from others at the table.

"I don't feel well." She pushed her napkin onto her plate and stood up. "May I be excused?"

The others nodded and Steven watched as she walked quickly down the hall to her bedroom.

It was getting worse.

She couldn't take a shower more than twice a week. She couldn't go outside. She could barely sleep.

She was scared to death, and her fear was ruining their relationship.

In the back bedroom she flopped onto the bed and started crying. The sobs tore at her heart; she couldn't stop them.

Oh, how can I live with myself? Can you ever forgive me, Missy? We left you up there, but it was worse than you thought it would be. They killed you and I didn't do anything about it.

Steven finished his dinner and stood up.

"I'm going to see how she's doing," he said. The others watched as he walked back to the bedroom. He could hear her sobbing before he opened the door.

"Come on, baby, you've got to let this thing go." Steven sat down next to her and stroked her hair. "You didn't do anything wrong. There's nothing you could have done to help her. Not with those two holding her down. They're much stronger than you."

"But I was there and I didn't even try to stop them!" It was almost a scream, and Steven held his finger to his lips.

"Shhh! You want everyone to know that you were there?"

She shook her head and buried her face in the pillow.

When she looked up, Steven saw more clearly than ever the fear in her eyes. "I know they want to kill me too. They don't want any witnesses and I'm afraid, Steven. I'm so afraid."

Steven nodded, taking her hand.

"Then we'll leave, baby. We'll go away. Maybe to Nevada or somewhere out of state. Would that help?"

She thought for a moment and nodded.

"Could we go to Las Vegas? They would never find me there."

Steven smiled at her. "Sure, honey. If you want to go to Vegas we'll leave next week. We can find work there and then maybe you can forget this whole thing."

She looked up at him and shook her head slowly. He still didn't understand.

"No, Steven."

Tears began streaming down her face and several seconds passed before she spoke again.

"We might be safer in Las Vegas, but I will never, never forget what happened that day. Never."

25

ROBERT LIBERSHAL REACHED into the ranger-station closet and pulled out his green jacket. It was going to be a long night. The weather was warm for a May evening, but the nights still dipped into the thirties, especially up at Camp Colby. The spot was at least four thousand feet above sea level, and it was always colder than the neighboring valleys.

Libershal stretched as he slipped on his jacket. He hadn't been looking forward to working late into the night and dealing with movie people. But the project could be interesting.

His supervisor had notified him earlier in the month that a production company planned to film a movie where the Camp Colby Bridge crossed Upper Big Tujunga Creek.

Ever since last October it had been a spot Libershal knew well.

The producer had loved the area, but he didn't know it was just a hundred yards downstream from where they had found the girl's body nearly eight months before.

Memories of that October day still haunted Libershal. The girl had been so tiny and so helplessly pinned beneath the log. It had been months since he'd heard anything about it in the press but as far as he knew, the killers were still at large.

Sometimes, when he thought about the girl, it seemed as if her murder had happened only yesterday. He had been on duty as patrol officer when he received the call from dispatch telling him to report to the creek. A couple of hikers had found a body.

Libershal remembered that the girl's position in the water had seemed almost surrealistic; how she lay, facedown with her legs crossed. All he had been able to make out was her blue jeans, white canvas tennis shoes, and one arm, stiffened behind her back. The log —a fallen tree trunk—pinned her face under eight inches of water.

He often wondered if the girl had still been alive when her killers placed the log on her back.

Libershal shuddered again, imagining the kind of cold-blooded people who would have heaved that log through the stream.

He sighed. Even now it was hard to forget the girl. Missy. Her name had been Missy. Libershal had read about her in the paper after they found her body. She had been the only girl in her family. Three brothers. He wondered how her family was doing now.

Libershal walked out to the truck and made his way up the forest service road to the bridge. The movie people knew nothing of the girl or her murder, and it would be nice to form a different kind of memory of the area.

He parked the truck and got out. The movie crew was just setting up and Libershal was glad. He might enjoy the night after all.

It was a full six hours before the movie crew was finally ready to begin filming. Libershal had enjoyed

Michele "Missy" Avila, at 17, just months before her murder on October 1, 1985. (Los Angeles *Daily News*, 1988)

Missy's family home in Arleta, California. (Karen Kingsbury)

Tree carving near the murder site in Angeles National Forest.
(Stephen Ellison/*People Weekly*, 1989)

Carving in a tree in Angeles National Forest, marking the "hangout" of Missy and her friends. (Stephen Ellison/ *People Weekly*, 1989)

Laura Doyle, 21, in Glendale, California, Municipal Court.
(Jeff Goldwater/Los Angeles *Daily News*, 1988)

Karen Severson during the jury selection in her trial.
(John McCoy/Los Angeles *Daily News*, 1990)

Karen Severson, center, and Laura Doyle, at their trial. (John McCoy/Los Angeles *Daily News*, 1990)

Missy Avila's brother, Mark, contemplates the loss of his sister at the creek where she was brutally murdered in the Angeles National Forest. (Stephen Ellison/*People Weekly*, 1989)

Missy's mother, Irene, at Missy's grave (Missy's face is etched in the tombstone). (Stephen Ellison/*People Weekly*, 1989)

watching the preparation and found himself amazed at the work that went into making a single five-minute film sequence.

He glanced at his watch. It was approaching midnight.

The crew was using floodlights and a beautiful full moon hung overhead. The ranger couldn't remember it ever being so light this late at night.

Libershal yawned. Just one more hour and the crew would be finished for the night. He turned his head back toward the road and watched as a light-colored oversized convertible bounced over the bridge and screeched to a stop in the middle of the dirt parking lot.

Strange time to be up here, Libershal thought. Then he made out the faces of the passengers—teenagers. They came up here at all hours of the night looking for a place to party. The kids piled out of the car and Libershal could see them clearly now. There were eight of them. A couple of boys and several giggling girls. They were talking loudly and heading toward the movie crew. Libershal had been asked to keep the public away from the filming, but he decided to let the teenagers watch as long as they didn't cause any trouble.

The group moved even closer and Libershal was just ten feet away from them when one of the girls began talking. She was very excited, moving her arms about and gesturing upstream. Libershal listened closely.

"Here it is!" the girl said, a strange, happy smile plastered across her face. "Right here. This is where my best friend was killed. See up the stream a ways? Well, it was right there."

Libershal moved a little closer. Did this girl know

about the murder? he wondered. As far as he was aware, no one else had been killed near the stream. He listened carefully as the girl continued.

"Can you imagine being killed up here? I mean, there's hardly any water in the stream. But this is the place. This is where she was killed. It was last October."

Libershal felt his blood run cold.

There had been just one girl murdered in the stream last October. He knew that much for sure. He didn't know the details of the police investigation, but he was certain that none of the news accounts stated specifically where the girl's body had been found. This girl knew.

Slowly, Libershal made his way over to her. Who was she? And why was she so happy about her best friend's murder? The girl moved away from the group and walked over to the car. Libershal met her there a few seconds later.

"Excuse me, miss," he said. "I overheard you say something about your friend being killed up here."

The girl nodded and looked at him curiously.

"I'm sorry to hear that," Libershal continued. "What was your friend's name?"

The girl ran her hand through her long, straggly hair and smiled sweetly at the ranger.

"Her name was Missy. Missy Avila. She was my best friend, and last October someone drowned her right up there in the stream."

Libershal listened as the girl made small talk for a few moments. She appeared happy, inappropriately so. And she seemed proud that her best friend had been killed in the stream. As though it made her important. Libershal thought it sickening somehow.

Minutes later the girl walked back to the group, and before Libershal could give the situation much more thought they got back into the car and drove off.

The girl was behind the wheel, and as Libershal watched them drive off she turned and stared at him. She had that same smile on her face, and a chill went down Libershal's spine.

There is something wicked about that girl, Libershal thought. *Something horribly wicked.* Yet he couldn't quite put his finger on what bothered him so. He considered writing down the license number, but now the car was making its way down the hill.

The crew finished up for the evening and Libershal drove back to the station. He couldn't stop thinking about the girl and the things she had said. He pulled out his daily log and signed the date and time. Then, almost on impulse, he pulled out a small notebook from the bottom drawer. It was a makeshift journal, a place where Libershal could keep track of the changes in the forest and other interesting happenings. He opened it up to the first blank page and scribbled the date. May 30, 1986.

Quickly, he wrote down the details of the girl's statements. He made note of the light-colored convertible and how the girl had been unnaturally happy —almost bragging—about her best friend's murder. He hadn't asked her for her name, but he remembered what she looked like and wrote down her description:

Average height. Dark, long, unbrushed hair. Overweight, with fleshy cheeks.

Libershal shut the journal and put it back in the desk. He made a mental note to tell his supervisor about the incident.

26

BY MID-JUNE every clue Catherine Scott and Dan Jenkins had run across in the investigation of Missy Avila's murder had dried up.

They still had their hunches. Both detectives believed the girl was killed by someone who knew her. And Catherine was still certain that a woman was somehow involved. When Karen Severson had brought up the name Christy Crawford, Catherine thought they might be on the right track. But when Christy had come into the station, she'd done little more than cry throughout the interview. Catherine knew from experience that Christy had turned to drugs and drinking to mask her grief. The girl's face was bloated and ruddy looking and her breath smelled of alcohol. As Catherine watched her talk about Missy, their fun times together and how badly they'd missed each other when she and her parents moved to Long Beach, she knew without a doubt that Karen was wrong—Christy wasn't involved in Missy's murder.

There had been other times when Catherine felt close to making a breakthrough in the case. Dan Jenkins had run across two dark-haired Caucasian boys driving near the outskirts of Arleta in a blue Camaro with expired license plates. He had brought the boys into the station and he and Catherine had grilled them. They said they knew Missy Avila, knew about her death, but that was all they could remember about her. They said they'd had nothing to do with it. Jenkins stared at the boys for twenty minutes in silence while Catherine called Laura Doyle down to the station. Through one-way glass Catherine asked Laura to look at the boys and identify them. If these were the two Laura had last seen Missy with, they were minutes away from making an arrest.

But when Laura looked at the boys, her face was completely blank.

"I've never seen them before," Laura said flatly.

Another dead end. Of course, each week Irene Avila was still calling with suggestions. Dan got so tired of the woman's constant need to know the progress of the investigation that he finally asked Catherine to take charge of her. Irene would have been pleased, because she certainly didn't mind being something of a pest. Someone had to keep Missy's name fresh in their minds, and Irene didn't care if she had to call once a week for the rest of her life. She wasn't going to give up.

Catherine, meanwhile, didn't mind the weekly conversations with Irene, because she was just as determined to solve this murder. She had never told anyone about the lock of Missy's hair she still carried with her. The promise she'd made to herself back in October was still just as important. Someday, no matter how long it took, Catherine Scott would make sure that justice was served for this terrible crime. It was the least she could do for Irene and Missy's brothers, and for Missy's best friend, Karen Severson.

Like any good homicide detectives Catherine and

Dan were trained not to rule out anyone as either a witness or a suspect in a murder investigation. Yet neither of them for a moment suspected that Karen Severson was involved in Missy's murder. Never in any investigation she'd ever conducted could Catherine remember such lies pouring forth from someone supposedly grieving about a murder. People who mourned like that could usually be counted on to tell the truth, because they loved the victim and wanted revenge. The thought never occurred to either detective that Karen might know more than she was saying, and so she was allowed to keep playing her twisted game.

By the summer of 1986 Karen Severson had completely transferred the Avila family's focus off Jimmy Mitchell. Once in a while she still talked about how much he had hated Missy and how he must have had something to do with her death, but Jimmy was no longer an obsession with her.

Jimmy never did understand why Karen had accused him of Missy's murder. The fight at Christy's house had been enough to convince him that his life was in jeopardy, and since then he had often considered moving. But each time he was tempted, Jimmy thought of his job as a mechanic and realized he couldn't leave. Missy's friends and family still didn't trust him, but he hoped that whenever the police did catch the real killers, the wounds would heal and the Avilas would welcome him as they had before. If Jimmy could have seen Karen's actions that summer of 1986, he would not have been surprised. Because Jimmy was well aware of the thoughts that welled inside Karen's mind.

That summer, the Avilas noticed Karen becoming

more than ever preoccupied with finding Missy's killers. Although the heat was now off Jimmy, there were others who were having car windows broken and tires slashed, others receiving death threats and mysterious phone calls.

In a desperate attempt to keep control of the investigation, Karen had come up with two others who might have been guilty. First it was Rob, a boy Missy knew from Mission continuation school. Karen had never liked the boy, and one day she was eating lunch with Irene at the Avila house when she brought his name up.

"You know, it seems clear to me that Rob had something to do with Missy's death." Karen took a bite of her sandwich. "Remember Rob? He was that guy Missy knew at Mission school and he always wanted to go out with her?"

Irene nodded. She had stopped becoming excited over every lead. There had been no clues for so long and the detectives had found nothing after months of searching for owners of blue Camaros. Even though she believed Karen was trying to be helpful, her hunches really didn't do any good. Missy was still gone. She would never come home, never graduate from high school, never have the wedding Irene and she had dreamed of. She noticed Karen looking at her strangely.

"I'm sorry, Karen. I wasn't listening. I know you mean well and I also want to see those murderers in jail, behind bars where they belong. But sometimes I just get tired of all the chasing."

"I understand. But listen, Irene. I really think Rob was involved." A look of excitement crossed Karen's face. "I just remembered something Missy told me a few weeks before she died."

Suddenly Irene looked interested.

"Missy once told me that this guy, Rob, had stopped her one day when she was walking home from school. Bobby Miller hated the guy because he always seemed to like Missy even though she already had a boyfriend." Karen stopped and tilted her head backward, as if trying to jar her memory. "Now I remember. She told me he was rude to her. He was mad because Missy wouldn't go out with him. He told her that one of these days she was going to turn down the wrong person and find herself in trouble."

Irene sat up straighter and began to catch Karen's phony enthusiasm.

"Did she say anything else about him? Maybe this is something the police should know about!"

Karen closed her eyes, relishing the drama of the moment. "There was something else, something Missy told me about him. She said he had scared her when he talked to her that day. She told me she thought he might try to hurt her." Karen paused and looked at Irene. "I didn't think about it until just now."

Irene felt the familiar rush inside her head. Maybe this was it. Maybe the killers would finally be found.

"Let's call the police and tell them. They said to call if we had any ideas." Irene moved toward the phone, but Karen stopped her.

"I know Rob, Irene. If he hears that the police are looking for him, he'll leave. I say we get him over here right now. I'll be able to tell just by looking at him if he did it."

Karen picked up the phone book and looked up

Rob. Within five minutes she had him on the line and was inviting him over to the Avila house.

There is no question that Karen was master of the game she played.

"Rob, this is Karen Severson." She was urgent. "I need to see you right away."

"Why? What's up?"

"Rob, I'm serious. There's no time to lose. You remember where Missy lived, don't you?"

"Yeah, but—"

"No!" Karen shouted. "I don't have time to talk about it on the phone. Just get over here as fast as you can. I'll explain later."

On the other end of the line Rob found himself agreeing to come. An hour later he walked up the front porch steps and rang the doorbell. Watching from the living room window, Karen whispered to Irene.

"Look at him, Irene. He's guilty. It's written all over his face. That's probably why it took him so long to get here."

Irene opened the door. She welcomed Rob inside, but the ruse lasted just a few seconds before Karen turned on him.

"Okay, Rob. You know why you're here and so do we. You thought we wouldn't figure it out, didn't you?" Karen reached out and gave Rob a quick push.

Rob wrinkled his brow and looked from Irene to Karen. Before he could speak, Irene reached across the living-room table and picked up a picture of Missy.

"Did you kill her, Rob?" Irene looked hurt and about ready to cry as she waited for the boy to answer.

Rob shook his head quickly. He was a rough-looking, muscular boy with tattoos along his arm and a wild look in his eyes, but he was shocked by what was happening to him now. Karen moved closer and screamed in his face.

"We know about what you said to Missy. You wanted her so bad that you killed her because she didn't like you. Why, why, Rob? Why couldn't you have just left her alone? What did she ever do to you!"

Karen's voice was rising, and Irene put an arm across her shoulders to calm her down. Karen stopped screaming and Irene turned to Rob. Her voice was much quieter than Karen's, and it sounded as if she was pleading with the boy.

"Rob, we don't know what happened to Missy, but if you killed her or if you know who did, it's time to come forward. The police are going to find out what happened someday. Why don't you tell us now and then it will be out in the open."

Suddenly, Rob seemed to realize what was happening. He was standing in a house he had never been in before and he was being accused of killing a girl he hadn't even dated. How had he allowed Karen to talk him into coming to the Avila house?

"I don't know what you guys are talking about, but I didn't kill Missy." Rob looked disgusted he shook his head as he turned toward the door. Before he could move, Karen grabbed his arm.

"You're not leaving that easy, Rob! You're lying about the whole thing. You killed her, didn't you?"

Rob was beginning to get angry. He had taken enough abuse for one afternoon. He shrugged loose of Karen's grip on his arm, glaring at her as he walked to the door.

"I don't know what has got into you, but I think you're crazy! You better never accuse me of this thing again or you'll really be sorry." Rob walked out the door and slammed it behind him.

Karen was burning with anger. Standing perfectly still, she watched Irene sink down onto the sofa, sobbing.

"Irene, he did it. And now he threatened me. Did you hear him? He told me I'd be sorry if I ever mentioned it again. What are we going to do?"

Irene couldn't talk. She had watched the boy's reaction and it was impossible to tell if he was lying. What had they been thinking, calling him over to the house? Of course he wasn't about to make a confession if he'd really killed Missy. If he was involved, he could even be dangerous, but it still didn't occur to Irene that they had reached a point that defied all common sense. And then, as Irene began to cry, Karen leaned down and patted her back.

"I'm sorry, Irene. I know how hard this is for you, but we can't just let it go. The police aren't working on the case like they should be."

One week later Karen forgot about Rob and openly began accusing Christy Crawford. Of course by then, Christy was mentally crippled by the numerous phone calls she'd received from someone calling herself Missy. She knew nothing of why she was being tormented, but she was positive she couldn't take much more.

Christy hadn't been around much since Missy's death, and that made her someone everyone might suspect. Karen planted the idea in Irene's mind later that summer, a month after suggesting it to the detectives.

"Maybe Christy is guilty, Irene," Karen said one day. "Christy was always jealous of Missy."

Irene angrily brushed off Karen's suggestion. She refused to believe that one of Missy's closest friends could possibly have anything to do with her murder.

"Drop it, Karen. We have to give up and let the police do the rest. Don't you see how it's tearing us up? Both of us loved Missy and now we have to go on. We have her memories, and I'd rather spend time thinking of the good times than chasing these endless leads."

Karen nodded, but she continued to make it clear that as far as she was concerned, Christy was involved. In the weeks that followed, Christy received numerous death threats and one morning awoke to find the word *murderer* scrawled across the sidewalk in front of her grandmother's home. This was the last straw, and eventually Christy returned south to Long Beach so she wouldn't go crazy.

Fifty miles away, just outside of Arleta, Karen Severson spent the anniversary of Missy's death in beauty school.

27

A WEEK BEFORE the anniversary of Missy's murder Karen Severson enrolled in the Modern Beauty Academy in Panorama City. After a lifetime of being far less than beautiful and a year of practicing makeup techniques on little Andrea, Karen had decided to become a beautician.

The beauty school was just a few blocks from the apartment she and Jimmy had shared more than a year before. It was ten miles outside Arleta, and even though there were beauty schools closer to home, Karen was familiar with the academy's success rate and thought it worth the drive. She had even talked it over with Missy one night and Missy had agreed. After all, Karen couldn't very well take Missy's place if she didn't first learn something about beauty.

Although Karen and Andrea had moved back home, Karen still spent nearly all her time at the Avila house; but now she had decided it was time for her to find a life of her own.

Lynne Robbins was among the students looking forward to the first day of beauty school. She had heard good things about the school and, after trying other occupational jobs, was certain she had finally found her niche.

At age twenty-four Lynne Robbins was a friendly girl with long dark hair and a pretty smile. She would have been happier if she could lose a little weight, but she still had an attractive figure and a beautiful face marked by high cheekbones. Lynne hadn't grown up in the Arleta area, but had moved there with her boyfriend. Now the two were engaged to be married. Lynne thought it the perfect time to be starting her career as a beautician. The past year had not been easy. Several months earlier Lynne's best friend, Amy, had killed herself. By now the shock had worn off, but Lynne still struggled with the haunting questions. Why suicide? Some nights, when Lynne couldn't sleep, she wondered if she could have done something to help her friend. Beauty school would be more than the beginning of a career for Lynne Robbins. It would be a turning point to help her put that horrible day out of her life forever.

Lynne found the school's address on the side of a large cement building and parked on the street outside. "Here goes," she mumbled to herself as she walked up to the receptionist's desk and picked up a packet of course materials. The receptionist said there would be at least twenty other students in the class. Lynne took a seat.

Five minutes later, while she was thumbing through the school's literature, a heavyset, frumpy-looking girl with greasy dark hair took the seat next to hers. Lynne looked up and flashed a nervous smile.

"Hi. I'm Lynne. You a first-timer, too?"

The girl nodded and Lynne thought she looked very confident, considering her appearance. She didn't really look like someone who knew much about beauty.

"I'm Karen. Karen Severson. And I'm here because I need a change."

Lynne laughed. "I know what you mean. That's part of why I'm here too."

"Not just a change in careers or anything." Karen looked Lynne in the eye and smiled. "My best friend was killed almost a year ago, and I guess it's just time to go on."

Lynne was shocked. "That's awful. Do they know who did it?"

Karen shook her head. "No. Sometimes I don't think they'll ever find the killers."

Her story made Lynne remember her own tragedy, and tears welled up in her eyes. She told Karen about Amy's suicide. When she'd finished, Karen made no comment. Instead she continued talking about Missy as if she hadn't been listening.

"We were best friends since we were eight years old. Her name was Missy," Karen said. "And then last October someone drowned her in a stream up near Big Tujunga Canyon. It was in all the newspapers. They even interviewed me in a few of them." Karen let out an odd laugh before finishing. "It was pretty exciting. But they haven't had any leads for a long time."

As Lynne listened, she felt sorry for her.

It was strange that she and Karen had so much in common. Each of them had come to the beauty school looking for a change and each had lost her best friend. But it occurred to Lynne that there was something strange about the way Karen talked about Missy. She seemed proud, as though she was important because her friend had been murdered and written about in the newspapers.

28

IT WAS A busy time of year for the Los Angeles County Sheriff's Department. During the holidays crime goes up: more robberies, more assaults, more rapes, and more murders. For Catherine Scott and Dan Jenkins this meant more work.

The bodies rarely bothered Dan Jenkins, even during the holidays. In fact, he liked to say that he and the other detectives could swap vacation stories over the bodies of most of their victims. Gang members, drug dealers, pimps, common criminals. It was easy to feel nothing for these victims because they had chosen their way of life. Occasionally, however, there would be a victim like Michele Avila. More than a year had passed since Michele was murdered, and even though it was no longer a priority case, the image of her dead body still haunted him.

Still, with the caseload increasing, it was impossible to spend much time on a fourteen-month-old murder with no hot leads. That didn't mean they were ready to give up on it. Technically, they never gave up on a murder, but as time went on they spent less and less time on it until it became nothing more than a file of notes they reviewed each year. By now they had long since exhausted every possible lead involving a blue Camaro.

The morning had gone by quickly and Catherine was looking forward to her vacation. Just a few more weeks of work and it would be time for a break. Grabbing her coat, she headed toward the parking lot. No blue Camaros there. Catherine shook her head sadly, realizing she had never been so concerned about the make and color of a car. Sometimes at night she dreamed about catching up with an elusive blue Camaro and making the arrest that would finally put an end to the Avila murder. The girl's mother still called every week, faithfully believing that one day the murder would be solved.

Catherine wondered how the Avila family was getting along, now that the shock had worn off and reality was setting in. Once in a while she asked Irene Avila how she was, but the woman remained quite stoic on the phone, concerned only about the investigation. Often the girl's mother would drop hints about possible suspects, and each time she and Dan would follow up on them. But there was never anything solid, no evidence linking anyone to the crime.

Most of the time the hunches came from Missy's best friend, Karen Severson. Catherine thought the girl was a little strange. She was always at the Avila house whenever Catherine or Dan dropped in with information; she seemed abnormally obsessed with the case. Catherine remembered her last conversation with Irene Avila. It had taken place a few days earlier, and the woman had spoken of Karen again. She said that Karen was trying to get Laura to remember more details. Irene said Karen thought Laura was lying about the story. Catherine and Dan both agreed. After hours of discussion they had agreed that Laura Doyle's story was suspicious. But they had nothing more than suspicion to go on. Maybe the girls had gotten into some trouble that afternoon and Laura didn't want to be caught by telling too many details. Maybe she was covering up for someone she knew. Something about her story just didn't sit well with the detectives.

Because of their suspicions they had called her in to be interviewed several times over the past year and her story never changed. In recent months Laura had been spending more time at her supermarket job in Arleta. She was going on with her life and seemed less and less interested in repeating the details of that fateful day.

Catherine turned into her bank driveway and parked the car. Maybe they would ask Laura Doyle in again, just to see if the details of her story remained consistent. Maybe they would catch her on a bad day and she would break down and tell the whole story. That's how detectives caught people in lies. When a person repeats a story—especially if it's a lie—sometimes there comes a day when the person can no longer remember the difference between what's fact and what's not. Catherine had noticed that when someone is lying, the details of the story never change. When the story is true, people tend to remember it in tidbits, not caring about the details, which sometimes change as time goes on. What didn't change was the sum of the story. People who told the truth had nothing to hide, but Catherine knew from experience that when a person was lying—unless he had forgotten his lie—the story was usually so perfectly prepared that it sounded like a broken record each time it was repeated. People typically didn't memorize the truth.

Laura Doyle's story had that kind of false ring to it, and Catherine made a mental note to get the girl back down to the station soon. Maybe after the holidays.

At the Avila home everyone was dreading the Christmas holidays. Missy had always loved Christmas. When she was a little girl, she would run down the hallway before the sun rose and announce loudly to her parents that it was Christmas morning and time to wake up. Irene would quickly dress and join her daughter, and the two would go about waking the boys. Then the festivities would begin. Stockings were emptied and toys from Santa Claus opened and assembled. The house would fill with delicious smells of cookies and roast turkey, and Missy would squeal with delight through all of it.

Karen Severson had been attending beauty school for three months and was making remarkable progress. She still spent most of her evenings with the Avila family, but these days she spent some of her spare time with Lynne Robbins. Yet even with her busy schedule at beauty school, Karen's apparent interest in solving Missy's murder was stronger than ever. Lately, she had talked about badgering Laura Doyle, calling her and yelling at her, trying to make her remember more details.

Karen sat across from Irene, satisfied more than ever that Missy's mother had no idea of the truth.

"Irene, I just know there's more to Laura's story," Karen said. She seemed so angry that her whole body shook as she spoke. "Don't you ever wonder about the boys and the blue Camaro. There must be more.

Maybe she's trying to cover up for someone she knows, someone involved."

Irene shook her head. "Karen, don't you think the police questioned Laura?" It didn't occur to Irene that the girl was always pointing a finger at people who knew Missy. After all, Missy could have been picked up by those boys and killed for any number of reasons. But Karen's odd theories went unquestioned. Irene looked at Karen and spoke softly. "Karen, I'm sure if there was more to her story, they would have gotten it out of her."

Karen thought for a moment and shook her head. "Not necessarily. Laura is good at lying unless you know her real well. One of these days, Irene, I am going to get the truth out of Laura Doyle. Wait and see."

Karen had become very close to Lynne Robbins, but in none of their conversations did Karen ever mention her suspicions about Laura Doyle. Instead, whenever Karen and Lynne were together, they talked about Missy. What Missy wore to school, how Missy talked, Missy's favorite pastimes.

Sometimes Lynne got tired of hearing about Missy, but she knew Karen needed to talk about her. It was part of the healing process. She was still going through it herself.

The week before Christmas break had been particularly busy. One afternoon Lynne had packed up her things and was about to leave when Karen approached her. She had a faraway look in her eyes and Lynne was worried. There was something in her eyes that was almost dead, as though she had no emotion. She asked Lynne over to her parents' house for dinner and although Lynne was tired, she agreed to go and make an early night of it.

Paula Severson's dinner was delicious, and it was almost eight o'clock when Lynne decided to head home. Suddenly, Karen jumped up from her seat and told Lynne there was something she had to show her in the back bedroom.

"Come on, I just got it all set up. You have to see it." Karen was excited and Lynne smiled. It was the first time she had seen so much life in Karen's eyes for a long time. She stood up and followed her down the hallway.

Karen reached the room first and went inside with Lynne right behind her. She waved a hand across the room and looked at Lynne.

"Well, what do you think?"

Lynne didn't know what to say. The room made her feel very uneasy. On Karen's dresser there was an oversized picture of Missy, and the walls were covered with snapshots of her. Missy as a little girl. Missy as a teenager. Missy with Karen. Missy with her brothers. There were newspaper articles, too, cut out and taped onto the walls.

It was like a shrine.

Lynne was silent and Karen was getting angry. Lynne was no better than Missy had been. She didn't really appreciate anything Karen did.

"You're not saying anything. Don't you like it? This is how I've always wanted my room to be. See the article over there." Karen pointed to a paragraph on one of the clippings that was highlighted by yellow marker pen.

It was an article written after Missy was killed, and Karen Severson was quoted saying that she wouldn't rest until she found the "animals that did this to her best friend."

Karen smiled proudly and looked again at Lynne.

"Uh, yeah," stammered Lynne. "It's great. I mean, this way you have all her memories around you." But there was no conviction in her voice, and she stepped nervously back toward the door. Suddenly Karen lost her temper and shouted.

"Just get out, if you don't like it! Who needs you in here, anyway? You're just intruding on my memories of Missy. These are my memories and I want you out. I never should have brought you here in the first place."

Lynne felt her hands begin to shake as she watched the enraged Karen. What had she done wrong? She liked the pictures, it was just that, well, there were so many of them.

"Hey, Karen. Listen, I'm sorry. It's just that I've never seen anything like this before, that's all."

Karen calmed down and apologized to Lynne before she left. But the scene in Karen's bedroom stuck in Lynne's mind as she drove home. Why would Karen want all those pictures staring at her every day?

A shiver coursed through Lynne's body as she pulled into her driveway and turned off the motor. Karen's preoccupation was unnatural. Somehow, in Karen Severson's bedroom, Missy Avila was still alive.

29

THE DESERT LOOKED like an unchanging sea of brown. Dry soil, rock formations, weathered cactus plants, desert brush, and the mountains off in the distance. The girl wondered how long it would take to reach their destination.

Summer was the worst possible time to travel through the desert, but they hadn't had any choice. It had been nearly two years since the murder, and finally she felt she would suffocate if Steven didn't get her out of Arleta. She needed to be somewhere else, where she could start over and where she wouldn't be terrified to take a shower. At first she had wanted to stay home, close to her friends and family. But the fear was eating away at her and she knew she couldn't take much more. She had made her decision last week, after the nightmare.

She had been tossing in bed, rolling from one side to the other and searching desperately for sleep. It was 3:00 A.M. when slowly she fell into a strange and terrible dream. She and Steven were walking along a stream, and then Steven disappeared and Missy stood before her.

"The worst thing you guys could do is leave me up here all alone!"

Missy repeated these words until they echoed inside the girl's head. She sat straight up in bed.

There was someone in the room, someone walking toward her. All she could see was the outline of the person's hair. Then she saw the face and screamed, hoping the image would disappear. Missy walked closer to the bed and stood right over her, staring at her face.

"The worst thing you guys could do is leave me up here all alone!"

The girl screamed again, but the image wouldn't leave and then she began to cry. Someone else entered the room—the killers.

Closer they came, and then Missy's face disappeared. First one and then the other began laughing and one yelled out, "Come on out here, Missy. It isn't that deep! Come on out here, Missy, it isn't that deep!"

Then they turned and looked at her, shivering in the bed, and moved closer.

The girl could feel their hands closing in on her throat and she knew they were going to kill her. She closed her eyes and fainted. The last thing she heard was laughter and one of them saying over and over, "Come on out here, Missy. It isn't that deep!"

It was six o'clock the next morning when the girl woke up and looked at the alarm clock. Steven lay beside her, still asleep. The room was just as it had been the night before. No one stood near the bed, and the door to the bedroom was still closed.

Sweat broke out over the girl's forehead. Of all the nightmares she'd been having lately, this had been the worst. Shaking violently, she slowly stepped out of bed and wrapped a bathrobe around herself.

She told Steven that morning over breakfast that

she wanted out. She had to leave Arleta before she went crazy or something terrible happened. Steven had agreed. He was relieved that they would finally be making a change. This way they would be far from the murderers, away from anyone who could hurt the girl he loved.

They had made plans to move to Las Vegas and now, ten days later, they were driving down the two-lane desert highway in search of a new life. The girl had been given a tryout to work for one of the big casinos as a lady wrestler. It wasn't the kind of work she wanted to do forever, but it offered a fantastic salary, which would help them get set up in an apartment.

A week after arriving in Las Vegas she got word from the casino that she had been hired. They had appreciated her thin, shapely body and pretty brown hair. She knew they weren't really looking for wrestlers but showgirls who were willing to play around in a satin-covered ring so men could have a good time. A month later, in September 1987, she had become one of the best lady wrestlers on staff. The trick was to look angry, as if you really were overpowering the other woman in the ring with you.

The work was easy for her. Every time she stepped into the ring she thought of her fears, the images of the killers and the drowned girl, which had held her back for so long. In the ring she could fight those fears and emerge victorious.

Only Steven knew the truth. She was still terrified. She didn't have as many nightmares as before, but she still couldn't take a shower by herself. He wondered how long it would take her to recover. After all, the girl had been dead for nearly two years.

* * *

In Arleta it had been a particularly warm summer. Irene Avila had had less and less contact with the detectives.

By then Karen Severson had finished beauty school and she and Lynne Robbins visited Missy's gravesite at least three times a week.

Catherine Scott had followed up on her hunch and Laura Doyle had been questioned again by the detectives. Her story remained unchanged, which bothered the detectives. But there was no new evidence.

That fall Laura Doyle was promoted at the supermarket bakery and was now making cakes. When she wasn't doing that, she was doing drugs. Karen had told the Avilas about Laura's drug problem, and it didn't surprise any of them that they almost never heard from her anymore.

30

AT NINE O'CLOCK in the evening, September 18, 1987, the phone rang in the Avila house. Irene, who had been folding towels, picked up the phone on the second ring.

"Hello?"

There was silence on the other end for a brief moment, and Irene wondered if this was a prank call. When the caller started talking, Irene recognized Karen Severson's voice. She was talking very fast; Irene had to strain to understand her.

"It worked, Irene!" Karen's words tumbled through the phone line. "She finally told the truth. I was over at her house and I was yelling at her, telling her that she had to tell the truth. She finally told me what really happened."

"Wait a minute, Karen. Slow down. What do you mean? Who told the truth?" Irene tried to speak calmly, but she felt her heart beat faster. Something had happened.

Karen spoke more slowly, and this time Irene understood everything she said.

"I'm at Laura Doyle's house. I've been here all evening and I finally got her to tell the truth. Now we can find out what really happened to Missy!"

Irene couldn't believe it.

October first was just two weeks away. Missy would have been dead for two long years, during which time the detectives had been working harder than anyone in the Avila family knew. But they had found nothing, and now, because of Karen Severson's diligence, they were going to know the truth. Laura had been lying after all.

"Can you bring her over here now?" Irene sounded hopeful, and she realized that a terrible weight had been lifted from her heart. She felt happier than she had in two years. She was going to find out what had happened to her little girl. Finally, Missy could rest in peace.

Karen placed her hand over the receiver and mumbled something to Laura. When she returned, she told Irene they would both be right over.

Irene hung up the phone and noticed that her hands were shaking. Why had Laura lied? Why had she kept the truth to herself for so long? What terrible information was she covering up?

Irene picked up the phone and made a call to the sheriff's station. She told the night deputy that there had been a breakthrough in the murder of her daughter, Missy Avila. The key witness, the last person seen with her daughter, was willing to tell the truth and she would like to bring her in immediately. The deputy put her on hold and, when he returned, told Irene that Catherine Scott and Dan Jenkins would meet her at the Van Nuys station at ten o'clock.

The detectives both remember driving to the station in record time. Catherine Scott was still shaking her head in disbelief when she pulled up and parked her car. They had been right about Laura Doyle. She was a liar and even though everything in their years of experience had told them she hadn't been telling the truth, they hadn't been able to get the girl to change her story.

Catherine smiled as she locked her car. This was going to be good—firing the questions at Laura, watching her squirm and finally spill out the truth. She'd come a long way from being Richard Scott's timid young wife, and as she walked into the building she couldn't wait for the show to begin.

Back at the Avila home Irene sat down on the sofa and waited for Karen's car to pull up out front. If ever there had been a time Irene Avila was thankful for Karen's constant involvement in Missy's murder investigation, it was now. Because of Karen's determination to see Missy's murder resolved, Irene believed they were about to find the truth. She glanced at Missy's picture over the sofa and the minutes melted away until suddenly she heard Karen and Laura walking up the front steps. Irene said nothing, and it wasn't until the girls were seated side by side in the living room that Karen finally spoke.

"Go ahead, Laura. Tell Irene what you told me." Karen stared at Laura and, when the girl didn't answer immediately, poked her sharply.

"Okay, okay." Laura looked up slowly and Irene realized that she had wasted away to almost nothing. Her face looked like little more than a skeletal frame and her skin had the cold, gray pallor of someone who was heavily addicted to drugs.

Drugs and alcohol were a way for Laura to escape the nightmare of real life, a way to escape the truth about October 1, 1985. Everyone knew Laura had become hooked on drugs and drinking, and they blamed these addictions on her parents' problems. But when Laura admitted she had been lying for two years about what happened to Missy, her addictions made more sense: she had been using substance abuse to distract herself from the ugly truth she had been hiding. Irene thought that if this was the case, telling the truth would help her put aside the drugs and alcohol and go on with her life.

Later, it would occur to Irene Avila that the night of truth telling did indeed mark a turning point in Laura Doyle's drug involvement: it got worse.

Irene and Karen sat side by side, waiting for Laura to speak.

"Well, I know I told you before that I dropped Missy off to talk to three boys." Laura's voice faded.

"Three boys in a blue Camaro, right?" Irene leaned forward, urging her to continue.

"Yeah. Three boys in a blue Camaro. Well, it didn't really happen like that. What really happened was, well . . ."

Irene sighed loudly. "Laura, just tell me what really happened. We have to get to the truth."

"Well, that afternoon, instead of going to the park, I took Missy to this church parking lot in Los Angeles and dropped her off. She told me she would get a ride home from this guy she was going to meet. She told me not to wait for her." Laura sat back and crossed her arms, looking down at the floor.

It took Irene a moment to realize that Laura was finished. There was nothing more, no great revelation. Irene began to grow pale.

"Laura, go ahead. Finish." Irene waited but Laura shook her head.

"That's all. That's all I can remember. She was going

to meet this guy there and she said she would get a ride home."

Karen Severson watched Irene's reaction. Irene wasn't believing the story because it had so many holes. Suddenly, Karen got angry and stood up, towering over Laura.

"Laura, you're just a no-good liar! There has to be more to the story than that." Karen grabbed the skin on Laura's arm. "Anyway, why should we believe that you can't remember the rest when it's taken you this long to come out with the truth?" Karen leaned toward the girl and pushed her. She winced, withdrawing to the corner of the sofa.

"I told you the truth. I'm sorry I waited so long, but now you know and that's all I can remember." Laura sounded adamant this time, and Irene slumped back in her chair. It wasn't much to go on.

"Why didn't you tell us all this before? The detectives have been looking for blue Camaros for nearly two years, Laura. Do you realize what you've done to the investigation? Now they might never be able to find out what happened to her." Irene stopped for a moment and thought of something.

"Was there a reason why you didn't tell us the truth?"

Laura looked up and Irene thought she had the eyes of a dead person. "Yes. I was afraid you'd be mad that we went to Los Angeles when we told you we were going to the park."

Laura sounded like a naughty child with a weak excuse. Irene could have taken the truth—if Laura's story was indeed the truth.

Now Laura was trying to convince Irene that she had jeopardized the investigation of Missy's murder because she didn't want Irene to be mad at Missy. Angry tears were rolling down Irene's face as she made an effort to speak.

"Okay. If that's all you can remember, then you can tell it to the police." Irene was angry, but her voice didn't give her away. They needed Laura now; everything she could remember was essential to the investigation.

Irene grabbed her purse and motioned to Karen to get her car keys. "Karen, you remember where the sheriff's station is, don't you?" Irene was halfway out the door with Karen right behind her.

"I remember. I'll drive us. Laura can sit in the front seat with me and you can sit in the back."

On the way to the station Laura asked Karen to pull into a drive-through dairy for some potato chips. Karen bought a soft drink for herself.

Even with her emotions churning in a dozen different directions, Irene thought the stop was strange. Her daughter had been murdered and the person last seen with her was finally willing to tell the detectives what really happened. And here they were stopping for chips and soft drinks as if it were just a night out on the town. Irene kept her thoughts to herself. They were just ten minutes from the station, and then the detectives could really begin to investigate Missy's death.

In the front seat Karen and Laura were munching their chips and giggling about something the radio announcer had said.

31

AT THE East San Fernando Valley police station it had been a slow evening, and the arrival of detectives Catherine Scott and Dan Jenkins had caused quite a stir among the night shift. It was common practice to let officers from the sheriff's department use the Van Nuys office to conduct interviews. In this case Van Nuys was just a few minutes from Arleta; it would have taken Irene, Karen, and Laura nearly an hour to drive to the sheriff's station in southeastern Los Angeles.

Catherine was waiting with Dan at one of the empty desks when a deputy walked up. "Three people are waiting for you in the lobby. Didn't give me a name, but I told them you'd be right out."

Catherine Scott smiled. She didn't need a name. She knew who they were and couldn't wait for the inquisition to begin. It was show time.

She walked out to the lobby. Irene Avila stood up to meet her.

"Laura has been lying," she said, starting to cry. Catherine reached out and took her hand. "Karen got her to tell the truth and now she wants to let you know what really happened to Missy that afternoon." Irene turned and motioned for Laura to stand.

Catherine looked at Dan and the two shared a famil-

iar look. They had been right all along. Laura Doyle
had been lying, which was why her story about the
blue Camaros had never changed any of the times
they'd questioned her. Catherine felt a familiar thrill
as she ushered Laura Doyle into the tiny room where
witnesses were questioned. A murder was about to be
solved, a murder that had stumped them for nearly
two years.

"Right this way, Laura." Catherine motioned to the
room and Dan followed them inside, shutting the
door.

While they questioned Laura, Irene paced in the
waiting area, nervously wringing her hands and glancing at the room.

"What's taking them so long?" she asked aloud.
Karen stood up beside her.

"They're probably trying to get more information
out of her. I know there's more to the story. That can't
be all she remembers, not after hiding the truth for so
long."

Twenty minutes later the door opened and an exhausted Catherine stepped out with Dan behind her.

Catherine walked over to Irene and shook her head
in frustration. "She tells us she took Missy to a church
parking lot in Los Angeles. She dropped Missy off to
meet some guy, and Missy told her she'd get a ride
home from him. That's it. She doesn't remember if
Missy mentioned the man's name. She doesn't remember if anyone was in the parking lot when she dropped
her off. She doesn't even remember where the church
was or what it was called." Catherine frowned. "I
think she's still lying. I think there's much more to the
story, and she's not telling us."

Karen stepped forward.

"Then let me go in there with her. Give me fifteen minutes. I know I can get the story out of her." Karen was so willing to help, and Irene was thankful again for her loyalty.

Catherine looked at Dan. The detective shrugged. There was something very odd about the role Karen was playing in all of this.

"Why not? We'll wait out here and you let us know if you find anything out."

Irene looked ready to pass out, and Catherine offered her a glass of water. "All we can do is wait and see what else she's willing to tell us." Irene nodded.

Dan watched as Karen joined Laura, and the wheels began turning in the corners of his mind. Something wasn't right. The new story felt even more like a lie than Laura's first story. Suddenly Dan wondered if maybe Laura might somehow be responsible for Missy's death. Her behavior certainly was strange. And now those two could be talking about anything in that room. For all he knew, Laura could be confessing everything to Karen.

Dan sighed. Maybe he was just jumping to conclusions, but more than ten years in the business was good for a hunch or two. Something about this whole scenario bothered him.

It was nearly eleven o'clock when Karen walked out of the room with a broad smile on her face. "It worked," she announced. "I got her to tell me the rest of the details."

Irene let out a deep breath and walked over to hug Karen. "I knew you could do it, Karen. How can I ever thank you?"

Laura left the room, her head down, and Catherine and Dan ushered her back inside where they, too, could learn the full details of her story. Dan listened as Laura told them that the church was Grace Brethren Community Church in Los Angeles near First Street. She had dropped Missy off to meet a drug dealer, someone she owed five hundred dollars for a previous drug sale. The guy was supposed to give Missy a ride home and Laura had left her there, waiting for him.

Catherine took notes on everything Laura said, but Dan kept his eyes fixed on the girl as she struggled to continue her story. There was still something wrong. He knew it intuitively, and there was nothing he could do but listen. When Catherine had finished her questioning he would have his chance, but he sensed that Laura wasn't going to change her story again.

When the questioning was over, the detectives and Laura Doyle joined Irene and Karen in the waiting area. By then Karen had explained to Irene what had happened when she and Laura were in the room. According to Karen, after several minutes in the room Laura had finally admitted that she was afraid to tell the truth because it involved a drug dealer. She hadn't wanted Irene to be upset because Missy was using drugs.

"That's crazy, Karen, and you know it." Irene looked ready to collapse. "I knew what Missy was involved in, maybe not everything and maybe not the extent of it—but that's no reason to lie about what happened."

Irene cried softly, but Karen stayed beside her, talking quietly to her, assuring her that Missy and she had shared a better relationship than most mothers and daughters ever dreamed of. Irene nodded through her tears and Karen leaned her head on her shoulder—just as Missy used to—comforting her, as she had for the past two years.

This was how Dan and Catherine found them when they returned to the waiting area. Karen comforting Irene, sitting beside her and holding her hand. Dan stood watching them for a minute, taking in the scene.

There was something repulsive about it.

Ten days later Laura Doyle's addiction to cocaine reached a fever pitch and on September 28, 1987, she checked into a treatment facility in the northwest end of the San Fernando Valley. There she spent thirty days drug free, and on October 26, 1987, Laura Doyle walked out of the center with a clean mind, if not a clean conscience.

The next day she began free-basing cocaine.

32

BY DECEMBER 1987 the leads that had been inspired by Laura Doyle's new story had all but dried up. At first, even though they doubted Laura's latest version of that October afternoon, the detectives were hopeful that some relevant clue could be uncovered. Dan Jenkins had checked out the neighborhood near the church, and Catherine Scott had talked to people who had worked at the church over the past two years. Nobody remembered anything unusual happening in October 1985. It was too long ago, the details too obscure, and even though it had been daylight when Laura dropped Missy off, no one remembered seeing the girls.

The detectives were not surprised. There was certainly nothing unusual about two teenage girls stopping in a church parking lot. However, the pastor at the church was surprised that anyone would meet a drug dealer in the lot. The church and its surrounding neighborhood had been given increased police patrol for the past three years, and the problems they once had experienced with drug dealers hanging around had disappeared by 1985.

Catherine Scott still kept Missy's lock of hair with her wherever she went. They still hadn't found anyone who knew about Missy's hair, how chunks of it had been cut off before she was killed. During each interview they hoped someone might mention the hair-cutting incident. But the new trail of clues Laura Doyle had given them only seemed to be taking them farther from the truth.

Since the day Laura had changed her story, the detectives had twice questioned the girl to see if she could remember anything else. Her story remained the same each time. Dan and Catherine were certain she was lying. There was something so cold about her, something that reeked of guilt.

By Christmas 1987 the hope that Irene had felt in September had also fizzled, and a gloom hung over the household as the holidays approached. It seemed to affect everyone, especially Karen Severson.

Strange things had started happening to Karen, and those who knew her wondered if she might be suffering from severe depression. Several times Irene had even told Karen that she should think about seeing a psychiatrist, but Karen had laughed at the idea. Karen knew what her problem was. She knew what had happened to Missy and she wasn't telling. So Missy wouldn't leave her alone.

Even Lynne Robbins had noticed Karen's behavior. Karen and Lynne had remained close friends after finishing beauty school, both with a license to do manicuring work. During the spring of 1988 Lynne grew quite worried about Karen.

Karen spoke constantly about Missy and her frequent visits to Missy's grave. Several times a week Lynne would accompany Karen to the cemetery, standing back while Karen sat on Missy's tombstone carrying on a conversation just as if Missy were able to hear her. Sometimes Karen would raise her voice and carry on, apologizing that Missy had died and not someone who deserved it. There were times when Karen would whisper to the picture of Missy's face etched in the stone. She would ask Missy to leave her alone and let her go on with her life.

Lynne found these actions strange and embarrassing, but what really made her nervous was the way Karen would turn around and look at her. If Lynne didn't have just the right expression on her face, Karen would lash out at her and tell her to stop intruding on Missy's memories.

One night at the cemetery Karen asked Lynne to go up to the stream where Missy had been drowned. Lynne instinctively felt that going with Karen Severson up to the murder scene would not be wise. She smiled politely and turned her down.

A week later Lynne visited Karen at her parents' home in Arleta. When she walked into Karen's room, Andrea was looking at her mother, smiling. She wore a party dress, Karen's high heels, and far too much makeup for a little girl. Karen didn't notice Lynne standing in the doorway, and for almost a minute she listened as Karen spoke to her daughter. She wasn't calling her Andrea. She was calling her Missy.

Lynne was convinced that Karen Severson was losing her mind. She told Irene about Karen's behavior, and later that month Irene again confronted Karen and again suggested the girl seek professional help.

It was nearly six o'clock and Karen was coming over for dinner. She was furious when she arrived. She said she had been talking to Laura again and that she still thought Laura was hiding the truth.

"I've got to get that girl to tell us what really happened to Missy!" Karen screamed, and Irene put her finger to her lips.

"Shhh. Don't yell, Karen." Irene spoke calmly. "I know you're frustrated, but we have to let the detectives do their job. It doesn't do any good to keep dwelling on what Laura says."

Karen grew quiet, a faraway look on her face. After dinner they went into the living room, and Irene cleared her throat.

"Karen, I think you really need to see a doctor." Karen wasn't listening. She had turned her head toward the sofa, her eyes growing wide. Irene followed her gaze, but the sofa was empty. When Karen spoke, it was as if from a trance.

"Irene, do you see her?" Karen pointed at the sofa and began to shake violently. Karen saw Missy walking toward her, holding a knife. "Do you see her, Irene?"

Irene felt a wave of anxiety as she looked again at the empty sofa and then back to Karen. The girl continued, her words even and measured.

"It's the same every night, before I go to sleep. She comes and watches me and never says a word. She scares me, Irene. But I never said anything about it before."

As Karen spoke, she never took her eyes off the sofa. Irene watched her, horrified.

"And every night she comes. I tell her I'm sorry, I tell her someone else should have died, someone who deserved it. But she doesn't say a word. She's going to haunt me forever, Irene. Just like she's doing right now."

Suddenly Karen turned from the sofa and looked at Irene. "Don't you see her, Irene? She was walking toward me, but now she's sitting on the sofa watching us."

Irene shook her head and despite her fear she managed to ask the question. "Who, Karen, who do you see?"

Karen turned her head slowly back toward the sofa and whispered, "Missy."

33

EVEN IN A town like Las Vegas most people were asleep at four o'clock in the morning. In the tiny two-bedroom apartment everyone was asleep except the girl. She had spent her worst night in months, forced to keep her eyes open to stop the killers from visiting her. They visited her often these days. Threatening her. Warning her. Telling her to keep her mouth shut.

After they left, laughing into the night, the dead girl would appear. Sometimes she would sit at the edge of the bed and sob, begging the frightened girl to help her, begging her not to leave her there, all alone. She couldn't help Missy now.

Her only solace was in the wrestling ring, pretending to fight, pretending to be angry. But it was not a game to her, and during those moments of concentration the fear was gone. She rolled over again, facing the alarm clock. Four-fourteen A.M. She wondered how long it had been since she had slept through a night or taken a shower without the suffocating panic that always engulfed her.

Then she heard a ringing sound. She sat straight up in bed, and Steven reached out in his sleep and picked up the phone.

"Hello?" he said, his voice groggy. Then he handed her the phone. "It's for you."

The girl began to shake as she took it from his hand. No one should be calling at this hour. Maybe it was the killers. Maybe they had found her and they wanted to do away with her too. Maybe this was a nightmare.

"Hello?"

"Hi, honey. It's Jack."

Jack. Her big brother. He was ten years older than she and they had different fathers, but he was always the one who looked out for her. Feeling a warm wave of peace wash over her body, she leaned back into the pillow. It was only Jack.

"It's so good to hear your voice." She spoke quietly because Steven had drifted back to sleep. "Why are you calling so early, Jack? It's not even five in the morning."

There was silence as Jack worked up the courage to go on.

"Honey, I've got some bad news for you. I had to call you now. I'm sorry, honey. So sorry."

Jack was crying now. He paused and the girl felt her heart begin to race again. So it was the killers after all. They had found her family and threatened to kill them too. Now they would all know that she had hidden the truth. The girl closed her eyes as Jack continued.

"It's Allen, baby. They found him an hour ago at his apartment. Honey, he killed himself. Oh, baby, I'm so sorry."

A new feeling consumed the girl. It started in her heart and worked its way through her arms and legs and ended up in her mind. It was something very different from the fear she had known for more than two years. It was pain. Raw, gut-wrenching pain.

Allen, her eighteen-year-old brother, was dead.

What had Jack said? Suicide. Her little brother had killed himself.

"Jack, are you sure? Are you sure it was Allen?"

In a house in Arleta, Jack Froman nodded. "Yes, baby. He's been depressed a lot lately, and we aren't sure what made him do it. Can you come home?"

The girl's head was spinning. Little Allen, her tagalong, her best friend, her brother. Dead. She had been too wrapped up in her own fears even to realize he was upset. He must have been hurting for a long time and she hadn't even noticed. She remembered the last time she had seen him and he hadn't looked as happy as he had in the past. But she hadn't noticed, and now he was gone. She felt strangled; a sob lodged itself in her throat. So this was what Missy's family had felt that afternoon in October. This was her punishment for having hidden the truth.

"I'm coming home, Jack. Tell them I'll be there."

Three hours later she and Steven were on the road, crossing back over the desert, four months after they had arrived looking for a new way of life. The two were silent for several hours before Steven spoke.

"Listen, I'm really sorry about Allen. If there's anything I can do, tell me, okay?" He looked over at her but she was staring out the window, in shock.

Steven looked away. Things had been so rough since the murder. And now this. He had always told her to keep quiet about the murder. Even now he believed that if she told the authorities, the killers would come after her. They were so much bigger. Bigger, stronger, and meaner. She wouldn't stand a chance.

He glanced at her again and realized the truth. She didn't stand a chance anyway. Now that Allen was dead, she was feeling the same kind of pain Missy's family must have felt, and he knew that among the tormenting thoughts that crowded her mind, she was thinking about Missy's family. She held the information that could give them freedom. He wondered if maybe someday she should tell the police and put the horror behind them.

Steven sighed and felt tears well up in his eyes. First things first. There would be the funeral and then he would have to see how quickly she recovered from the shock. But when the healing process began, he was almost certain she would ask him again about the murder. This time he would give her different advice. He would tell her to call the police and give them the truth about what had happened to Missy. Even if that revelation jeopardized her safety, at least she would have some peace of mind.

34

DETECTIVE CATHERINE SCOTT was frustrated. Although the spring of 1988 had been a good season, with relatively few murders and several of the tough long-standing ones solved, there was one case that bothered Catherine like none other. During the slow nighttime shifts the Michele Avila murder took up permanent location in her mind.

First she would review the facts. They never changed, but she was comforted that they existed. Then she would think about the possibilities, allowing herself an open mind, and consider even the most absurd scenarios. After all, Michele Avila was dead. Someone had killed her. She hadn't wound up facedown in a shallow stream by herself. No accident had caused a log to be placed over her back, and she hadn't driven up to the remote mountainside area by herself. She and Jenkins agreed that Laura Doyle was lying. If they'd doubted her before, they were certain something was wrong with her story after she had changed it.

Catherine stood up and walked to the hallway for some water. She would spend the rest of the evening thinking about the Avila murder, but later that night when she went home she had a sickening thought that it would never be solved. The worst of it was that somewhere, that very night, the people who had killed Michele Avila were free.

Nearly twenty miles away, in a cemetery near Arleta, Karen Severson steered her parents' van over the winding, narrow roads. She knew her way—even now, in the pitch dark. She spotted the tree, her landmark, and pulled the van over, turning off the engine.

It was time to visit Missy.

Karen pulled a six-pack of beer from behind her seat, separated one from the rest, and popped the top. She stepped out of the van and pulled her sweater tightly around herself. The nights were cold, especially here by Missy's grave.

She walked over to the stone and looked down at it. *In loving memory of our precious Missy, 1968 to 1985.* Karen read the words over and over and took a long swig of beer. She turned her head slightly and her eyes settled on Missy's face, etched into the stone. She was so pretty, even in death.

Slowly, Karen bent down and traced her finger across the etchings. Missy's pretty eyes, her perfect face, and gorgeous long hair. Karen looked away and stared at the sky.

"Missy, I'm back. I've come to talk with you again. How have you been?"

Karen paused, looking back down at Missy's face in the stone. She waited for an answer.

"Why are you mad, Missy?" Karen waited again. "I know. I know. I've told her to stop coming around. She's butting into our memories, which I don't like either."

The wind whistled through the trees and a coyote began to howl. It was almost midnight. Karen kept talking.

"You know she doesn't mean anything to me, Missy. Lynne and I are just friends from school. Missy, you don't know how much I miss you."

Karen waited, tilting her head, listening to imaginary voices.

"That's not true. I'm so sorry. It should have been someone else. I had nothing to do with it, Missy, can't you let me go? I have to go on with my life."

Suddenly the coyote was silent and Karen could hear the sound of leaves crunching in the distance. She took another gulp of beer.

"Okay, okay. I'll stay away from her. I don't want her around anyway because it ruins what we have. She even told me she thinks it's wrong for me to come here and meet with you."

A look of fear crossed Karen Severson's face and she spoke quickly.

"I have to go now, Missy. I'll talk to you later."

Karen crumpled the empty beer can, tossed it near Missy's grave, and walked quickly to the van. She stepped inside and turned the key.

It was dead.

Karen tried it again. Silence. The wind began to rustle and Karen could hear Missy talking.

"Missy, let me go! I'm sorry! Why won't you let me go!"

Karen banged her hand on the steering wheel and tried it again. The key turned, but the engine was quiet.

"Missy, let go of me! I have to get out of here! I'll come back, I promise!"

Karen's screams could be heard across the cemetery now, and she began to shake. Quietly, she whispered her final plea.

"Missy, I'll do anything you say. Please let me go!"

This time, when she turned the key, the engine started.

Later that same night Lynne Robbins was sleeping soundly when the phone rang. She woke up instantly and looked at the clock. It was just after two o'clock in the morning. She picked up the phone and muttered a tired hello.

"Hi, Lynne. Just wanted to warn you to look out for yourself."

Lynne was wide awake now, and she sat up in bed. She didn't recognize the voice, but it was a female who knew her name. She waited for the caller to continue.

"Are you there, Lynne? You need to look out behind you. Stop intruding where you are no longer welcome."

Lynne was scared now, but she still couldn't figure out who the caller was.

"Who is this? What do you want?"

The caller laughed.

"I want you to stay away from Karen Severson. Stay away from the memories. Do you understand?"

Lynne wondered if she should wake her husband, but she stayed perfectly still, too frightened to move.

"Tell me who you are. Why are you calling?"

The caller could hear the tremor in Lynne's voice and she snickered.

"You know who I am, Lynne. Don't act so innocent."

There was a pause and Lynne wondered if she should hang up. Then the caller spoke again.

"This is Missy."

35

ALLEN HAD BEEN dead for almost four months when the dreams returned. At first they were brief and the girl could make them go away by forcing herself to wake up. Then, during the summer of 1988, they grew worse than ever before.

The killers would walk up to the bed and laugh. Then they would vanish and a black-hooded creature would appear. She knew the creature represented death. The same death that had taken Missy and Allen was trying to take her too.

For five months she continued in a state of terror, afraid to sleep, afraid to shower, and afraid of dying.

Finally, on July 25, 1988, she could no longer stand it. That morning she told Steven she would go to the police. Whatever they did to her would be preferable to living amid a cloud of fear.

Steven listened as she announced her decision. Tears rolled down her cheeks, and his heart went out to her. He took her into his arms.

"It's okay, sweetheart. I understand." He stroked her brown hair and felt her sobbing against his chest. "And after you tell the police, we can put it all behind us. Maybe one day we'll get married and this whole thing will just be a bad memory."

The girl nodded, grabbing a tissue and wiping her face. She walked over to the phone and dialed Jack's number. Cindy Silverio had always thought of Jack as her brother even though they had different fathers. Jack's father was a police officer and he would know whom she should contact. She waited nervously while the phone rang.

"Jack Froman." He was at work and sounded very official. She forced herself to speak.

"Jack, it's Cindy. I have to talk to you. Can you meet me after work? It's important."

Jack was confused. Cindy sounded desperate; he wondered what had happened. Maybe she was just lonely, but she sounded particularly urgent.

"Sure, baby. No problem. I'll meet you at your apartment as soon as I leave here. About five-fifteen. That okay with you?"

"Yes. See you then. Thanks, Jack."

When Jack Froman arrived at his sister's apartment, she answered the door and ushered him inside. Steven sat nearby and the girl remained standing.

"Okay, so why am I here?" Jack smiled, but his sister stared down at the floor. Her face was deathly white, and Jack couldn't imagine what had caused her such distress.

"Jack, I know about a murder. It happened a long time ago. Almost three years now."

Jack couldn't believe his sister's words. At first he thought she must be kidding, but he could tell by her expression that this was no joke. He waited for her to go on.

"You remember that girl I went to school with? Her name was Missy Avila."

Jack thought for a minute and then he remembered.

Of course. She had been drowned in a stream up in the Angeles National Forest and the killers had never been found.

Jack nodded.

"Well, I know what happened to her. I went up there with the people who killed her and then I got scared and ran back to the car. They told me they killed her, and I never said anything because I was afraid they would kill me too. Oh, Jack. What should I do? I want to tell the police what happened. Can you help me?"

The girl began to cry. Jack stood near her, taking her hand.

"There, there. It's okay. Did anyone know you were there besides the people who killed her?"

She shook her head, then remembered. "Just Steven. I told him right after it happened, but we both decided it would be better not to say anything."

Jack understood. Even now he was worried about his sister's safety, but she must have thought over the danger before she came to him. Now she was ready to talk to the police.

"Why did you wait until now, baby?"

The girl dropped her head into her hands and began to sob. "Because of Allen. I wasn't going to say anything about it, but then Allen died." She struggled to finish. "Then I understood what Missy's family went through, how they must have suffered. How they still suffer. I couldn't keep it in any longer."

Jack nodded. "It's okay. I understand. I think I know whom you should call."

He reached for the phone and got the number for the Foothill police station in the northeast San Fernando Valley. Arleta was part of the Foothill station's jurisdiction, and Jack was certain someone from the station would be willing to talk to them.

He dialed the number as the girl sat down on the sofa and tried to stop shivering. This was it. There would be no turning back once she talked to the police. The operator put him on hold and it was nearly two minutes before someone got on the line.

"How can I help you?"

Jack cleared his throat.

"Sir, this is Jack Froman. I live in Arleta and I'm at my sister's house. She just told me that she is a witness to a murder that happened three years ago. I think we should come down and let her give you the details."

The officer sounded bored when he answered.

"That's something for the day shift," he said. "You'll have to call back between nine and five."

Before Jack could respond, the officer hung up. Jack stood holding the phone and watched his sister's reaction.

"Well, what did they say?" She looked at him with fear in her eyes.

"They said to call back tomorrow during business hours." Jack was livid. Here was someone ready and willing to come forward as a witness to a murder and they didn't have time for her.

By 9:30 the next morning it was a hundred degrees in Arleta. Jack Froman was determined to help his sister, but he wasn't about to call the Foothill police station. If they didn't want to talk to her, fine. He would call the bigwigs. He looked through the phone book and found the number for the district attorney's office. The deputy who answered the phone was polite and asked which murder his sister had information about.

At first the officer didn't remember the case. Then he remembered. It was the one the sheriffs were working on—they'd conducted their interviews out of the Van Nuys station because it was closer to the people they were interviewing. The officer sorted through his desk and found the sheriff's card: Catherine Scott, homicide.

He picked up the telephone and began dialing.

It was seven o'clock when Catherine Scott arrived at Cindy Silverio's apartment in Arleta. The building was one of those that developers throw up in a few weeks with a couple of truckloads of plasterboard and two-by-fours. You could sneeze in one of these apartments and the guy three doors down might yell, "Bless you!" The building was just one of dozens like it in that particular neighborhood, with graffiti scrawled on some of the signposts and brick walls. But Catherine was used to conducting interviews in such places.

Cindy's apartment was on the third floor, and Catherine walked the stairs quickly. She had spoken to the girl briefly on the phone, long enough to be certain this visit would be worth her while even if it was her day off.

Catherine knew exactly what she was looking for. For three years the detectives had skillfully kept quiet about the fact that someone had cut Missy's hair before they killed her. If this girl was the real thing and she had been up at the murder scene the day Missy was killed, then she would certainly know about the hair. And if she hadn't been there, if she was just another of Missy's friends trying to be helpful, then the hair would never come up. It was that simple. Silently, Catherine prayed the girl would know.

Before she knocked on Cindy Silverio's apartment door, Catherine Scott reached into her pants pocket and pulled out a folded piece of paper. It was yellowed by now, wrinkled from the number of times it had been moved from one pocket to another. She opened it slowly, careful not to disturb the contents. There, nestled inside, was the tiny lock of Missy's hair. Catherine folded the paper back together and held it in her fist for a minute. She put the folded paper back into her pocket, took a deep breath, and knocked on the door.

Inside, Cindy was expecting her and answered quickly. The girl looked terrified and Catherine forced herself not to seem overanxious.

The apartment had a simple floor plan: one bedroom and a small bathroom off the main room, which was really something of a living and dining room in one. Cindy introduced her boyfriend, Steven, and her brother, Jack, who were seated on a couch in this room. Catherine nodded and followed Cindy toward a three-legged table in the corner.

"My sister told me she knows the details of a murder. She wants to tell someone about them," Jack said. Steven, sitting next to him, nodded in agreement.

"Thank you for your help," Catherine said, and looked around the room. You never knew about someone calling with case-breaking information, but Catherine was almost positive these people were sincere.

It was a humid July night, oppressive and stuffy inside Cindy's apartment, which was not equipped with central air conditioning. Instead, a small fan sat on the kitchen counter and a wall unit chugged at full speed from one of the two windows in the room. The machinery, which was doing very little to ease the uncomfortable heat, made it hard for Catherine to hear Cindy.

The detective placed her notebook in front of her and leaned as far across the table as she could.

"I'm afraid," Cindy said over the whirring of the fan behind her. "I don't know what's going to happen to me. What if they send me to jail too?"

The girl was scared to death, and Catherine stopped her from saying anything else.

"Before we start, let me ask you one question. Did you participate in the actions that led to Missy's death?"

Cindy shook her head adamantly and her lower lip began to quiver.

"Did you kill Missy?"

"No. But I was there, and I never came forward till now with information. They can send me to jail because of that, can't they?"

"No, Cindy. Not for being afraid to talk." Catherine opened her notebook. "Why don't you tell me what happened."

Cindy swallowed hard and started talking. It wasn't the most professionally articulated bit of information Catherine had ever heard, but it was sweeter than anything she'd listened to in a long time. Her pen raced across the page, trying to capture every detail.

On October 1, 1985, Cindy Silverio had gone with Karen Severson to a park where they met Laura Doyle and Missy Avila. Karen and Laura began yelling at each other, pretending to fight, and before long Laura and Missy took off driving toward the mountains. They drove forty-five minutes up a winding mountain road to a place called Wicky-up, which was actually Camp Colby Ranch in the Big Tujunga Canyon of the Angeles National Forest. Throughout the drive Cindy and Karen were in Karen's car close behind.

Up at the mountains Karen and Laura suddenly told Missy they were only pretending to be mad at each other. The person they were really angry with was Missy. Then the four girls walked up a footpath into a wooded area near a stream that ran through the canyon. When they came to a clearing, Karen and Laura directed Missy toward a rock on the shore of the stream. There they called her names and screamed at her until finally, unable to take any more ridicule, Missy began crying.

Cindy paused and Catherine Scott held her breath, waiting for the girl to continue.

"Then Laura grabbed Missy's arm and Karen pushed her into the water." Catherine felt a sinking feeling in her stomach. Cindy had passed over the single detail she needed to remember.

"Cindy, did they do anything else to her?" Catherine leaned even farther across the table, straining to hear what she wanted the girl to say. But Cindy's face was blank.

"Think hard now. Did they do anything else to humiliate or degrade her?"

"You mean like pinching her? They didn't pinch her," Cindy said.

"No. Not like pinching. Did they do anything at all to degrade Missy?"

Suddenly Cindy's expression changed and she dropped her head into her hands. When she looked up, there were tears streaming down her face and she was nodding her head slowly.

"They cut her hair," she said, and she began to sob. "They cut off chunks of her hair."

There it was, the real thing. Catherine Scott was absolutely sure about it. Karen and Laura had killed Missy, and this girl leaning on the Formica table across from her was the only witness. Even with the heat in the apartment Catherine felt herself shiver. If Cindy hadn't made the phone call, if she hadn't come forward, there was an excellent chance no one ever would have known what had happened to Missy Avila.

It took about two hours before Catherine had enough information from Cindy Silverio to file a case with the district attorney's office. By then Catherine was sure she had the truth. Of course, there were still a few details to work out and the matter of convincing a jury. And she still didn't understand the motive: the hatred that had led two teenage girls to torture and kill one of their friends. Nevertheless, at that moment, as far as Catherine was concerned, the murder was solved.

And that evening before Catherine climbed into her car and headed home, she took the piece of paper from her pocket, unfolded it, and let the lock of Missy's hair blow into the breeze, a few strands at a time.

36

ON JULY 27, 1988, the day after Cindy Silverio told the truth about what had happened to Missy Avila, Catherine Scott came to work more rested than she'd been in years. She could hardly wait to sit down with Dan Jenkins.

An hour later Dan was still trying to believe it. "I never would have guessed it, never in a million years." Dan sipped his coffee and shook his head. "There we were chasing blue Camaros across the city, and we had the killers right under our noses."

Catherine nodded. "They sure had us going. Made us out to be complete fools. Now, Laura I can understand. There was always something suspicious about the way she told her version of the story."

Dan laughed. "Make that versions. Remember, Laura changed her story last year."

"You're right. But Karen Severson? The girl moved in with the Avilas, led them on chases, pretended to comfort them, and every day played the role of the grieving friend. We're dealing with a very sick individual, Dan. We must get those girls in here this morning and start the thing rolling to the district attorney's office."

By ten that morning the detectives had a plan of

action regarding the arrests of Karen and Laura. Catherine called Karen from one office while Dan called Laura from the other.

"Karen, Detective Scott here." Catherine sounded very casual. It was part of the plan. For the first time in years Karen wasn't in control of what was about to happen. "We'd like you to come down to the station. We have a few questions for you."

Of course, this request didn't surprise Karen Severson. The detectives had been relying on her false leads ever since they'd started investigating Missy's murder. Karen smiled graciously. "Why, certainly. What time would you like me to come?"

"Try to be here by eleven o'clock."

In the other room Dan Jenkins was having an equally easy time with Laura Doyle. She had been scheduled to work that day, but she woke up with a nosebleed and she was exhausted, having done two grams of cocaine the day before.

"Laura, this is Detective Jenkins," Dan said, forcing himself to sound routine. "We'd like to have you down at the station to answer a few questions, if that's okay with you."

Laura was tired of the interviews, but Karen was right. If she didn't cooperate, the police would figure something was strange and then soon enough they'd both wind up in jail. She sighed loudly. "Sure. I'll come down. When do you want me?"

"It's ten o'clock now. How about in an hour, at eleven?"

When Dan hung up, Catherine was waiting for him out in the hallway.

"All set?"

"All set." He put an arm around Catherine. "Good work, Detective."

Catherine looked straight at him. "Don't thank me. Thank Cindy Silverio."

Side by side they walked into the break room and worked out the details of their plan. They had become better friends while working on the Avila case. Jenkins was divorced, but he had been seeing someone for two years, and occasionally, since they'd been working on the Avila murder, Catherine had joined them for dinner or a movie. Most of the time she kept her socializing separate from work, but Dan was special.

Karen was the first to arrive. She walked in with Andrea—who by then was five years old—and her new boyfriend, Larry, whom she'd been dating for a few weeks. Catherine met them in the lobby and asked them all to take a seat. This was part of the detectives' plan. Karen and Laura needed to see each other for it to work. Catherine couldn't wait to see the look on Karen Severson's face when Laura Doyle walked in the door. It took five more minutes for her to arrive. Catherine was watching as Laura opened the door and walked inside. For a moment neither girl noticed the other. Then Karen gasped.

"What are you doing here?" Just as Karen started to stand up, Catherine walked into the lobby with Dan Jenkins right behind her.

"Karen, why don't you follow me." Catherine motioned toward a small room just off the lobby and Karen followed her reluctantly. There was no denying the hatred in her eyes as she glared backward toward Laura. Seeing Laura at the station was not part of Karen's plan.

After Catherine and Karen had left the lobby, Dan

Jenkins ushered Laura into an adjacent room. Then, just as they had planned, Catherine and Dan left the girls alone in their separate rooms. They met in the hallway, signed out, and went to the cafeteria for some lunch. It would be the longest hour in either Karen's or Laura's life. Catherine laughed out loud as she and Dan sat down with their food.

"Those two are going to be climbing the walls by the time we get to them," Catherine said. The plan was simple. After an hour had passed, both detectives would visit first one girl, then the other. They would tell Karen that Laura had come clean with the entire story, and when they interviewed Laura, they would blame the confession on Karen. It didn't really matter, since they already had the truth from Cindy Silverio. Only, her name would not be brought up. Not today, anyway.

Finally, shortly after noon, Catherine and Dan walked into the room where Karen Severson sat. She looked desperate, like a caged animal. When she heard the first question, it took her exactly one minute to start bawling like a baby.

Catherine did the talking. Dan watched Karen's behavior, her eye contact, and took notes on everything she said.

In the back of Catherine's mind she hoped that this might be one of those times when the pressure had grown so strong that the suspect might just come clean. It didn't happen often, but when it did, it was an investigator's dream. The questions start coming and before the suspect realizes what's happened he begins talking about what he was feeling and why it happened and the entire story unfolds in a matter of minutes.

But Catherine was fairly certain that after three years of lying—to everyone including, quite possibly, herself—Karen Severson wasn't about to stop now. No matter how bad she looked, she would probably keep lying.

"Karen, we have the facts. We know what happened and all we need now is your side of the story. We know you killed Missy Avila."

Karen's face went ash-white and the tears began streaming down her cheeks.

The most disgusting thing about those tears, Catherine Scott would later say, was that they were shed not out of grief but self-pity. All along Karen Severson had thought she was too smart to be caught, that somehow she was invincible to prosecution.

"I don't know what you're talking about," Karen shouted, her voice shrill with indignation.

"Don't bother with the lies anymore, Karen." Catherine sounded eternally patient and Karen squirmed in her seat. Actually, Catherine was furious, but she would never let Karen see her feelings.

"Laura told us everything. Where do you think we've been for the past hour? She told us how you set Missy up and took her up to the stream that afternoon. She told us that you called Missy all those names and then you hit her and slapped her and cut her hair." Catherine spoke slowly, emphasizing each word. "Finally, with Missy sobbing and begging you to stop, you pushed her into the water. Then you forced her face into the stream, smashed it down, and held her there."

Karen was crying harder now and shaking her head, but Dan noticed she was no longer trying to say anything.

"Then, when Missy stopped moving, you had to be

sure she was dead. So you picked up that log and laid it across her back. That's really what happened on October 1, 1985. Isn't it?"

Catherine sat back and waited for Karen's reaction. For several minutes Karen buried her head in her hands and said nothing. The only sounds that echoed off the walls of the closet-sized room were her blubbering and the ticking of the clock.

"We aren't going anywhere, Karen," Catherine said after ten minutes had passed. "We'll just sit here and wait for you to tell us your side of the story. Because the way Laura tells it, this whole thing was your idea."

Those words pushed Karen over the edge. She looked up, her eyes swollen and red, her face distorted in anger. "Laura is a lying bitch! It was all her idea. She organized it, she drove Missy up there. She was the one who started calling her names."

Their plan was working, and quietly, Dan scribbled the word *Bingo* on his notepad.

"What else, Karen? What else did Laura do?"

Karen sniffled dramatically and tried to sit straighter in her chair. Maybe there was still a chance. Maybe, if she worded her response just right, Laura would take the rap for the whole thing.

"Well, once we were up there, Laura cut Missy's hair. Then after that, Laura pushed Missy into the water and held her under until she looked like she was probably dead. That's when Laura put the log across Missy's back."

Catherine raised one eyebrow. "And what were you doing while all this was happening to your best friend?"

"Well, I was, I was sort of paralyzed by fear," Karen

said, convincing herself as she created the answer. "I just stood there and didn't do anything."

Catherine nodded sarcastically. "I see. And all this time, for the past three years, even though you knew what had happened to your best friend and you yourself were innocent, you never said a word to anyone. Is that what you want us to believe?"

Karen looked uncomfortable again and seemed to be shrinking. "Well, you see, I wasn't sure what would happen to me if I said anything."

"Oh, well, then it all makes perfect sense," Catherine said, turning toward Dan. "Make sense to you, Dan?"

"Yes, perfect sense," Dan said without looking up. Catherine was enjoying herself now, and Dan didn't want to crack a smile, so he kept his eyes focused on the notepad.

"Well, then, tell us this, Karen. How many of you were there up there that day?" Catherine leaned slightly closer to Karen and looked directly into her eyes.

Karen thought about it for a minute. "Three of us. That's it. Just Missy, Laura, and me."

Catherine sighed. "We aren't interested in playing games with you, Karen. If you have something to say, make it the truth or don't bother."

Karen's eyes grew wider. They really did know the truth. She was going to spend the rest of her life in jail, and the realization made her start crying all over again. Five minutes passed before Karen decided to come clean with one more bit of information.

"Four. There were four of us. But I can't tell you the name of the fourth girl, I just can't."

Catherine watched as Dan scribbled another word

on the notepad: *Double-Bingo*. She smiled. Dan was right. Karen's admission that there were four girls at the murder scene meant that Cindy Silverio had been telling the truth. Karen didn't want the detectives to know her name. After all, Cindy knew what had happened. It was bad enough that Laura had turned against her. The last thing she needed was for them to haul Cindy down to the station. If that happened, if they ever got hold of Cindy's story, Karen knew it would be all over.

"What's wrong with giving us her name, Karen? Worried she might know too much?" Catherine waited.

"I just can't tell you, that's all."

"Well, we're going to be together in here for an awful long time then. But that's okay. We work here. And you probably don't have much else going on, either, right?"

Karen was getting very angry and, in a single burst of emotion, shouted one word. "Cindy!"

Dan wrote the name on the notepad and Catherine offered Karen a tissue for her tears. "Now, Karen, this is your last chance to tell me what really happened that day. Do you have anything else to say?"

Karen slammed her fist onto the table. "Just that I'm innocent and you're both going to be sorry for putting me through this. Laura's lying. You've got to believe me. Missy was my best friend in the whole world."

"Yes, we know." Catherine stood up, looking very disgusted. "Well, then, if that's all you have to say, I'd like you to stand up."

At this point, for the first time since she'd arrived at the station hours earlier, Karen smiled. They were going to let her go. As soon as she got out on the street she was going to go as far away from Arleta as she could. But instead of opening the door and thanking her for her time, Catherine walked over to Karen and grabbed her wrists behind her back. In an instant the detective slapped steel handcuffs on her.

"You are under arrest for the murder of Missy Avila," Catherine said, glaring into Karen's beady eyes. "You have the right to remain silent. . . ."

Meanwhile, Dan Jenkins had called a couple of bailiffs into the room and asked them to book Karen Severson on suspicion of first-degree murder.

They were ready for Laura Doyle.

Catherine and Dan walked into the room and found Laura staring at the wall, her expression completely blank. She'd been in the room for two hours now and she sensed that this was going to be a very different kind of interview. The detectives sat down and Catherine began speaking.

"Laura, we know you killed Missy. We just got finished talking to Karen and she told us everything." Catherine waited to see Laura's reaction, but there was absolutely none. In fact, if Catherine had had to sum up the look on Laura's face, she would have called it indifference. Laura hadn't even acknowledged the detectives once since they'd walked into the room.

"Laura, Karen tells us that you drove Missy up to the stream that afternoon, called her names, cut her hair, beat her up, and then pushed her into the water."

As Catherine spoke, Laura turned to look at her. Her expression was completely blank and unwavering with no response whatsoever to the statements Catherine was making.

"We know the rest, too, Laura. Karen told us you held Missy's head underwater until she stopped moving. Then, just to be sure she was dead, you placed that log over her back. The only thing we need now is your side of the story."

Catherine sat back in the chair and waited. Laura stared straight ahead, not moving or even blinking for nearly ten minutes. Then Laura began swallowing in an odd reflexive way, as though she were choking on words.

"We can wait here a long, long time, Laura," Catherine said, breaking what had been a deafening silence.

Laura said nothing. Instead, she continued to make loud, overexaggerated swallowing motions every few seconds. Catherine wondered if the girl was going to faint.

Fifty minutes ticked by, one at a time, while Catherine and Laura stared at each other and Dan doodled on his notepad. They were used to playing the waiting game.

"Okay, Laura. If you aren't talking, then we'll have to believe everything Karen said. That's fine with us. You don't have to give us your side of the story."

Suddenly, a sound came from Laura's throat and she began to speak. Her voice was a dry, unfeeling monotone, and the detectives had to strain to hear her.

"It wasn't my fault." Laura shook her head slowly and continued to stare straight ahead. "Karen made me do it. Karen said we had to teach Missy a lesson and she made me pick up Missy that afternoon. Karen made me drive her up there."

Catherine lowered her voice. "What else, Laura? What else did Karen make you do?"

Laura swallowed again. "Karen made me take Missy to the stream and Karen cut her hair. Then Karen pushed Missy into the stream and she made me come along. Karen held her down and I had to help her. Karen made me help her."

"What about the log, Laura? Who moved the log onto Missy's back?"

Laura's eyes opened wider than they had been before, but she still had no expression on her face. She looked completely unmoved. "Karen saw the log. She tried to move it but it was too heavy so she made me help her. It was all Karen's idea. It wasn't my fault. I loved Missy. She was my friend."

Catherine nodded. "Was anyone else up there? Besides Missy and Karen and you?"

Laura looked down at her hands and swallowed hard. "Yes. Some girl named Cindy. I don't know her last name."

"Was this Cindy involved, did she help Karen kill Missy?"

Laura shook her head. "No. Cindy left, she went back to the cars before it happened."

Catherine looked at Dan and he nodded. Catherine stood and walked over to Laura, motioning for her to stand up. She snapped the handcuffs on her wrists.

"Laura Doyle, you are under arrest for the murder of Missy Avila. You have the right to remain silent. . . ."

By the time Catherine finished reading Laura her rights, Karen Severson had been booked, photographed, and fingerprinted. Catherine told the bailiffs that both girls would be going to Sybil Brand Institute —a maximum-security facility for women.

"This one has a request." The bailiff motioned toward Karen Severson, sitting on a nearby bench where she was still crying loudly. "She wants to say good-bye to her little girl out in the lobby."

Catherine thought about it. There was no reason to show any kind of mercy to someone like Karen. But at the same time, it wasn't the child's fault. Catherine stared at Karen and said, "Follow me."

Out in the lobby Larry and Andrea were still waiting. When they saw Karen in handcuffs, Larry jumped up and ran to her.

"What the hell . . ."

Karen shook her head before he could say anything else. "They've arrested me. They think I killed Missy." Karen began sobbing all over again.

"That's ridiculous! Why in the world would you kill her? She was your friend, don't they know that?"

Catherine stepped forward and broke up the discussion. "You have one minute to say good-bye. Make it quick."

Karen called Andrea to her and bent down. "Andrea, Mommy has to go away for a while, but you just remember I love you."

Larry picked the child up so she could kiss Karen. "I'll be in touch," Karen told him. "This is all a mistake, so tell my parents not to worry. Tell them I'll try to be brave."

Catherine could hardly believe it as she listened to Karen. It was as if she were going off to serve her country, not to serve time for killing her best friend.

Down the hall the bailiffs had finished booking Laura Doyle. Unlike Karen, Laura had no one waiting for her in the lobby and although they offered her the use of a telephone, Laura said she had no one to call.

Catherine and Dan stood together near the main desk while Karen Severson and Laura Doyle were ushered out of the station and into a waiting police transportation bus. Both girls were handcuffed. Both were being charged with first-degree murder in the death of Missy Avila.

There was only one more thing to do—break the news to Irene Avila.

It was well into the afternoon before Catherine had finished the paperwork and finally had some time to drive to the Avila home. She could have called them on the telephone, but after three years of investigating Missy Avila's murder, Catherine wanted to tell these people in person what had happened. The news would be almost as devastating as Missy's death had been.

At three o'clock that afternoon Catherine Scott parked her car in front of the Avila house. She walked up to the front door and rang the doorbell. Irene answered, pushing her hair out of her face and smiling at the detective.

"Oh, hi! I didn't know you'd be coming by this afternoon," Irene said. "Come on in."

Catherine walked inside and Irene motioned for her to sit down. "Can I get you something to drink?"

The detective shook her head. "Irene, you need to have a seat. I have some news for you."

Irene grew very still. She moved slowly to the sofa. The detective's voice told her that she had important news. She wanted to think they had solved Missy's murder, but she couldn't bring herself to hope.

"What is it? Did you find out who killed Missy?"

Catherine nodded, and Irene felt her head beginning to spin. Finally it was over. They could make an arrest and the agonizing uncertainty would be finished. But Irene couldn't understand why Detective Scott didn't look happier.

Catherine looked down at her hands and then up at Irene before she continued.

"Irene, we made two arrests this morning. Dan Jenkins and I feel very confident that we've got the killers. Someone came forward and told us what happened that day."

Irene's heart began to soar. She had almost given up hope. But by now, more than two years after her daughter's murder, even she had doubted it would ever be solved. This was tremendous news. Not only did they have the information, but they had already made the arrests. And they had a witness.

Catherine cleared her throat and continued, her voice lower and softer than before.

"Irene, we arrested Laura Doyle and Karen Severson."

For what seemed like nearly a minute, Irene did nothing but stare at Catherine Scott. Then, slowly, Irene began shaking her head.

"What? Are you crazy?" This had to be a joke. "That's impossible, Detective." Irene was shaking her head harder now. "You're wrong. This is all a mistake. Not Karen. Karen and Missy were best friends. And Laura. There's no way Laura was involved. She and Laura were so happy when they left the house that day. You must be wrong."

Catherine shook her head and reached for Irene's hand. "Irene, this isn't a mistake. One of their friends came forward and told us she had been up there with them that day. They did it, Irene. Karen Severson and Laura Doyle killed Missy."

Irene put her hands over her ears. "Stop. Don't say

anything else. It can't be true! I can't hear any more. Go away. Get out of this house right now. It's all a lie."

Irene was shouting, and Mark and Chris came into the room. Catherine looked at them and told them what had happened. "We've arrested Laura Doyle and Karen Severson for killing your sister," she said. Mark turned quickly toward his mother, but it was too late. He could see the color draining from her face and he knew she was going to pass out.

Irene reached for his hand as she started to fall.

At that moment Irene's mind tried desperately to convince itself that Detective Scott's accusation wasn't true. Karen couldn't have killed Missy. And then Irene began drifting backward in time, back to the days when Karen and Missy were best friends. Karen and Missy holding hands. They were eight years old and they were happily playing together. Now they were older . . . teenagers . . . and Karen was standing in the kitchen promising to watch out for Missy. Irene felt a sense of peace washing over her. The detectives were lying. Missy had loved Karen, she had trusted her. They were best friends.

Irene collapsed to the floor. Mark ran to the phone and called the paramedics and Catherine knelt at the woman's side. The detective had been right. It had been every bit as bad as telling Irene about Missy's death. This, too, was a death, like losing a second daughter. The woman had loved Karen Severson, treated her like one of the family.

But not anymore. Catherine knew that when Irene realized the truth and accepted the fact that Karen had indeed killed Missy, Karen Severson, too, would be dead.

37

THE PARAMEDICS HAD been gone for hours, and Irene Avila lay on her bed lost in a world of sedation. A deathly quiet hung over the house. Missy's brothers had gathered with other family members in the living room. No one talked. There was nothing to say, really. The news was still too shocking.

Mark Avila sat staring at the floor, remembering the time Karen Severson had taken the group up to the stream. She had talked about having a strange feeling and even felt she knew where Missy had been killed. Mark began to shiver. She had taken them right to the spot where she and Laura had killed his sister and she hadn't shown one sign of remorse. She was psychotic, a cold-blooded liar. He closed his eyes, but all he could see was Karen's smiling face. "I'll lead the way and we'll all look for clues. We have to catch the animals who did this to Missy." Her crazy smile wouldn't leave his mind. He thought of how she had tried so hard to convince them that Jimmy was the guilty one. Mark felt an intense anger growing out of his shock.

Chris, now fourteen years old, felt sick. He thought of the times when he and Karen had gone to the market together or run errands for his mother. She could have killed him too. What if she got out of jail and still wanted to kill him? He knew he should feel brave, but he was scared to death.

Ernie junior sat near his wife, his head buried in his hands. Karen Severson had blamed everyone but herself for the past three years, and now she was in jail. He had never been close to Karen, but he was crushed by her betrayal. Especially considering his mother had treated her like another daughter. He wondered if his mother would be able to take in the reality of what had happened. He decided to check on her and walked softly back to her bedroom. She was asleep; quietly, he shut her bedroom door. He hoped she would sleep for a long time. The news wouldn't be any easier to take tomorrow, when the sedatives wore off.

From somewhere in the recesses of Irene Avila's mind, she heard her son look in on her and shut the bedroom door. She tried to scream, tried to stop him from leaving, but her mouth wouldn't work. She was trapped in the nightmare.

It was a constant dream and completely evil. It scared Irene to death. It was coming again and Irene tried to shake it away, but it was relentless.

It was 1976. Missy was walking home from school. She was eight years old and she was in her favorite blue school dress.

There she is. I can see her. It's Missy, my sweet little girl. But why is she walking so slowly? She never walks this slowly when she comes home from school. I can see her clearly now. Walking toward me. Cheerful smile, pretty long brown hair, and sparkling blue-green eyes. But wait. What is it? That black shadow behind her. It's growing bigger and bigger and . . . wait . . . it's not a shadow it's another girl . . . a heavy girl . . . and she is closing in on little Missy. . . .

Then Irene could see the girl carrying a butcher knife, smiling. She was going to stab Missy in the back, killing her with a smile on her face.

I have to get to the door, I have to save her.

Irene raced to the front door. It was locked and she was trapped inside. She stared out the window, desperately shouting at Missy, trying to warn her. But the girl was closing in and the knife was growing larger. Then everything froze and Irene could make out the girl's face.

It was Karen Severson.

Irene tried to scream, but the second cycle had started and Irene knew she was helpless to stop it. Slowly the pictures began to fill her mind. She saw herself in the kitchen and the phone was ringing. Irene knew who the caller was but picked up the receiver anyway.

Suddenly the lights went off in the house and she was standing in pitch darkness. A cold chill hung in the air and a voice filled the house. It sounded like Missy.

"Hello, Irene. I've got a message for you. Missy is gone. Missy is gone. Missy is gone."

Irene groped around in the blackness looking for the voice and knowing it had to be Missy. "Missy, where are you? Come here, honey. It's Mommy. I miss you, honey. Don't scare me like this."

Her words echoed through the house and she realized she was no longer in the kitchen, but in the depths of a dark, dank cave. Then the voice began to laugh. This time it sounded different, angry and evil.

"She's dead. Stop looking for her because she's dead. I killed her and she's never coming back."

The voice grew louder and Irene knew the person was closing in on her. She had killed Missy and she was going to kill her but the cave was so dark, she couldn't tell where the voice was coming from.

"I killed her, Irene. I killed her. I killed her. Look out, Irene, I killed her."

The laughter grew louder, and Irene began to recognize Karen Severson's voice.

The third cycle was starting and it was the worst of all.

Irene could see the car coming into focus and she could make out Missy's face. She was in the car with two girls, laughing and having a good time, but she couldn't see their faces. All she could see was Missy, but Missy was crying and looking at Irene.

Irene could hear her voice now, and from deep in the nightmare Missy started to cry.

"Mom, can you hear me? Help me! I'm trapped and there's no way out. Mom, I need you. Please help me, Mom. Please."

Irene ran over to the car and tried to open the door, but it was locked. The girls were laughing harder now, laughing at Missy. Irene couldn't make out their faces because they were shrouded in dark hoods. One of the girls put her hand on the steering wheel and Irene could see talons appear. Sharp, hooklike claws. They were evil and they were going to hurt Missy. Irene knew it but there was nothing she could do and Missy was still screaming for help.

"Mom, I'm trapped. They're going to kill me, Mom. Help. Please open the door and get me out of here. Help me, please."

Missy was trying desperately to get out, to get away from the girls. They were laughing even louder now.

Irene picked up a steel crowbar and tried to smash the car windows, but they wouldn't break. Now the hoods were pulled back and Irene could see the faces of Laura and Karen.

Irene rolled over in bed, trying to bring herself out of the dream, but she was helpless. Slowly, the dream started over again.

The nightmare was absurd, because Karen Severson and Laura Doyle were Missy's friends. Irene knew in her heart they wouldn't hurt Missy. But somewhere deep in Irene's heart she was convinced they had killed her.

38

IT WAS MID-AUGUST 1988 and detectives Dan Jenkins and Catherine Scott were delighted with the preliminary hearings. Catherine had no idea what defense the girls' attorneys would put forward when the case got to court, but she knew one thing for sure: If she were given the distasteful job of defending someone like Karen Severson, she would definitely plead not guilty by reason of insanity. Of course, Catherine hoped that wouldn't happen, because she wanted to see Karen behind bars for a long time. But really, when one considered the stunts Karen had pulled after murdering her best friend, she had to be a very sick individual.

Karen and Laura's evil trickery in luring Missy up to the mountain stream had shocked the judges in both preliminary hearings. Both commented on the callous nature of two teenage girls who had been cold and calculating enough to kill their best friend. One judge had called it an execution-style murder, one in which the killers had led their victim up to a remote spot and then tortured her before killing her. During this stage of the proceedings a judge made the crucial decision that Karen Severson would be tried as an adult despite the fact that she'd been a few months from her eighteenth birthday when the murder took place. Had she been tried and convicted as a juvenile, Karen's sentence would have been considerably lighter.

It was determined during those hearings that jealousy was the official motive for the killing and the girls were ordered to remain at Sybil Brand Institute for Women in East Los Angeles. The judge had refused to set bail for Laura Doyle and he set Karen Severson's at $1 million, because she was a minor when the murder happened. Catherine and Dan were satisfied. Karen and Laura would not be getting out of jail for a long time.

Sybil Brand Institute was set up in such a way that prisoners could stay at the facility for up to one year or until sentencing. Most of the women admitted hoped for a speedy trial.

When the girls had been at Sybil Brand for two weeks, they were visited by a reporter. She had been researching the story and was fascinated by its many twists and turns. After talking to the family members and officials involved, she drove to the jail determined to interview Karen and Laura, though she knew there was a good chance the girls would refuse. After all, by now they probably had attorneys advising them. A lawyer would not want to read about his client's story in the press before it had been told in court.

It was ten o'clock that morning when the reporter turned onto the city road that led to the prison. It was adjacent to a male prisoners' colony and for several hundred yards her car ran beside fifteen-foot-high brick walls topped with loops of barbed wire. Occasionally, a group of prisoners could be seen gathered on the roadside picking up trash while a supervisor watched closely. Graffiti covered many of the walls.

The reporter knew this was a tough area. Gang violence claimed several lives each day in this part of Los Angeles.

She pulled into the parking lot and tried to ignore the fear that welled up inside her. This wasn't the best place for a well-dressed young female reporter to spend much time alone. Outside the entrance to Sybil Brand a receptionist's office was housed in a brick cage. Steel bars crisscrossed the only window, the place where visitors checked in. Under the window was a rusty metal sign that advised visitors to leave all firearms with the receptionist.

The reporter swallowed hard and looked at the waiting area.

There were two long, dirty benches under an aluminum overhang. Waiting there was a pitiful group of people—a shaggy-haired man in dingy clothing who had a desperate look in his eyes, and others pacing nervously, almost certainly strung out on rock cocaine or heroin. The reporter looked at these characters and realized their role. They were here to visit friends who had committed crimes, and she wondered how many were themselves simply criminals who hadn't been caught yet.

There were other visitors too: pathetic clusters of grandmothers and small children waiting to see their beloved inmates. The grandmothers looked sad but hard. They had been here before and they were used to waiting four hours for a twenty-minute chat with their daughters. It was easy to see that the light in their eyes had long since gone out. The children were the only ones oblivious to the desolation. They ran about and played on the grassy area in front of the jail,

squealing and laughing. This was life for them—visit
ing Mommy in jail.

The reporter checked in and sat down to wait. Sh
began to notice that every hour or so, a woman woul
be escorted to the prison's front gate and released. Sh
would be carrying a small plastic bag full of belonging
—toothbrush, comb, and makeup, some pocke
change. She would step outside and blink severa
times, unsure which way to go. Then she would wal
slowly, taking shaky steps, toward the bus stop. Th
was how the previously incarcerated reentered soc
ety.

Finally, at just after one o'clock that afternoon,
handful of waiting visitors, including the reporte
were called to the front gate. She had asked to se
Karen Severson first and now she was being whiske
through the front gates. She couldn't believe her luck

The group were escorted across a garden patio are
into another building, where they had to walk singl
file into a visiting area. It was a long, narrow corrido
flanked with what looked like phone booths. The re
porter was told to sit in booth number 14.

Carefully, she sat down on the metal stool and se
her notepad on the tiny shelf. There was a thick pan
of glass separating her from the seat opposite. This wa
where Karen Severson would sit when they brought i
the prisoners. There was a phone on each side of th
glass divider. The reporter was surprised. Some jai
allowed the inmates to talk through holes in the glas
Others didn't even have glass dividers. But this was
high-security facility designed for only the most dar
gerous criminals.

Five minutes passed before Karen Severson was le
into the waiting area. She sat down at the booth. Sh

was grossly overweight and her brown hair hung in oily strands that fell unevenly on her blue jail dress. She wore no makeup. Looking surprised and angry, she picked up the phone.

"Wait, who are you?" she asked into the phone. "They told me my mother was coming to see me. I'm expecting my mother and I can only have one visitor a day."

Karen Severson stood quickly and grabbed the supervisor's arm. "Can I go back to my cell? I don't want this visitor. I'm expecting my mother today and I thought this was going to be her."

The woman shook her head. "Nope. This is it. Enjoy the visit." She turned her back on Karen.

Slowly, Karen sat back down and faced the reporter. "Who are you?"

She sounded even angrier than before, and the reporter steadied herself before she proceeded.

"I'm a reporter. I'm writing a story about Missy's death and I wanted to get your side of the story." Karen sat perfectly still with her arms crossed, the phone wedged between her ear and shoulder. She looked strangely satisfied with herself but said nothing.

The reporter continued. She knew how to get the girl to talk.

"The press is making you look guilty, Karen. No one's asked you for your side of the story, so I just wanted to give you a chance to say something for yourself."

This time Karen shook her head. "No. I can't talk to anyone right now."

But the reporter was persistent, and five minutes into the visit Karen Severson began talking.

"I can't really tell you all the details. They'll come out in court," she said. "But I will say this. Missy wasn't as innocent as everyone thought."

The reporter was confused. As far as she knew, Missy hadn't been blamed for anything. She asked Karen to elaborate. "You mean Missy hurt you and Laura, she tried to beat you up?"

Karen shook her head and flashed a disgusted look at the reporter. "No. Nothing like that. But she moved in on my boyfriend one too many times and I couldn't take it. But I wouldn't kill her, you know."

Karen ran a hand along her fleshy arm and the reporter noticed bruise marks on it.

The reporter realized how rough life must be behind the glass divider. Girls could be vicious, especially when an inmate accused of killing her best friend entered their midst. That didn't go over well with the jail crowd.

Karen cleared her throat and tried to explain. Her words were filled with pride and indignation. "It's like I said before. Missy wasn't as innocent as everyone thought."

They continued their conversation, and the reporter asked if she and Laura had planned to take Missy up to the stream that afternoon.

"I can't say," Karen said, tilting her head a bit higher and refusing to admit her involvement. The reporter had an idea—maybe if she reworded the question.

"Let me ask you this. Did Missy know you were taking her up to the stream that afternoon?"

Karen shook her head. "No, Missy didn't know."

The reporter scribbled down her answer and found herself amazed at the girl's stupidity. She was basically admitting her guilt to a reporter she had never met

Just then, the supervisor walked back into the room and summoned the prisoners. Twenty minutes had flown by. The reporter looked over her notes. They weren't much, but they would be enough. Karen stood up and joined the others in a straight line, giving the reporter one more chance to see how large she was. Missy Avila had been so tiny.

The reporter gathered her notes and headed back to the front gate with the other visitors. It was time to talk to Laura Doyle. The reporter put in her request and sat down to wait, but thirty minutes later she heard her name called over the loudspeaker.

The receptionist told her that Laura Doyle had refused to be interviewed. That was okay. She had already talked to Laura's friends and learned about her and Karen's admission from the district attorney's office. Besides, Karen Severson was the more interesting interview of the two. She was the one who had grown up with Missy, been her best friend, and then moved in with her family to help her mother find the killers. The district attorney had already said she thought Karen was the mastermind behind the crime.

39

DURING THE SUMMER of 1989 Deputy District Attorney Tamia Hope was assigned the task of prosecuting Karen Severson and Laura Doyle.

Some people spend half their lives deciding what profession best suits them. Others, like Tamia Hope, are born knowing. In 1950, at the tender age of four, Tamia knew with no uncertainty that she wanted to be a lawyer. Nothing special had happened when she was four—it was simply as far back as Tamia could remember.

The daughter of a successful general practice attorney who loved his job, Tamia spent much of her childhood and adolescence watching her father work in his Orange County office and dreaming of the day when she, too, would be handling cases. This wasn't a passing phase. In the mid-sixties, when other teenagers were hanging out at the local fast-food joints or attending sock hops, Tamia was poring over legal books and preparing for college entrance exams.

Still, for all her focus on the legal profession, Tamia never once considered being a trial lawyer. In a Beach Boys era when every southern California girl was supposed to be blonde, tan, and ready to ride a surfboard, Tamia had short dark hair, fair skin, and a love of horses. She was also classically beautiful, but she didn't recognize that any more than did most of the other teens at her high school. As a result, right up to the moment she graduated, Tamia was one of the shyest girls in the school.

For this reason, although she had the grades to go wherever she wished, Tamia chose to attend Mills College in Oakland, an all-women's college. For the first time in her life Tamia wasn't worried about what others thought of her. She found herself thriving, raising her hand and purposefully joining in class discussions with her female classmates. Under these circumstances Tamia first considered being a trial lawyer. Four years later, when Tamia enrolled at Hastings Law School in San Francisco, she was certain of her calling.

Conditions were a little different at Hastings. Suddenly, after spending her entire undergraduate career with women, Tamia found herself thrust into an environment that was ninety-five-percent male. But by then Tamia had added to her repertoire of talents the single one she had lacked prior to attending Mills College—self-confidence. She graduated three years later in the top third of her class.

Several good things came out of Tamia's time at Hastings. First, between her second and third years she took a job with the district attorney's office. Second, she received such a good legal education that when she attempted the California State Bar Exam she passed it with flying colors on her first try. Third, Tamia found a man. He was her Prince Charming. Handsome and self-assured. Never once did he feel threatened by the fact that they were both equally qualified for the legal profession. Tamia loved being with him because he shared every interest she'd ever had in her life.

In January 1972 they celebrated twice: first when she was sworn in as a deputy district attorney, and again when he took a prestigious position with the U.S. attorney's office. But the biggest celebration of all came later that year at their wedding.

For the next six years the happy couple lived something of a storybook life-style. Each had a car, a business wardrobe, and a successful career. By 1978 they had purchased their first home together and were blessed with a beautiful baby girl. The dream was coming true. It wasn't until four years later that life began to unravel.

Somewhere along the way both attorneys began devoting more time and energy to their careers than to each other. In fact, other than their honeymoon and a few other vacations, they hadn't gone away together in ten years of marriage. By 1982, days before their second daughter was born, Tamia Hope was feeling fat, bloated, and undesirable, though she wondered if her husband even noticed. During this time it occurred to Tamia that her marriage was in deep trouble. She decided that what she and her husband needed was more dating, such as they'd done back in law school. On their first date, when their second daughter was seven weeks old, Tamia had more fun than she'd had in years. A week later she felt bold enough to ask her husband the one question every woman hopes she never has to ask. Was there someone else? The answer was yes. By the end of the night Tamia's dream of living happily ever after was dead.

The separation came two weeks later, but it took much longer for the blinding pain and devastation to wear off. As Tamia would say later, you get over the guy so much quicker than you get over the dream of this storybook life.

What Tamia didn't realize then was how the pain of losing her husband to another woman would contribute to her ability as a deputy district attorney. Suddenly, she could empathize with her witnesses and the families of victims in a way she had never been capable of before. In late 1983 Tamia Hope was transferred to Pasadena's Superior Court to prosecute murder suspects. In this arena she found that everything about the pain of her own experiences could be used to her advantage. In fact, one reason Tamia Hope was so effective in court was that she was so sincere. A single mother of two children prosecuting some of the worst criminals in the city, Tamia was thankful for her job because she was able to make a difference.

Without a doubt the biggest challenge in Tamia Hope's career was the task of prosecuting Karen Severson and Laura Doyle. First, it would be especially emotional because Irene Avila was a single, divorced mother who had lost her daughter. By then Tamia was forty-three and knew the role a child can play in the life of a divorced mother. Children were your reason to hope, to survive, and end up with a better life.

Second, Tamia could relate to Cindy Silverio. One of the reasons Cindy had come forward was that, with her brother's suicide, she was finally able to feel the pain Irene Avila had been feeling for three years. It had taken Cindy six months to come forward. After her divorce Tamia understood the kind of grief that could consume a person, even stop a person from talking about a murder she had witnessed.

Tamia Hope could feel for these people. So from the

beginning she put all her resources into preparing for the trial.

She thought over the key aspects of the case.

There was Cindy Silverio's testimony, certainly. And in the past weeks she had rounded up several people who could testify to the jealousy that consumed Karen Severson and Laura Doyle. They had Christy Crawford on their side, and Victor Amaya, Laura's former boyfriend. Of course, Irene Avila would testify, and Missy's brothers. The family would tell the story of Karen's manipulations and deceptions since the girls were children. They would tell how she had pointed her finger at several others in an attempt to keep the blame away from herself.

Then there were the professionals. Catherine Scott and Dan Jenkins; the coroner; and the forest ranger. They would probably ask the hikers to make a statement in court as well. But as she looked over the evidence list, the district attorney knew which part of the proceedings besides Cindy's testimony would be most effective: the pictures.

The pictures taken at the scene of the murder were bound to have a profound impact on any common jury. In her years as a deputy DA, Tamia had come to know what would and wouldn't affect a jury. She used her own emotional barometer as an indicator, and by now she had seen a variety of crime scenes. Over the years there had been pictures of bodies contorted in many different ways, but none had affected her like the pictures of Missy Avila.

Maybe it was her size. She had asked the photo lab to blow up the pictures and she had them mounted on giant poster board. She wanted every one of the jurors to be able to see just how completely the tree trunk covered the tiny girl. All that could be seen was Michele's legs and one of her arms. Tamia pulled the color pictures out and looked at them again. Someone had held Missy's head facedown, smothered in the tiny pebbles and rocks that lined the stream bottom. There, the girl had suffocated and drowned in just eight inches of still water. But the deed had taken two people—Missy's feet told that much. The picture showed how, when the body was discovered, her feet were still crossed and pushed partly down into the sand. It had taken one person to hold her feet and one to hold her head and her arms. Missy had probably tried to kick free of her killers, but she had simply been overpowered.

When she had stopped struggling, they had walked a few feet away and heaved the log onto her back. The act was so brutal. She knew the jurors would be disgusted, no matter how young the accused killers were.

She was thankful that the courts had decided early on to try both girls as adults, even though Karen Severson had been only seventeen at the time of the killing.

Tamia thought about her own daughters, both approaching their teenage years. One, Michele, reminded her of how Missy must have been. They even spelled their names the same way. Her Michele was sweet and pleasant and everyone in her class enjoyed her friendship. According to Irene, Missy had been the same way.

The district attorney looked over her notes and tried to surmise what angle the defense would use. Karen Severson's family had hired a private attorney, William Andrews, a quick-witted man with years of experience. He had a friendly smile and spoke with his hands, often convincing confused jurors of his arguments regardless of the validity of the prosecution's assertions. Tamia knew he would be hardest on Cindy. The Silverio girl was no match for the likes of William Andrews, but Tamia only hoped her honesty would prevail. Tamia believed Cindy Silverio was telling the truth. Maybe not the entire truth, but she was telling the truth.

Laura Doyle had a court-appointed attorney— David Thomas. He, too, was sharp. His forte was emotional appeal, asking jurors to be forgiving and allow his client to have a second chance. Together, the two would make a very tough team.

But Tamia had just won the first battle when the judge agreed to try Laura and Karen together, in one trial. This would prevent Tamia's witnesses from having to go through the ordeal of a month-long trial twice. In addition it would prevent Andrews and Thomas from catching the inevitable discrepancies that crop up when people are forced to give virtually the same testimony two times. Best of all, with the girls in the same courtroom there was always a possibility that one of them, whichever one thought she was less at fault, would grow frustrated and demand to be heard on the witness stand, or blurt out something incriminating.

Naturally, Andrews and Thomas had asked for separate trials because neither counselor wanted his client side by side with someone else accused of murder.

Tamia doubted that either Karen or Laura would say anything in her own behalf. They had the right to remain silent, of course. But if she could get one of them up there, the finger pointing would begin and the jury would see the crime very clearly. It would then be easy to convict both girls. Andrews and

Thomas were no fools, and Tamia was certain that by now they had counseled Karen and Laura to remain perfectly calm during all court proceedings.

Their silence wouldn't really matter. Tamia was fairly confident that the jury would convict them anyway. She would present witnesses who would make the decision easy if everything went right.

Tamia knew that her witnesses had their shortcomings. Andrews and Thomas would certainly notice that many of them were not the most wholesome group of all-American kids in the world.

But that was part of Missy Avila's story. She had fallen in with a rougher crowd because she had followed Karen to continuation school, because her friendship with Karen had been the most important part of her life. And even though they were a little rough looking, her witnesses were believable. They had no reason to take the witness stand and make up stories.

The only person missing was Jimmy Mitchell, and no one knew where to find him. It seemed that after Karen's constant harassment, Jimmy had taken off to find a new life for himself. With a common last name like Mitchell, Tamia doubted whether they would find him in time for the trial. Without Jimmy there really was no motive for Karen Severson to kill her best friend. The testimonies from Missy's family about Karen's bizarre behavior did not prove a motive, and so Tamia knew any defense attorney would tear their stories apart. At least they had Victor Amaya, who could testify about Laura Doyle's motive.

Tamia had only one choice—to find Jimmy Mitchell. If she found him, she was almost certain to get a conviction on Karen Severson. He was worth looking for.

40

THE FALL OF 1989 was unseasonably warm in Seattle, Washington, despite the frequent rains. The colors were changing, and families spent the weekends picnicking in the park and playing in their large backyards. Jimmy Mitchell was pursuing a full-time computer-programming education at Griffin College.

Jimmy loved Seattle. It was a big city with a small-town heart, clean and gentle, the perfect place to find a new way of life. Best of all, Seattle was a place Karen Severson had never visited. She would never think of looking for Jimmy Mitchell there.

After he had recovered from the fight in front of Christy Crawford's house, Jimmy had tried to resume his life working at the tire shop and keeping a low profile. However, Karen had been relentless, even after she had told the Avila family that Jimmy was not responsible for Missy's murder. They never knew how she had continued to harass him. There were constant death threats and strange phone calls. Sometimes the calls would come at work, and finally, one day in December 1987, his boss had confronted him. He told Jimmy that he valued him as an employee, but that the phone calls had to stop.

Jimmy had gone home that evening desperately

troubled. He knew Karen was behind the continuous torment, but there was nothing he could do to stop her. When he changed his phone number, she found out the new one by tricking one of his co-workers into giving it to her. There were also the times when strange cars cruised by his house late at night. Sometimes Jimmy wondered if Karen might actually try to have him killed.

He thought over his options and decided he had just one. He would move and start over again. He would get a job and go to school to learn a trade. He would never set foot in Arleta, California, again.

One week later Jimmy packed everything he owned into a pickup truck and headed north. He had heard a lot about Seattle from a girl who had never been a part of Karen Severson's group, and he believed with all his heart that he would love his new city. After he paid for the motel his first night in town, the man behind the desk shook his hand and welcomed him. From that moment on Jimmy knew he was home.

Now, almost two years later, life was treating Jimmy Mitchell better than he could have hoped. He was happily involved in a relationship with a girl who loved him dearly, and he had finished two semesters at Griffin College. He looked healthier than ever, he was wearing his dark brown hair in a short, conservative style, and, most important to him, he had found the Lord. To Jimmy, Christianity meant giving up the drinking and partying and instead making God his number-one priority. In Christ, Jimmy had found peace, comfort, and purpose; and a kind of love he hadn't known existed. The days of Karen Severson and a town full of people pointing fingers at him were behind him now as though a different person had lived them.

He had enjoyed a particularly pleasant morning. His courses had gone smoothly, and he was making better grades than he had the previous semester. But he needed some time alone to think about his term project. He decided to visit the campus library, and there he settled into a large overstuffed chair by a window overlooking the green hills.

Two hours later Jimmy grew tired of studying and glanced at a nearby table covered with magazines. He grabbed the first one he saw, opened it to the table of contents, and scanned the list of articles. There was a story about Jim and Tammy Bakker, one about the latest gossip in Hollywood, and a piece about Japan's royal bride.

Then he saw it.

The article was in the back of the magazine, in the crime section. Her name caught his eye—Missy Avila. It had to be the same Missy Avila he knew. Jimmy felt his heart skip a beat. He swallowed hard and read the caption:

> *After Missy Avila's death, her friend Karen Severson couldn't rest until the killer was found; now she's charged with the murder.*

Jimmy felt his face losing color, and he leaned back in the chair. He realized that all the accusations against him, the slashed tires, the times he had thought he was being followed—could have been arranged by Karen Severson.

A shiver ran down Jimmy's spine as he realized what Karen had stood to gain by killing him. He was someone on whom she could blame Missy's death. Then people would figure he had killed Missy and they would stop looking for other suspects. Jimmy finally understood how very close he must have come to dying.

The magazine was dated September 18, 1989—the newest issue. They had just found her out after all this time. He flipped to the article and began to read. The story described Irene Avila's grief and how Karen Severson had vowed to comfort her and help her find the animals who had killed Missy. Jimmy found himself agreeing with the description of Karen and Laura as having been intensely jealous of Missy. He read Irene's words:

> *Not a night goes by that I don't cry for Missy. It will never be all right.*

His heart went out to her, and he felt his eyes sting with tears. Poor Missy. She had been so trusting. Tears were streaming down Jimmy's face now, and he thought how terrified she must have been. Missy never would have suspected that Karen Severson would kill her.

Jimmy sighed. The final piece of the puzzle was in place: Karen Severson had killed Missy and she had used him as a scapegoat.

Suddenly, Jimmy had an idea. He searched the article again and found what he was looking for. The trial hadn't started yet. Maybe it wasn't too late, maybe he could make a few phone calls and testify against Karen. After all, he had witnessed Karen's intense dislike for Missy's popularity. Maybe his testimony could help put her away.

He wiped his eyes and picked up the magazine, made two copies of the article, and then headed home. It was not quite six o'clock that evening when Jimmy looked through his old address book and dialed the Avila number. He sat down to calm his nerves. What would the family say after all this time? Maybe they still thought he'd been a party to the crime and wouldn't want to hear from him. That didn't matter. Jimmy knew he had to make this call for Missy, for whatever good might come of it.

"Hello?"

Irene had answered. Jimmy took a deep breath. "Hello? Irene? This is Jimmy Mitchell."

"Jimmy! Where are you? How are you? Oh, Jimmy. We're all so sorry for blaming you about Missy. . . ."

Irene spoke very fast, and Jimmy began to laugh with relief.

"I'm calling from Seattle. I live here now and I just saw the story in the magazine. I can't believe they killed her, but I want to do whatever I can to help."

Irene was stunned. Jimmy's call was too good to be true. He was the missing link, the person Tamia Hope had been looking for. Here he was on the phone, like a gift straight from God. There was still time for Jimmy to go to court.

Irene lowered her voice and brushed back the tears that had started rolling down her cheeks.

"Thank God, Jimmy. Thank God you called."

Jimmy smiled. "Yes, Irene. I think He had a lot to do with it."

41

THE NEXT TWO months dragged by, with one court delay after another. Since Karen and Laura were going to be tried together, their attorneys argued that they needed more time to prepare for their two clients.

Irene hated the delays. They had been going on since Karen and Laura were arrested back in July 1988, and now it was more than a year later, almost time for the Christmas holidays again. She had complained about the continuances once to Tamia, but the district attorney had made it very clear that they were necessary. If William Andrews and David Thomas didn't have enough time to prepare for their clients, the prosecution might later be saddled by an appeal, which they couldn't risk.

By then Irene Avila had lost more than thirty pounds and the continual delays were taking their toll on her health. She was still very beautiful, but the dark hollows under her eyes told people how she was really feeling. She was having trouble sleeping and the nightmares about Missy, Karen, and Laura were more real than ever.

The summer of the arrests Irene had finally reached a point where she could think clearly. She had taken every picture of Karen and Missy together and ripped Karen out. Coming across a picture of Karen by herself, she would tear it into tiny pieces before compressing it tightly in her fist and slamming it into the trash can.

Sometimes her anger was palpable. They had used her, lied to her, and killed her daughter. Karen was especially loathsome. How could she have moved in and acted so concerned about finding Missy's killers? Four years after Missy's death the charade those two had played was foremost in the Avila family's thoughts.

Their only comfort was knowing that Karen and Laura were in prison.

In November 1989, while Irene and her sons were losing sleep, weight, and faith in the justice system, Laura was busy taking computer programming courses. Three months earlier she had received her high-school diploma courtesy of the tutors at Sybil Brand Institute for Women.

Karen, meanwhile, had also received her high-school diploma behind bars and was enjoying some of the extracurricular classes the prison staff offered, in particular a parenting course.

In Pasadena, at the district attorney's office, Tamia Hope was finally ready for the case against Karen Severson and Laura Doyle. She had Jimmy Mitchell now, and that would make a tremendous difference in the outcome. His story was sweeter than any Tamia had heard since she'd started working on the case, and she was looking forward to watching Karen Severson's face when Jimmy Mitchell paraded up to the witness stand.

Jimmy knew something the others didn't, the part Karen had always hidden from the Avilas. According to Tamia's talk with him Karen had hated Missy for years—hated her because she was thin, pretty, and trusting—and Missy had never known it.

Jimmy remembered that Karen had been up to the murder site—Wicky-up, they called it back then—many times before Missy's death, even though she told the Avilas that she had never been there in her life. He could also testify about the death threats and the time when he had nearly died on the street in front of Christy Crawford's house.

It hadn't been easy preparing for this case. First Tamia had spent hours listening to Irene Avila's story. Somehow, Tamia had to find Karen's cruel behavior after the murder relevant. After interviewing Irene she searched and found a case that showed guilt could be proven if the defendant used "deliberately false and misleading statements after the murder." This was a gold mine. If those types of statements could be used to prove guilt, then everyone who had ever heard Karen say anything deliberately false or misleading could be brought into court to talk about it. That way, in case the jurors didn't believe Jimmy's testimony, they could find Karen guilty because of her many lies after Missy's death.

Next Tamia had gathered the relevant characters, everyone from Vic Amaya to Jimmy Mitchell, Brian Taylor, Katy Vincent, and Lynne Robbins, who could testify about Karen's strange behavior at Missy's gravesite.

Tamia had tossed and turned at night thinking about what it would be to lose one of her daughters. She knew that she positively wouldn't rest her case until the jury understood how Karen had been jealous of Missy since the girls were eight years old. Of course, Catherine Scott and Dan Jenkins would be very helpful in making this picture complete. Catherine had called several times and offered to help. Each day during the proceedings either Catherine or Dan would be present. At some point Tamia wanted to get Catherine on the witness stand.

The jury would learn about the time when Karen was pregnant and Missy stayed by her and helped her, how Missy had even transferred to continuation school because of her. Whatever role Missy may have played in aggravating Karen and Laura by flirting with the boys at school, there was no question about one thing: Missy was loyal to her friends, especially Karen Severson.

There was the time in Missy's first year at continuation school when she had been attacked by a group of girls. The jury would hear how Karen had told the girls that Missy had been sleeping with their boyfriends. Tamia had queried several of her witnesses and Missy seemed innocent of these charges. Rather than blame Karen for setting her up, Missy had told the girls never, ever again to tell such awful lies about her friend. Missy didn't believe Karen Severson would do anything to hurt her.

Tamia would then tell the jurors about the time Karen had ordered Missy out of her apartment because Jimmy had made a move on her. By then, Tamia was certain the jurors would see Karen Severson's jealousy and how it had grown like a cancer for nearly a decade.

If the tapestry of manipulation and deception didn't really include as much about Laura Doyle, that was all

right with Tamia Hope. Laura Doyle wasn't the mastermind in this crime. If Laura had refused to have any
part in Missy's murder, Karen would have found someone else, as Tamia intended to show.

Tamia would tell the jury about the time Karen
Severson and Cindy Silverio had come by the Avila
house accusing Missy of sleeping with several guys.
Irene had told them to tell Missy to her face.

They had done that, all right. They had taken her up
to a remote mountain creek and drowned her.

By now Tamia Hope had what she thought was a
fairly accurate portrait of Missy Avila. The picture
showed Tamia that Missy was in many ways a typical
teenager, someone who wasn't perfect but wasn't a
troublemaker either. She had been dabbling in drugs
and drinking and she had been sexually active, which
at seventeen wasn't so unusual for her generation. In
grade school and the first part of junior high, Missy had
been a good student and something of a Goody Two-
shoes, the kind that seems too pretty and smart to be
true. But after her parents' separation Missy had
turned into a troubled teenager, lonely, fearful, and
willing as never before to go along with the crowd. For
the most part Missy's crowd catered to the bossy dic-
tates of Karen Severson.

But more than anything else, more than her experimentation with drugs or her presence at Stonehurst
Park, more than her real or concocted reputation with
the boys, Missy was remembered for her looks. She
was a slim, clear-skinned, green-eyed beauty with a
warmth that the other girls couldn't imitate.

The only pictures the jurors would see of Missy
would be those taken after she had been killed, but
Tamia was going to do her best to paint the living

picture of Missy Avila for the jury. They needed to feel as if they had known her, and they needed to understand her vulnerability to Karen and Laura.

To prove that vulnerability Tamia would point out how just before they killed her, Karen and Laura had separately made their peace with Missy. Missy, naturally, had believed them. Never for a minute did she think that her best friends were secretly planning to kill her when they took her up to the stream that day, all the while pretending to be angry, not at her, but at each other.

Then there was the charade Karen and Laura had played after Missy's death. The jury would learn of the two-faced comfort Karen Severson had given to Irene Avila, and they would find out about Karen's bogus investigation. It was a story that would give the jurors nightmares.

Cindy's testimony was going to be quite graphic, and the story she had to tell included details of Missy's death that Irene didn't know, details she should never have to know. Tamia thought Irene shouldn't sit in the courtroom during Cindy's testimony, and she had told her as much a few weeks earlier.

Cindy's story was the single reason Tamia Hope believed she had enough to go on for murder in the first degree. It was harder to prove than second-degree murder, but Tamia thought the charge was applicable in this case. First-degree murder meant that the accused had killed the victim intentionally and with malice aforethought. Murder one carried with it a sentence of twenty-five years to life in prison.

If the jury was not convinced, they would almost certainly convict the girls of second-degree murder. Second-degree murder lacked premeditation. Tamia believed she could eliminate the possibility of second-degree murder. After all, if they had only wanted to hurt Missy or scare her, they would have taken her to the park. That was their usual hangout, and it would have been the perfect place to settle an argument. But they had driven for thirty minutes up a winding road into the mountains—altogether a forty-five-minute death march—before leading Missy up a dusty path to the site of her execution.

Now only a few more weeks remained before the murder trial of Karen Severson and Laura Doyle would begin.

42

SOMETHING WAS DIFFERENT about this warm January day in Pasadena's oldest court building. The empty-eyed drifters and mothers rounding up runny-nosed children could sense it: an excitement that could not be ignored as they watched the crowd gathering in front of Division J, Judge Jack B. Tso's court-room.

Irene Avila stood fifty yards down the hall, surrounded by her sons and other relatives. They wanted to be far away from the reporters studying their notes and checking batteries in their tape recorders. Amid the commotion photographers clamored for position, waiting for the doors to open. This wasn't yet a media event, but there were many local newspapers that didn't want to miss a thing.

The day had finally arrived. Missy Avila's best friends were about to be tried for first-degree murder —the murder of Missy Avila.

It was about time. There had been an unusual number of delays in taking this case to trial, and on December 18, 1989, Judge Tso had agreed to give everyone a two-week break for the holidays. Then there had been an additional week granted upon the return to court. After that Judge Tso had warned the defense that there would be no further delays in his courtroom. Andrews and Thomas knew they had pushed him to the limit and finally, with jury selection just finished, the trial was about to begin.

Tamia Hope understood the strategy of delaying the trial as long as possible. Back in December every one of her witnesses had been ready, but if the defense could delay the trial, there was always a chance that something would happen. Time often caused witnesses to disappear or change their minds. If the defense got extremely lucky, a witness might die of natural causes.

Then there had been the jury selection. Even with the delays requested by the defense, the trial would have started sooner if the jury selection hadn't taken so long. All three attorneys used the maximum number of peremptory challenges allowed by law, and on January 9, when there was just one more juror seat to fill, two of the prospective jurors backed out. After lunch they handed notes to Judge Tso requesting to be dismissed because they "couldn't handle sitting in on a murder trial involving a girl who might have been killed by her best friends."

It was now January 10, and it had taken till midday before they had finally picked a complete jury with two alternates. By then the attorneys had grilled more than ninety-two jurors.

Tamia's questions had been fairly routine: Do you believe that women can commit first-degree murder? Even very young women?

The defense attorneys had been more subtle, asking jurors who, in the history of time, they would most like to have dinner with and why. Tamia knew they were hoping to reveal personality traits in the jurors that might affect their judgment. They also asked the jurors if they believed that sometimes, in the heat of the moment, it was possible to do something awful and then instantly regret it.

Tamia Hope was surprised by their questions. Unless they were hiding something, she could tell that at this point they had very little to go on.

Through it all Tamia watched Irene Avila grow more and more despondent, more doubtful of the legal system. Tamia had been spending more time with her own daughters since taking on the Severson-Doyle case. Sometimes she even tried to imagine what life would be like without them, the pain she would feel if she were being dragged through defense-attorney delays awaiting the trial of her daughter's killers.

While Karen Severson and Laura Doyle were dabbling in extension courses at Sybil Brand Institute and Tamia Hope was waiting for the trial to start, Irene Avila had joined a support group for parents of murdered children. Through them Irene finally found some understanding. Several members of the support group had promised to be there at various stages of the trial.

Now, on January 10 at 12:30 in the afternoon, the Avila family needed only each other for support. In thirty minutes the trial would begin.

Finally, it was nearly one o'clock and one of the court reporters unlocked the courtroom doors. It was time to hear opening arguments in the case of the *People* v. *Karen Severson and Laura Doyle.*

In the hallway Mark Avila—in every way a living testament to his sister's good looks—straightened his dark suit. He would be the first to take the witness stand, and afterward his mother would testify. He entered the courtroom and took a seat.

Except for Irene the entire Avila family were present in the courtroom. Even Ernie senior—who until now had been unable to attend any of the proceedings —was there, though seated off to the side, removed from the others. Outside in the hallway Irene paced the shiny floor, smoking one cigarette after another. She thought how unfair it all was that they should be in this Pasadena courtroom today, one month before what would have been Missy's twenty-second birthday, waiting for Missy's best friends to be tried for her murder. Irene knew that she would have no problem getting on the witness stand, looking into Karen's beady, frightened eyes and testifying against her. She clenched her jaw, opened the courtroom doors, and made her way quickly to a seat in the front row.

She was still such a pretty woman, despite the mark of tragedy that never left her face. She wore a dark red suit that molded her petite figure perfectly. Her raven-colored hair was cut short and it hugged her neck in a fashionable manner. People who knew them could see how much Missy had looked like her mother. Spectators who recognized Irene from the newspaper articles whispered in hushed tones as she sat down. She saw none of them; instead, her eyes were fixed on two girls being led into the courtroom.

But something was wrong. Irene's face went pale and she fought the urge to gasp.

The girls had changed. Someone had worked with them, and now their appearance was nothing like what it had been back in 1985 when they'd killed Missy. Karen had lost weight, fifty pounds or more. She was still heavyset, but she wore a tight denim jean skirt and a baby-blue sweater. Her hair was cut to the shoulders and hung in a neatly brushed veil. She wore very little makeup, but the pale pink blush across her cheeks and the subtle eye shadow made her look as sweet and innocent as a kid in the church choir. Then Karen looked over her shoulder at Irene. Their eyes held for a few seconds and Irene saw her smirk.

Karen didn't appear worried about the outcome of the proceedings. She smiled coyly toward the jurors. She was probably sure there wasn't a person in the box who would believe Cindy's story, and that they were bound to see that Missy was a slut who had deserved what she got. A look of excitement lit up her eyes as she turned around, straining to see the reporters and cameramen waiting outside the courtroom door. Missy had never got this much attention. Karen turned forward again and leaned back in her chair.

Irene felt sick to her stomach; she clutched her sides as Mark put an arm around her. Laura was just as difficult to look at. The girl had gained weight, a little too much for her figure, but at least she didn't look skinny and angular and evil as she had before. She, too, wore an outfit Irene had never seen her wear, a black skirt that hung to midcalf and a light pink sweater. There was a large pink bow clipped to the back of her head, pulling her hair back from her face. Irene felt her nausea grow.

Laura looked strange and uncomfortable in the pretty outfit, but she sat perfectly still, her expression blank and unmoving. As far as she was concerned, this was all Karen's fault. She never should have agreed to be part of the whole plan. It was a stupid mistake. But there was no point getting emotional about it until a decision had been made. Laura knew there would probably be some kind of sentence to pay. But with any luck the jury would see that Karen had masterminded it, and in a year or two she'd be home where she belonged. Laura took a deep breath and adjusted the bow fastened to a section of her red hair.

"I can't believe it," Irene whispered when Tamia Hope approached her. "They have those two looking like Mary Poppins, and my daughter is dead. It isn't fair."

Tamia knew it was part of the game. If the defense could make their clients look attractive enough, perhaps the jury would be a little easier on them. Tamia had to admit that they didn't look much like cold-blooded killers the way they were dressed today.

Tamia bent closer to Irene. "Irene, you have to leave. You can't hear any of the proceedings until after you testify." Tamia had warned Irene that this would probably happen, and Irene nodded as she stood and left. It would be more peaceful out in the hall, anyway.

Suddenly, Judge Tso entered the courtroom. He had gray hair, a kind face, and round glasses. He chuckled a lot and looked like the kind of man who would be wonderful with his grandchildren. His eyes, though, conveyed his essential toughness. Judge Tso had a no-nonsense reputation for handing out some of the most stringent sentences in the district. Tamia was thrilled that he would be hearing the case.

The deputy district attorney straightened her notes and approached the microphone, looking intently at the jury. She wasn't dressed like most businesswomen —in a suit with sharp-looking heels. Instead, she looked neat and trim in a matronly dress with flowers and a sash that tied in the back. Her black hair was short and straight. She looked like a pretty young mother, emanating trust and loyalty. Tamia knew she was someone jurors tended to believe. She had picked up more than a few subtle devices of her own over the years, and her style was no accident.

It was time for her opening argument, and she knew she would have to catch the jury's attention right away. It was an interesting group. Of the twelve jurors only one was a woman. The others were, for the most part, retired men. Tamia had no preconceived ideas about this jury. It was too soon to tell. But she would work them as best she knew how, painting the pictures so that they wouldn't be able to think of anything else until the trial was over.

She cleared her throat and began.

"On October 1, 1985, Michele Avila was seventeen years old. She was a very popular young lady—just four feet eleven and ninety-seven pounds. She had long brown hair, pretty green eyes, and she was petite. Her friends called her Missy.

"The only problem on that fateful day was that she was also very popular with the boys. And it drove the defendants—Laura Doyle and Karen Severson—crazy."

Tamia paused and turned toward Karen and Laura. The jury followed her eyes, craning their necks to get a look at the girls. Karen and Laura appeared cold and unremorseful, which Tamia thought the jury saw too.

During the next twenty minutes Tamia told the jury about Victor Amaya and Jimmy Mitchell and how jealous their girlfriends—the defendants—had been. She told them about Cindy's tormenting guilt and she described what Cindy remembered about that afternoon. As she spoke, Tamia Hope was pleased to see the eyes of several jurors grow wide with horror. Before she was finished she'd told the jury about Karen's strange behavior after the murder and how she had pointed the finger at so many others.

"And so we are in this courtroom today because Cindy Silverio could no longer live with the knowledge that Missy's murderers were allowed to be free. She is here for the same reason you are, to see that justice is done.

"Everyone loved Missy, and because of that, her two best friends decided to kill her. In this country that is first-degree murder, and we will prove to each of you before this trial is over that Karen Severson and Laura Doyle must be convicted and put behind bars for a long, long time."

Tamia was satisfied as she sat down and waited. It was time for the defense lawyers to give their opening arguments, and everyone in the courtroom guessed the tack they would take. As far as Tamia was concerned, it didn't matter what remarks the defense attorneys made, as long as they said something. It was much easier to try a case when you knew what you were up against. Otherwise, the defense—which was within its rights to waive its opening statement—might have a surprise witness or a strategy that the prosecution had completely overlooked. It would be like fighting an unknown opponent.

The courtroom was silent for a moment and then Judge Tso nodded to the defense attorneys. "The defense will give its opening statements now."

David Thomas stood and said, "I waive my opening

statement on behalf of Ms. Doyle." He sat down quickly.

William Andrews rose from his chair, smiling amiably toward the jury. "And I also waive my opening statement on behalf of Ms. Severson."

43

IT WAS JANUARY 11, 1990, just after lunch, and Mark Avila was on the witness stand being cross-examined by William Andrews. He had started his testimony the day before, and Tamia had given him just one piece of advice—stay calm.

She knew the hatred and anger Mark harbored against Karen and Laura. He and Missy had been very close, and Tamia was afraid that an outburst from him might jeopardize the case. But if Tamia could have crept inside Mark's mind, she wouldn't have been concerned. Even though his hatred was as intense as ever, there was nothing in the world he wanted more than to see Karen and Laura convicted.

Whatever Andrews or Thomas asked him, he was going to stay calm. Tamia had already questioned him once, and she was waiting for the chance to question him again in the redirect. From where she sat, Tamia thought Mark looked the perfect picture of a grieving brother. Tamia liked to think the jurors shared her view. He was conservatively handsome in a black suit and starched white shirt that set off his lightly tanned skin and dark hair. On several occasions during the testimony his eyes overflowed with tears.

Andrews was centering on one line of questioning:

beer drinking. Earlier, Tamia had asked Mark about the times the group of friends had gathered at the Avila house and, at Karen's request, gone looking for clues at the murder scene. That gave Andrews the opportunity to ask Mark who was drinking at the get-togethers. Part of Andrews's skill was the way he asked a question so many different ways, it began to sound like the truth regardless of what the person on the witness stand was saying in contradiction. He was playing that game now.

"Were you drinking beer on those occasions?" Andrews smiled as he waited for Mark's answer.

"Yes, a little bit."

"And what's a little bit? Say, a six-pack? Two six-packs?"

"Maybe a six-pack, I'm not sure."

"Was Victor drinking beer?"

"Yes."

"Not much, though, right? Maybe just a six-pack or two, right?"

"I don't know, maybe more than a six-pack."

"How about Brian Taylor? Was he drinking beer?"

"Yes."

"And what about your mother? Was she drinking beer?"

"No. My mother doesn't drink."

"Okay. But everyone else was, is that right?"

"No. I don't think Christopher was drinking beer. He was there sometimes."

"But everyone else was, is that right?"

"Yes, I guess so."

The questions were endless, and it wasn't until Andrews was finished and Tamia stood up that the whole story came out.

Tamia asked her question quickly and with a directness that told the jury the defense's line of questioning was pointless.

"Mark, who suggested the group go get beer?"

Mark caught on immediately and realized that the truth would erase whatever damage the defense questioning had caused.

"Karen Severson."

"And who paid for the beer?"

Mark refrained from smiling as he answered. "Karen Severson."

"And how much did Karen Severson buy each time?"

"A case of beer."

"And how much beer did Karen drink?"

"More than half the case."

"She drank more than twelve beers, Mark?"

"Yes. Sometimes much more than that."

Tamia had just one more question for him.

"Mark, you told us earlier that some of the details are difficult for you to remember because you were in a terrible state back then. Why were you in a terrible state?"

Mark leaned forward toward the microphone and stared Karen Severson and Laura Doyle in the eyes. When he finally answered, his voice cracked with emotion. "Because. I loved my sister very much and someone had taken her away from me."

At 2:40 that afternoon Irene Avila was called to the stand.

She had hoped to make it up the day before, but the proceedings had gone on longer than Tamia had expected. Now, after a sleepless night, Irene appeared shaky and distraught as she took the stand. Tamia

brought her a glass of water and a box of tissues and
started the questioning.

Irene spoke softly, answering each question as politely as possible. Several times during her testimony
Karen Severson glanced in her direction, but Irene
never noticed her. She was focused on Tamia Hope
and the jury. They were the ones who needed to know
the story now.

During the next hour Tamia eased the story of
Karen and Missy's childhood friendship out of Irene
Avila. The jury heard about the details of October 1,
1985, and how Missy had never come home. Just before the break Tamia asked Irene a simple question.

"Did Karen Severson say anything to you the day of
the funeral?"

Irene nodded, tears streaming down her face. Finally, she turned and looked across the courtroom at
Karen and Laura.

"Yes. She said she would stick by me and help me.
Now that Missy was gone, she told me she would never
let me down."

It was time for the break, and Mark Avila knew from
experience that his mother was about to faint. He rose
to meet her at the swinging gate that separated the
spectators from the courtroom action. She collapsed in
his arms, and Tamia ushered them both into an adjoin-
ing room.

The questioning resumed fifteen minutes later, and
Irene managed to climb back onto the witness stand.
There would be a four-day weekend after testimony
finished for the day, and Tamia wanted to save the
most emotional parts for the end of the afternoon.

At 4:15 Tamia asked Irene if Missy had been wearing jewelry the day she disappeared, Irene nodded.

"Did the police ever ask you to sketch what those pieces of jewelry looked like?"

Again Irene nodded. "But I couldn't remember everything exactly."

Tamia continued. "And did someone else remember everything exactly?"

"Yes."

Tamia held up a piece of green notepaper with drawings on it. "Did that person then sketch the jewelry on this paper and offer it to the police?"

"Yes."

"Who was that person, Irene?"

Irene closed her eyes when she answered.

"Karen Severson."

The jury looked shocked and several of the men shook their heads. The single woman on the panel dropped her head into her hands.

Judge Tso dismissed the jury and ordered all parties to return to the courtroom January 16 at eleven o'clock in the morning.

It was a long four days for the Avila family, but finally they were all back in the courtroom and Irene was again on the stand. She wore a black dress with a pretty gold chain, and she was watching as Tamia Hope gingerly lifted a blue denim purse out of a box.

"Is this Missy's purse?"

Irene let her head fall into her hands, and a loud sob escaped before she could control her emotions. She looked up and nodded. "Yes."

It was the first time Irene had seen the purse since Missy disappeared that afternoon in October. Before Tamia was finished, Irene was asked to identify each of the belongings inside. It was a torturous process and several jurors had tears in their eyes by the time it was finished. The cross-examination was next, and Irene stood up stoically under the defense lawyers' intense questioning. Finally, they were through with Irene and she took a seat next to her sons.

The forest ranger was next. Tamia wanted to set the stage for what was coming afterward, and by midday January 17, they had all they needed from him. He had spoken about the body and how it had been found, and he had talked about the depth of the stream. He had also testified about a time he was overseeing a movie shoot and a group of teenagers had come up to the Camp Colby Ranch area near the murder site.

"The girl seemed to be bragging about her best friend's murder," he said calmly. When Tamia asked if he could identify the girl as someone sitting in the courtroom now, he pointed to Karen Severson.

"That's her. Of course, she looks much more glamorous today."

It was the perfect answer and one that hadn't been planned. Tamia was thrilled. As the ranger spoke, every juror turned and looked at Karen. Suddenly she didn't look so pretty and innocent. She looked like a phony.

The ranger was dismissed just before lunch, and now the courtroom buzzed with anticipation. Everyone knew who the next witness was because she had been standing with her boyfriend, Steven, out in the hallway. In just a few minutes the truth about what had happened to Missy Avila would be made public.

The next witness was Cindy Silverio.

44

ON JANUARY 17, just after noon, the rain stopped and the sun broke through overcast skies. This was appropriate, as if the doubt that had clouded the courtroom was also about to clear. After today there would be no more guesswork, no more speculating about what really had happened to Michele Avila. Cindy Silverio was about to testify.

Reporters and photographers clamored for a spot in the tiny courtroom, just as they had on the first day of the trial. Every one of the forty-eight theater seats was filled by the time Judge Jack Tso took the bench. Tamia had advised Cindy to remain in a side room until she was called, because she didn't want her talking to reporters or members of the Avila family. If she had, the defense attorneys would come back later and accuse them of collaborating on their testimonies.

Tamia was more nervous than she had been at any other time during the trial. The entire case rested on Cindy's testimony, and she wondered if the girl would remember important details. The district attorney hadn't coached her about what to say because she believed the girl was telling the truth. Tamia didn't want her sounding like a broken record, rattling off a prepared speech. No one would believe that. Instead, she wanted her star witness to sound just as she had that afternoon when she'd spilled the story to the detectives.

The judge had ruled earlier that Mark and Irene would have to sit outside during Cindy's testimony in case they were called to the witness stand again.

The courtroom buzzed in anticipation as Deputy District Attorney Tamia Hope walked up to the microphone and called her next witness.

"The people call Cindy Silverio, Your Honor."

Suddenly, two bailiffs ushered Cindy into the courtroom as every head turned her way. The girl looked simple and demure. She wore her long, wavy brown hair pulled back in a ponytail and her face had a glow that suggested she'd been out in the sun. She looked like a college coed, dressed in a pretty white sweater and pink slacks. There was nothing hard about Cindy's appearance, nothing to suggest she was anything but a distraught girl who needed to tell her story. She looked like the real thing, and Tamia Hope had to suppress a smile as she took the stand. Suddenly it was easy to see the facade of pink bows and soft sweaters that Karen and Laura were using.

Cindy swallowed hard as she took the witness stand.

Tamia planned to be gentle and sympathetic in her questioning. For the most part she would let Cindy do the talking because, after all, her story was the reason they were in the courtroom that January afternoon. In addition, she wanted to give her a break, since the defense attorneys were probably looking forward to her cross-examination as children look forward to Christmas.

Tamia had already warned Cindy about their likely tactics. She had said they would probably jump from one topic to another, trying to confuse her. They would probably question her motives and her integrity and definitely her version of the story. They might even accuse her of killing Missy. As she climbed into the witness box, Cindy tried not to think about her performance. She knew it would be hard to tell the jury what had happened, but she would have found it harder to remain silent.

Tamia Hope cleared her throat. The easy questions came first.

Cindy testified that she had known Karen, Laura, and Missy since 1982. She said she had been one of several in the group of friends that had hung out together at Stonehurst and Branford parks in Arleta. She added that sometimes the group gathered at another spot—Strathern Park.

Tamia paused a moment, sorting through her notes.

"Cindy, have you ever seen Karen physically hurt Missy Avila?"

"Yes. At Strathern Park about a month before Missy was killed. Karen was angry at Missy because she thought Missy was seeing Jimmy."

Tamia interrupted her. "That would be Jimmy Mitchell?"

"Yes. Jimmy Mitchell. Anyway, Karen walked up to Missy and shouted at her. Then, before anyone could stop her, she smacked Missy in the face."

The first surprise was out. There were several muffled gasps from the courtroom as Missy's brothers shared looks of confusion. Chris shook his head and formed his fists into tight balls. Missy had never mentioned the incident to any of them, probably because she was too loyal to Karen.

Tamia continued, jumping to the day of the murder.

Slowly, the jurors began to tune out Tamia's questioning and listen only to Cindy's story.

On October 1, 1985, Cindy Silverio and her boyfriend, Steven, had been living with Karen Severson for two days. Karen and Steven had been friends for several years and the arrangement seemed ideal. Karen needed a roommate and the couple needed a place to live, somewhere they could be on their own.

That morning, Steven had gone to work. Karen Severson approached Cindy and asked if she wanted to go with her to her grandmother's house for dinner that evening. Cindy decided to go.

"I didn't know Karen very well, really, but I thought it would be a good chance to get to be better friends so I told her I'd go," Cindy said.

The jurors were leaning forward, anxious to hear what had happened next.

Cindy continued. She and Karen had left the apartment at about two o'clock that afternoon in Karen's white Chevrolet. Karen was driving and a few minutes later the girls pulled into Stonehurst Park. There, Karen pointed to Laura's Volkswagen stopped alongside the park. Missy was sitting in Laura's passenger seat.

"Karen turned to me and said, 'There's Laura and Missy.'"

Cindy stopped and took a sip of water as the jurors waited.

"Karen drove her car next to Laura's and started cussing at her. She was really mad. Then Laura started cussing back at Karen."

Cindy seemed to drift back in time.

"At that point Karen and Laura yelled at each other for several minutes," Cindy said. "The whole time,

Missy was looking at them from the passenger seat. I think she was confused by their fighting. Then, suddenly, Laura pulled back out into traffic and Karen pulled out after her. Karen chased Laura's car through Arleta to the Big Tujunga Canyon.

"Laura was driving very fast and we were keeping up with her," Cindy said softly. "Then Karen looked at me and told me it was all a trick. She said she wasn't mad at Laura, and Laura wasn't mad at her. She said they were going to scare Missy."

The courtroom was completely silent and Karen Severson glared at Cindy. But Cindy had gone too far to stop now, and she looked straight at Tamia as she asked, "Cindy, did you observe Missy doing or saying anything as Laura Doyle was driving her up the mountain road?"

"Yes. She would put her head in her hands and then she would turn toward Laura and then she would put her head back in her hands. She looked upset. Like she was trying to tell Laura something."

"Did you see Laura Doyle doing anything when Missy made those movements?"

"No. Well, I could just see her head move back and forth. Not like she was saying no, but like she was just glancing over at Missy and then watching the road and . . ."

Cindy's voice drifted off and she seemed about to cry. Tamia moved on.

"Did Laura Doyle or Karen Severson stop at all on the way up the mountain?"

"Yes. Probably after about ten or fifteen minutes of driving they pulled over to a picnic area and got out of their cars."

"Did you see them say or do anything once they

both got out of their cars?" Tamia's voice grew softer with each question, and the jurors had long since tuned her out. In their minds they could almost see the winding road and the confusion on Missy's face as the cars pulled over.

"Karen and Laura walked over to each other. Maybe they said something, but then I didn't hear it. Afterward they just got back in the cars. Laura took off first back up the hill and Karen followed her."

"Missy was still in Laura's car and you were still in Karen's car, is that right?"

"Yes."

"What were you doing at this time?"

"I asked Karen what was going on and she said something like 'We're just going to scare Missy.' "

Tamia nodded, and the jurors watched as she walked back to the table and flipped through some notes. Several seconds passed before she asked the next question. In the audience Chris Avila dropped his head in his hand. The charade was coming to light. He was glad his mother and Mark were out in the hallway.

Tamia started asking questions again, but this time her voice had changed. She no longer sounded sadly sympathetic, but incredulous. She had transformed herself into Cindy's friend, someone who was hearing the details of that October day for the first time. It made the jurors and everyone else in the room think they had stumbled onto a private conversation, and they sat mesmerized as the questioning continued.

"What happened next, Cindy?"

"Laura turned right onto a narrow, single-lane dirt road up in the mountains and Karen followed her."

Suddenly the judge interrupted.

"I think this is a good time to take the noon break. We will reconvene at two P.M."

By two o'clock Karen and Laura were back in the courtroom and the jurors were in place. The defendants watched as Tamia called Cindy back to the witness stand. She looked a little more distraught than she had earlier in the afternoon. Tamia started her questions almost immediately, and instantly the same mood descended on the courtroom. People sat rapt, listening in on an honest and horrifying private conversation between two people.

"Cindy, do you recall how long it took to drive from the park up to the area you described where Karen Severson and Laura Doyle turned off onto the dirt road?"

"Approximately forty minutes."

"Where did Karen and Laura drive to once they turned onto the road?"

"Well, we drove over a little bridge and then we stopped in this open parking lot. It wasn't paved, just a dirt lot."

"What happened then?"

"Karen and Laura got out of their cars, and I think Missy slid over to the driver's side of Laura's car so she could hear what they were saying."

"And what were they saying?"

"They were still yelling at each other, calling each other names like they had at the park."

"And what tone of voice were they using, do you remember?"

"Yes, it was sarcastic."

The jurors followed Tamia as she turned and looked at the defendants. Her gaze was fixed on them as she asked her next question.

"And what happened then?"

"At that point they turned toward Missy and said something like 'We're not really mad at each other, it's you we hate.' "

Someone in the back of the courtroom muffled a gasp and Ernie junior and Chris seemed to sink a few inches deeper into their seats. They were caught up in the truth now, and they felt compelled to hear it out.

"Do you recall whether or not Karen Severson or Laura Doyle indicated why they were mad at Missy?"

Cindy swallowed hard and stared down at her hands. "They said it was because she had slept with their boyfriends."

"And what happened then? Did Missy say or do anything?"

Cindy was growing more nervous. She hated having to relive that day, after years of suppressing the truth. And the ordeal was only going to get worse during the cross-examination.

"She started to cry."

Tamia paused and let Cindy's words sink in. Several of the jurors looked disgusted. Suddenly, Chris Avila stood and left the courtroom. He had told himself he could take the truth—he wanted to hear what had happened to Missy that day. But this story was too hard. They had tricked her and tortured her. He couldn't imagine what other horrors might be revealed in Cindy's testimony.

Tamia continued her questioning.

"Then what did Karen and Laura say to Missy?"

"They were just . . . they were naming off boys' names—boyfriends and friends they said she had slept with."

"What was Missy doing?"

"She was crying, she really didn't say much."

"Cindy, can you tell us what this particular area is called?"

"Wicky-up."

Tamia pulled out several poster-sized drawings. For the next several minutes Cindy showed the distance between Karen's and Laura's cars and other basic details of the place the teenagers called "Wicky-up."

The jurors looked impatient. They didn't want diagrams and penciled-in drawings. They wanted the truth about what had happened to Missy that afternoon, and Tamia quickly returned to her previous line of questioning.

"After Karen and Laura turned on Missy, and Missy was crying, what happened then?"

"After they finished yelling at her, one of them, I believe it was Laura, said, 'Let's take a walk.'"

"And what did Missy do then?"

Cindy stared down and shook her head. It was all coming back to her and she started crying.

"What did Missy do then, Cindy?"

"Missy looked up at me and she said, 'The worst thing you guys could do is leave me here all alone.'"

Cindy was crying, and Tamia gave her a moment to compose herself. Tamia knew from interviewing Cindy that those words had haunted the girl these past years. Missy had been wrong. The worst thing they could do was yet to come. Tamia took her time asking the next question.

"And did you do anything to help her?"

Tears were streaming down Cindy's face now, and she shook her head. "No. I put my head down and looked away. But she kept looking at me like maybe she wanted me to help her or something."

Tamia glanced at the jurors again. Experience told her that the jury knew how badly the guilt had eaten away at Cindy. After all, Cindy had been the last person Missy had reached out to, the only one who could have helped her. Tamia knew from the looks on the jurors' faces that each of them was spellbound, caught up in the horrible truth of what had happened to Missy Avila. It was crueler than any of them had imagined.

Tamia asked one more question before continuing. "What was Missy's expression like when she was looking at you, Cindy?"

Cindy seemed in pain when she answered. "She was crying and she had, like, kind of like an innocent look on her face. And I didn't do anything. I just let her cry."

Cindy took a tissue from the box on the witness stand and wiped her cheeks.

"And when Missy said, 'The worst thing you can do is just leave me up here all alone,' what happened then?"

"Then they told her, 'Let's go.' And I believe Laura grabbed her by the wrist and pulled her up out of the car. I don't know how she did it, but after that Laura got her to walk toward the path. We walked down the path, I believe it was Missy, then Laura, then Karen and me."

"And what was Missy doing as she was walking along this path?"

"I believe she was still crying." Cindy had composed herself now and she looked like a brave child recounting the frightening details of a nightmare.

"Then, after you all walked up the trail, what happened?"

"We got to an opening and we stopped. There was a

stream on the left side through the opening and there was a large rock on the shore of the stream."

"When you got to the opening, what did Missy do then?"

"I know she was still crying at that time, and she went over toward the rock."

"What did Laura Doyle do then?"

"She forced Missy to sit down on the rock, and Karen moved over beside them. After that she and Laura kept yelling at Missy and naming boys' names, telling Missy she had slept with all of them."

"Do you recall any specific names that Laura named?"

"Vic."

"And do you recall now any specific names Karen named?"

"Jimmy."

"And what did you do during this time?" Tamia's voice was soft. There was no need for dramatics now, not with Cindy providing them on the stand.

Cindy stared down at the microphone and tried to remain composed as she spoke. "All I did was stand there with my arms crossed, listening to them yell off the names. They just kept going on and on."

Tamia was directing Cindy's testimony like a master conductor, and the music was beautiful to the prosecuting attorney. By then the jurors could see Missy crying on the boulder. They could imagine the terror that must have filled the girl's heart as she realized the friends she trusted more than any others really hated her.

"And what happened then?"

"Well, I saw Laura grab Missy's hair with her fist and

pull her head back. Then she screamed something at Missy."

"Do you recall the exact words Laura screamed at her?"

"Exact words?"

"Yes, the exact words."

"She said, 'You screwed my . . . you screwed my boyfriend.' "

"And did Karen do anything at that time?"

"I don't recall."

"Did you see anything happen to Missy's hair?"

"I didn't see anything happen, but I did . . . at one point I glanced up and saw there was hair on the ground."

The next few minutes were frustrating for Tamia. In the preliminary hearing and during an interview by one of the investigators, Cindy had said that she saw Karen pull out a knife and use it to cut off chunks of Missy's long brown hair. But now, in front of the jury and a packed courtroom, Cindy was having trouble remembering the details.

"Did you ever see Karen Severson near Missy's head or hair?"

"I'm sorry?"

Cindy was getting very nervous, and Tamia tried desperately to correct the situation and give the jurors a clear picture of what Cindy thought had happened.

"Did you ever see Karen Severson near Missy's head or hair?"

"No, not to my knowledge, unless I'm not understanding your question. I'm sorry."

Tamia steered her questions to another track.

"At what point did you see hair on the ground?"

"After Laura had grabbed her."

Tamia pulled out an enlarged photograph of chunks of hair lying near a rock. They were photos taken by the sheriff's deputies when Missy Avila's body was found.

"Cindy, have you ever seen what is shown in that picture before?"

"Yes. On the ground that afternoon near the rock."

Tamia had an idea and she smiled politely.

"Did you ever see something in Karen's hand as she and Laura stood near Missy and the rock?"

"I did see her hold something but right now I can't clearly recall what it was she was holding."

Tamia was patient as she asked her next question.

"Do you recall talking to an investigator in 1988 and at that time do you recall naming an object that you saw in Karen's hand?"

"Yes. At that time I believe I described the object Karen was holding as a knife."

Determined to make the point, Tamia gave Cindy a copy of her interview with the detective. But the effort was a futile one.

"Now that you've read the report do you recall that when Laura pulled Missy's head back, Karen took out a knife and cut Missy's hair?"

"See, I don't actually recall it. I think when I was telling the detective that—since I had put it behind me for so many years—I think when I had mentioned the hair on the ground I was assuming it was a knife and that Karen had cut her hair. I do remember seeing the hair on the ground."

Tamia turned back toward the table. This would have to do. The jurors wanted the rest of the story, not this tedious testimony about hair chunks. The prosecuting attorney continued.

"Okay. After you saw Laura Doyle grab Missy's hair and accuse her of sleeping with her boyfriend, and after you then at some time saw chunks of hair on the ground, then what happened?"

"Laura let go of Missy's hair and then she walked over to the stream; into the middle of the stream."

"And what did Laura Doyle do or say as she walked to the middle of the stream?"

"She glided her hand across the water and said, 'Come out here, Missy. The water isn't so deep.'"

"And did you see how deep the water was at that point?"

"When Laura was in there she had tennis shoes on and it came to, well, I guess you could call it her lower shin or just above her ankles."

Tamia was the artist now, directing Cindy's testimony like vivid colors across a sheet of canvas. The jurors seemed to be completely involved in the story and none of them remembered they were sitting in a drab, unfeeling courtroom. They had been transported during the course of questioning to shoreline seats and now each of them could see Laura Doyle leaning over the water, beckoning Missy toward her. Tamia was aware of the effect the testimony was having on everyone in the courtroom, and she continued.

"And as Laura Doyle walked out into the middle of the stream and put her hand over the water, what did she say?"

"She said, 'Come on out here, Missy. The water isn't so deep.'"

Tamia spoke softly as she asked the next question. "And how did Missy respond?"

"She didn't say anything, she didn't move. She was still crying."

For just a moment Laura Doyle looked down at her hands as Cindy spoke, but when she looked up her expression was the same as before—completely void of emotion.

"Did Karen do anything then?"

"Yes. Karen put her hand on Missy's shoulder and pushed her off the rock. Then she nudged her toward the stream."

Throughout the questioning Tamia had moved closer to Cindy until it really seemed as if the two were simply sharing a heart-to-heart conversation. But now, with Tamia just a few feet from the witness box, Judge Tso called her back to the table.

"Yes. Thank you, Your Honor." Tamia took a few steps back and without skipping a beat turned toward Cindy. "Where did Missy go after Karen pushed her off the rock and nudged her toward the stream?"

"Missy started to walk into the water."

"How far did you see her get?"

"I saw her go a couple of steps into the water and then Laura walked toward her, reached out, and grabbed her by the wrist."

"And was Karen doing or saying anything at that time?"

"Karen was standing at the edge of the water where she had nudged Missy into the stream."

"What happened then?"

Cindy began wringing her hands nervously. "That's when I got scared and started running up the path."

"Why did you do that?" This was the question the jurors would be thinking, and Tamia wanted to voice it before they could.

"I didn't like what I was seeing. I was nervous. I started running up the path and Karen came running toward me. She wanted the car keys and I gave them to her. I just wanted to get away from them."

"Okay. Once you got back to the cars in the dirt lot, what did you do?"

"I went to the cars to see if they were locked. They were, so I ran back to the stream to see if I could borrow the keys. But by the time I got to the foot of the path, I heard Missy scream."

"What did you do when you heard Missy scream?"

"I just . . . I can't remember exactly. I just freaked out and I ran back to the cars. I sat between both cars crying for a long, long time."

Cindy began to cry again. Everyone in the courtroom could hear Missy's last scream, her last gasp for a single breath of air. They could picture her helplessness and they could see the horror in her eyes when the reality hit her. Her best friends didn't just hate her. They were going to kill her. In the spectator section of the courtroom Ernie junior began to cry softly. If only he had been there, if someone had been there. Tamia paused long enough for Cindy to compose herself.

"How many times did you hear Missy scream?"

"Just once."

"How long after you heard Missy scream did you see Karen and Laura?"

"I don't remember exactly how long. It seemed like about two hours, but I'm sure it wasn't too long. Karen came back toward the cars by herself and I asked her what happened."

"And what did she say she had personally done?"

Both defense attorneys were on their feet, but it was Andrews who objected first. Even if there weren't grounds, there had to be some kind of break in the testimony. It was simply too damaging to their clients.

"Objection, Your Honor. That's leading and suggestive."

But Judge Tso wasn't buying the tactic. "Overruled, you may answer."

"I don't remember her exact words, but Karen said that she had . . . that she had to hide or cover the body. Then she got into her car and drove off, leaving me there by Laura's car."

"Okay. After you saw Karen leave in her car, what did you see Laura Doyle do, if anything?"

"Laura came back from the path and she started panicking. First she tried to take off her shoes and she was trying to take her seat covers off and put them in the trunk of her car."

"Why did she say she was taking the seat covers off?"

"She said she was afraid she'd be caught."

Tamia stole a glance at the jurors. They looked horrified at what had obviously happened to Missy.

"What was the condition of Laura's shoes when she took them off?"

"Her pants and her shoes were wet. I told her I wanted to drive but she wouldn't let me. I thought I should drive because at that time Laura was just . . . she was panicking. She was . . . she was just going crazy."

"What happened then?"

"Laura got into the car and I got into the passenger seat and we started driving down the canyon. Laura was swerving a lot. She wasn't staying within the lines very well and I told her to calm down."

"Did you ask her what had happened?"

"I believe I did, yes."

"What did she say that she had personally done?"

"She said that she had killed Missy."

Several spectators gasped and the dozen reporters began scribbling notes furiously. A few jurors glanced over at Laura Doyle, but the indifference never left her face. It was as if the story being told were about someone altogether different.

"Did she indicate why she had killed Missy?"

"Because Missy had slept with her boyfriend."

"And did she indicate how she personally felt about having killed Missy?"

"I don't recall."

It wasn't the answer Tamia wanted. She tried another approach.

"Did she indicate whether or not—"

David Thomas was on his feet.

"Just a minute! I am going to object to all that as leading the witness. She has said she does not know."

Judge Tso shook his head. "Let's hear the next question."

Tamia took a moment and looked at her notes.

"Okay. Cindy, how many times did Laura Doyle tell you she had killed Missy?"

Now Cindy understood.

"A couple times. She told me in different ways with different personalities."

"What do you mean with different personalities?"

"Well," Cindy began. "First she'd say it with a really evil laugh—"

Again David Thomas was on his feet.

"Objection, Your Honor. I don't think there is such a thing as an evil laugh. Maybe it can be described better than that."

Judge Tso nodded. "Sustained."

Tamia welcomed the opportunity.

"Cindy, could you describe what you mean by an evil laugh?"

"Well, she would say, 'Ha, ha, ha. I killed Missy.' Then she'd say it like she was scared, like 'Oh, my God, we killed Missy.' Then she'd slam on the brakes, stop the car, and say, 'Maybe we didn't. Maybe she isn't dead.' "

"What happened when she slammed on the brakes?"

"She said she wanted to go back and check. To make sure she was dead."

"And what did you say then?"

"I said no, keep driving. I said it because I was afraid. I wanted to get home and get out of that car."

At this point in the testimony it was important that the jury feel sympathy for Cindy and understand her fear as she was captive in Laura's car. Later, both defense attorneys would tear to pieces her testimony by contending that she was more concerned about getting home than helping her friend, Missy, who at that time, according to Laura, might still have been alive.

During the next two hours Cindy described what had happened when she and Laura reached the bottom of the canyon. First, they went to Karen's grandmother's house, where Cindy took her purse from Karen's car. Afterward, Laura and Cindy drove on to a friend's house so Cindy could use their bathroom. After that, which would have been about an hour after Missy's murder, Laura dropped Cindy off at her apartment. Of course, it was also Karen Severson's apartment. Tamia skimmed over Cindy's willingness to return to the apartment she shared with Karen, but the defense was certain to dwell on it. Why, if Cindy was so scared of Karen, was she willing to spend the night with her? Especially when her testimony had already pointed out that she had at least one friend in the area, whose house she stopped at to use the bathroom.

Cindy also testified that she and Karen said nothing that evening about what had happened earlier in the day up in the mountains, even though at one point they were alone together in one of the apartment rooms. Tamia could see confusion clouding the faces of several jurors. She could just imagine what the defense would do with this part of Cindy's story.

Cindy went on to say that later that same evening, hours after Missy's murder, there was a fight among Karen, Cindy, her boyfriend, Steven, and his friend, Troy. According to Cindy the fight was not about what had happened earlier in the day up in the mountains. In fact, neither the prosecution nor the defense ever probed into what that fight might have been about.

Cindy testified that sometime during the fight Steven threw Karen out of the room and minutes later Karen returned with a kitchen knife and threatened to kill Cindy. Troy, Steven's friend, then grabbed the knife and Karen tried to stab Troy till Steven intervened.

According to Cindy Silverio that was the end of her relationship with Karen Severson. Steven's family came to pick him and Cindy up that night and she never saw Karen again until some time later at Branford Park. On that occasion there were no other people near them, yet still neither girl made any reference to the incident involving Missy Avila.

For obvious reasons Tamia Hope also did not dwell

on that chance meeting at the park, because according to Cindy, it was fear of Karen Severson that had kept her quiet about the murder for so long. But if Karen was so intimidating, why hadn't she threatened Cindy on the two occasions after the murder when the two girls were alone?

Cindy also testified that she didn't attend Missy's funeral. "I didn't think it was right, knowing what I knew."

When Tamia asked Cindy why she hadn't gone to the police right away, Cindy stared down and bit her lower lip.

"I was afraid for my life. I thought if they could kill Missy, they could also kill me."

"But you did go to the police eventually, right?"

"Yes. After my younger brother died. He was only eighteen, and after he died I suffered a lot of pain and I finally knew how Missy's family was feeling. Before then, I didn't understand. I had never felt that kind of pain before."

For an hour Cindy described how she had gone to her older brother, Jack, and how he had called the police for her. Eventually, the detectives on the case had arranged an interview and she had told them everything she knew.

There was just one more thing Tamia wanted to ask Cindy. She wanted the girl to identify the pictures of Missy's body. It might be important for her to identify the clothes Missy had been wearing and testify that the place in the stream where her body lay was the same spot Cindy had last seen Missy alive. The color pictures were blown up poster size and were very vivid. The jury had already seen them, and Tamia had been right about their impact. The jurors had been glued to the pictures, looking at them for as long as they could stand it, then looking away and finally looking back again.

Tamia carefully picked the pictures up and turned them around toward Cindy.

"Do you recognize—"

But Tamia never got a chance to finish her question.

Cindy Silverio screamed and began sobbing for the district attorney to take the pictures away. Her eyes closed, Cindy crossed her arms in front of her body, hugging herself tightly and rocking back and forth, sobbing and screaming. It was a moment of truth.

Karen Severson and Laura Doyle had shown no reaction when the pictures were first introduced, as if there was nothing surprising about seeing their friend lying facedown in a stream with a log across her back. Suddenly the jury understood their complacency— Karen and Laura had seen the image before, in real life.

For more than four years Cindy had only pictured how Missy must have looked after they'd killed her. The image had haunted and tormented her and now that she was being faced with the actual sight, it was too much for her to take.

Five minutes went by before Cindy regained control of herself, and then Tamia Hope made one simple statement.

"No further questions, Your Honor."

Cindy's reaction had said it all.

Tamia was satisfied, despite the fact that no one really understood why Karen and Laura would take Cindy up the mountain road with them to witness a murder and despite the lack of details in much of Cindy's testimony. They had a motive—jealousy—and they had their witness. Four of them had gone up to the mountains that day and three had returned.

Judge Tso nodded. "It's getting late. Why don't we break for the afternoon? We will resume tomorrow morning at nine o'clock."

The defense attorneys stood quickly and left the courtroom together, whispering in tones no one could have heard. But one thing was obvious: They couldn't wait to start tearing holes through Cindy Silverio's testimony.

45

HAVING HEARD THE details of Cindy's testimony
from her sons, Irene spent that evening at home
grieving in a way she hadn't since Missy first disappeared. She finally felt the terror her little girl had
known in the last moments of her life. How frightened
Missy must have been as her best friend held her face
under water. The poem Missy had written about being
afraid of the ocean, afraid of drowning, came back to
her. Who would have thought she'd drown in eight
inches of water? And at the hands of her best friends.
Irene knew it was time to accept the truth. Karen had
hated Missy. She had killed her, and then for three
years made a mockery of her family's grief. Irene
could feel a hatred for Karen growing until she could
picture herself killing the girl if they ever met face to
face again. She prayed that would never happen.

Since his divorce from Irene, Ernie senior hadn't
really been included as one of the family. He had chosen his life-style and he understood Irene's need to go
on without him. But Missy was his only daughter, his
little girl. He had learned about her death after work
one day and he hadn't been the same since. When
Ernie had first seen the pictures of his daughter lying
in the stream, pinned under a log, he'd looked at them

for only a moment and then stared down at his shaking hands, clasping them together. He never returned to the courtroom, not even for Cindy's testimony. Nothing would bring Missy back.

That same night, across town, Cindy Silverio lay still in the arms of her boyfriend, Steven, trying not to wake him. Her demons were gone now. No more bedside conversations with ghosts, no more nightmares. Showers no longer scared her. But sleep didn't come any easier. Testifying was the hardest thing she'd ever done—sitting up there in front of everyone and telling the truth while Karen and Laura stared at her from just a few feet away. Still, seeing them in person was no where near as frightening as seeing them in her dreams, and one day it would all be over. Cindy closed her eyes and tried to sleep.

That night in her prison cell at Sybil Brand, it is doubtful that Karen Severson shed any tears for Missy Avila. But the confidence she had shown when the trial first started had to have been replaced by a cool desperation. There had to be some way to stop that stupid Cindy Silverio from doing more damage up there. Perhaps she wondered for a moment if her attorney would let her take the stand and clear things up, tell the world that no one should be allowed to have as much as Missy Avila. It wasn't fair. She probably thought her present circumstances were all Missy's fault.

In another Sybil Brand cell, far away from Karen's, Laura Doyle was probably wishing she'd never met any of them. Not Cindy Silverio, not Missy Avila, and especially not Karen Severson or Victor Amaya. No guy was worth wasting your life for in a prison cell. And after Cindy's testimony Laura must have had a pretty good idea that she would be spending the next few years in prison.

Tamia Hope spent that night alone, her stomach twisted in uncertain knots. It wasn't Cindy's testimony that bothered her. The girl had been believable and emotional, which was all Tamia had hoped for. Of course, there was still the cross-examination to go through, and no doubt the defense would give Cindy a tough time. But what bothered Tamia that evening had nothing to do with Cindy's testimony or cross-examination. It had to do with Thomas and Andrews. As often as Tamia tried to imagine the line of defense they'd take, the fact still remained: She was presenting her case, playing her entire hand—without the slightest idea of theirs.

Victor Amaya visited the cemetery that evening. Every week since she died, Victor had been visiting Missy's gravesite. Sometimes he would take flowers he picked in the nearby hills. Pretty yellow and orange wildflowers, the kind Missy had loved when she had been alive. Victor had been disgusted by the trial's revelations, and he couldn't help feeling somewhat responsible. He knew how angry Laura had been with Missy, but he hadn't said anything. Victor sat at the foot of Missy's grave. He ran a hand over his shoulder, tattooed with the words *Missy, Rest in Peace*. Missy had loved and trusted those girls like sisters. He remembered the day Laura had driven by his house and seen Missy talking to him. As Vic sat in the quiet cemetery, Laura's words from that evening long ago played over in his head. "I'm going to kill that bitch. I'm going to kill that bitch. I'm going to kill that bitch."

Why couldn't he have seen that she was serious? Tears rolled down Victor's face, and he looked up to where the sun was setting in the clear blue sky. Sometimes he felt that Missy was still with him. He would think about her bright smile and trusting heart when he took the stand in a few days to testify.

46

THE CROSS-EXAMINATION of Cindy Silverio took place on January 22, a crisp, cold day when the only storm clouds for miles were those brewing inside Judge Tso's courtroom.

The courtroom was even more packed than it had been the day before. Tamia expected the defense to fire biting questions at Cindy like so many deadly missiles. Defense attorneys loved using their arsenal of dramatics, especially when the witness was so young and the story she had to tell already four years old. Tamia only hoped the jury wouldn't forget the convincing aspects of Cindy's story.

David Thomas had opted to go first. He appeared eager to attack Cindy's testimony.

"Good morning, Miss Silverio," Thomas said, proffering a sarcastic smile in Cindy's direction. Thomas was dressed to perfection in an elegant pinstriped black suit. "Is it fair to say that Missy Avila was your good friend?"

In contrast with Cindy's appearance the previous day, she looked scared, jittery, and wide eyed. She almost winced at the questions David Thomas asked.

"She was one of my good friends, yes."

Whereas Tamia had asked her questions slowly and

deliberately, Thomas spewed them out angrily, one after another in rapid fire.

"And you saw her up there in the mountains and people were pushing her around, is that correct?"

"Yes."

"Screaming at her?"

"Yes."

"And you didn't stick up for her, did you?"

"No, I didn't."

"Now, on other occasions you befriended her like a little sister, didn't you?"

"Yes."

"And now you didn't—"

"Excuse me." Cindy was clearly flustered as she interrupted Thomas. "Can I please explain why I didn't defend her that day?"

"Yes!" Thomas spoke as if he were accepting a tremendous job offer, waving his hand and shaking his head excitedly. Several jurors snickered. "Take your time, Miss Silverio."

"Well, one of the reasons I didn't defend her was I had no idea Karen and Laura would kill her; two, I was very afraid of Karen at that time."

"I see." Thomas nodded sarcastically. "You were so afraid of her you spent the night at her house, didn't you?"

"I was living there, yes."

"Yes." Thomas chuckled and looked directly at the jurors as he spoke. "You weren't afraid of her then, were you?"

"I had my boyfriend with me."

But Thomas had made his point, and he jumped to another topic.

"Now, when you came down the hill, based on what

Laura Doyle told you, you didn't know whether Missy was dead or alive, did you?"

"No, I really didn't."

It was the wrong answer, and Tamia tried not to cringe as Thomas pounced on Cindy's words.

"And did you go back up there later that night to see about your good friend?" Thomas spoke the last two words as if they were poisonous, and in the witness box Cindy seemed to be shrinking.

"No."

"Did you go to the police?"

"No."

"One of your brother's friends was a police officer, is that correct?"

"Correct."

"But you didn't start talking about going to the right person in the police department until about three years later?" Thomas sounded amazed, and Chris and Ernie junior squirmed in their seats. The attorney was making Cindy look ridiculous.

"I believe so, yes."

"Let me ask you, Miss Silverio, were you taking any notes when you were coming back down the hill with Miss Doyle?"

"Taking any notes?"

"Did you take any notes as to what she was saying?" Thomas lowered his head and spoke at her directly, as if talking to a child. "You didn't, did you?"

"No."

"All right. Later on, did you write down what she said?"

"No."

If this had been a tennis match, Thomas would already have won the first set with that point. How could Cindy have remembered what had been said, word for word, some five years ago? After all, and Thomas had just driven the point home, Cindy hadn't taken notes.

Next, Thomas pointed out the first of several minor discrepancies between Cindy's testimony of the day before and that given during her preliminary hearing months earlier. They dealt with the order in which Cindy remembered the four girls walking up the path that October first. Was it Missy, Laura, Karen, then Cindy? Or was it Laura, Missy, Karen, and Cindy? Then he noted that during the preliminary hearing Cindy said it had taken about fifteen minutes to walk up the path and the day before she had recalled it as taking only three minutes.

Before the hour was up, Cindy was so confused, she was asking more questions than Thomas.

The questioning took most of the day and finally, just before the afternoon recess, Thomas turned to Cindy and abruptly asked her whether she had told anyone what had happened to Missy, before going to the police three years later.

"All right." Thomas was having fun with her now, aware that he had Cindy Silverio talking in circles. "Now, that day, you told one of your brothers what happened, didn't you?"

"Which day?"

"October 1, 1985, the day when you came back down the hill with Miss Doyle."

"No, I didn't. I told my fiancé, Steven."

"I see. And what did you tell him?"

"I don't remember exactly what I told him."

"You don't remember what you told him?" Thomas sounded incredulous, and from where she sat at the attorney's table, Tamia Hope glanced at the clock. Thomas still had enough time to make one final point before they were dismissed for the lunch break.

"Now, you indicated on direct examination that you were beating Miss Severson up. Do you remember testifying on direct that you were beating Miss Severson up?"

"Yes, I did."

"Tell us when was that?"

"That was October second, at the apartment."

They were talking about the incident involving Karen, Cindy, Steven, and his friend, Troy. Tamia knew where Thomas was taking his questions, but she could only sit by and watch.

"All right." Thomas turned slowly toward the jurors, a smile plastered on his face. "You weren't afraid of Karen then, were you?"

"No." As Cindy spoke she realized what had happened. She had just contradicted herself and she quickly added, "Well, not until after the fight."

But the damage was done and Thomas turned to her angrily. "This fear that you had of Miss Severson was overcome by October second, is that right?"

Cindy hung her head. "That's correct."

The judge looked at the clock on the wall and ordered that all parties be dismissed until after lunch. When they returned, Thomas took up where he had left off. He was in the middle of a line of questioning that cast doubt on Cindy's fear of Karen Severson when he suddenly turned and walked angrily toward the witness stand.

"Now, let me ask you this"—Thomas's nostrils were flaring in rage and his voice fairly shook the courtroom as he continued—"isn't it true, Miss Silverio, that you are lying about Miss Doyle; isn't that true?"

Cindy sat back in her chair, willing herself away from the angry man coming her way. Her voice was barely audible, and the jurors leaned forward to see the confrontation. "That I was what?"

"That you are lying about Miss Doyle; isn't that true?"

"No, it is not true."

"Isn't it true that you killed Missy?"

A collective gasp echoed through the courtroom, and Tamia glanced at the jury. She was flooded with a sense of relief. They weren't buying Thomas's reasoning. In fact, their faces indicated that a few of them were even angry with the way Thomas was treating Cindy Silverio. It was up to Cindy now. She could either buckle under the pressure or stand up to it. If she was telling the truth, as Tamia thought, then she should be able to handle even these questions.

"It's true, isn't it? You killed Missy Avila?"

"No, that's not true." Cindy sounded more composed now that the initial shock of Thomas's accusation had worn off.

"And that's why you didn't report it for three years, isn't that true?"

"I was afraid."

"You were afraid of whom?"

"I was afraid for my life. I was afraid of Karen and I was afraid of Laura."

"So afraid that you spent the night—"

"No!" Cindy wasn't going to let him manipulate her again, and she interrupted him. From where they sat in the courtroom, Chris and Ernie junior muffled a laugh. Cindy was standing up to him.

"I spent the night with my boyfriend."

Judge Tso released a deep sigh, bored with the inter ruption, and turned his head toward Cindy. "It will b up to the court to ask the questions, Miss Silverio."

Cindy nodded as tears began streaming down he cheeks. "I'm sorry. I really am sorry."

Thomas cast a mock look of sympathy toward Cindy "Do you need a few moments to compose yourself?"

"No." Cindy shook her head. "Go ahead."

"And isn't it true that that's why you can't remem ber the details of what you have told the court o other occasions—because you are lying—isn't tha true?"

"I'm sorry, what do you mean?" Cindy looked tire and worn out from the questioning, and now Tami was certain the jury was beginning to sympathize with her. If they were lucky, Thomas's antagonizing ques tions would backfire on the defense.

"Well, I mean this." Thomas struggled to maintain calm voice as he continued. "Sometimes you remem ber one thing, sometimes another. Sometimes the girl are in one order as they walk up the path, sometime another. Sometimes you remember it taking fifteen minutes, sometimes three minutes. And these differ ences are all because you are lying, isn't that right?"

Cindy shook her head. "No, that isn't right."

Thomas shrugged and rolled his eyes in the direc tion of the jury. His body language made him look a though Cindy Silverio's words were bold-faced lies.

"Okay. You used to stick up for Missy because she was a friend of yours, isn't that correct?"

"She was a friend of mine, yes."

"You treasured her friendship and the friendship of her family, didn't you?"

"Yes."

"But now, after observing all those things happen-ing to her on October 1, 1985, and even after you thought she might be lying up in the mountains dead or near dead, you didn't call Missy's family at all, did you?"

"No, I didn't."

"It was three years later that you finally said some-thing about what happened, is that correct?" Thomas sounded like an irate parent questioning his teenage daughter's version of why she'd crashed the family car.

Cindy nodded. "Yes, approximately three years later."

"I have nothing further." Thomas spat his last words in disgust and turned to sit down.

Judge Tso ordered a short break and when everyone had returned to the courtroom, Cindy Silverio looked five years older than she had when she'd arrived ear-lier that morning. Tamia Hope had told her the de-fense would be ruthless.

William Andrews, whose tactics were much gentler if not easier than those of David Thomas, questioned her next. Andrews spent the first half hour establishing again the lack of common sense surrounding the idea that Cindy would be scared of his client, Karen Sever-on, and then still spend the night of the murder in the same apartment with her. He also, by means of several questions, established that Cindy was more afraid of Karen than of Laura at the time immediately after the murder.

"Now, as you were driving down the mountain road, Laura said, 'Maybe Missy isn't dead, maybe we should go back,' do you remember that?" Andrews smiled at

Cindy, sounding like a man conducting an employ
ment interview with the favorite candidate for th
job.

"Yes."

"You discouraged her from doing that. You said, 'N
no, no! Let's not go back!' Is that right?"

"That is correct."

"You weren't concerned about whether or not Miss
was safe or whether she was injured or dead; yo
didn't care, did you?"

"No." Cindy was no longer fighting the question
but just answering them as they came.

"And you weren't afraid of Laura at that time, wer
you, afraid that she'd physically harm you?"

"I guess at that point I was."

"You guess. But you aren't sure, are you?"

"If I can recall right, I was very afraid."

The interviewer had found a flaw in the candidate
resume. "But you told us just a moment ago that yo
were more afraid of Karen than you were of Laura.

"That was later, after we'd gone down the hill."

"Well, you didn't go back up to check on Missy late
that evening, did you?"

"I was too scared, I was afraid of seeing something.

Thus the cross-examination continued throughou
the afternoon. Neither defense attorney really ha
anything to go on, but both men wanted Cind
Silverio to look like a girl with low moral standard
one who lied, cheated, and had held a grudge. The
wanted to establish that perhaps Cindy might hersel
have held a grudge against Missy. (Otherwise wh
would she have stood by while Karen said rude thing
about Missy at the Avila home three weeks prior to th
murder?) They wanted the jury to think that the rea

son Cindy came forward was to protect herself, that perhaps she was just as guilty as the girls she was accusing.

In the late afternoon Andrews asked Cindy about her time in Nevada and, inevitably, about her stint as a lady wrestler.

"So, you're pretty strong, aren't you?" Andrews flexed his arms and smiled toward the jury. Several members snickered before Cindy had a chance to answer.

Andrews wasn't going to tamper with the image the jury now had of Cindy as a strong wrestler. He changed topics. This time he accused Cindy of being afraid she'd be blamed for Missy's murder.

"You thought you'd be blamed for Missy's murder and that was why you were quiet about it for three years, isn't that so?"

"No."

"But that was on your mind, wasn't it?"

"No."

Andrews acted as if he hadn't heard Cindy's last answer as he turned to the judge and said, "I have nothing further."

It was Tamia's turn again, and she wasted no time getting to her feet.

"When you were a lady wrestler, were you the same size and shape you are in now?"

"No, I was a little smaller than I am now."

"How tall are you?"

"I believe I am five six and a half."

"And how much did you weigh approximately on October 1, 1985?"

"One hundred and fifteen. Maybe 125 when I was a lady wrestler."

"Okay. And were you fighting for your life when you were a lady wrestler?"

Cindy relaxed and giggled softly. With Tamia asking the questions she was instantly transformed back into the sweet college coed. "No, I wasn't fighting for my life. It's just a show."

"And did you ever participate in wrestling as a teenager in high school?"

"No." A few jurors snickered and Tamia was satisfied. She changed the subject, but she had made her point. Cindy Silverio's wrestling had had nothing to do with her ability to defend herself.

The end of the day was nearing, and Tamia was watching the clock carefully. The importance of getting a significant point in at the end of the day was immeasurable, and Tamia had this one planned perfectly.

"Cindy, did you know that Karen and Laura intended to kill Missy that October first up in the mountains?"

"No."

"Did you know it was necessary to save Missy's life at any point that afternoon?"

"No, I didn't."

"When did you realize it might be necessary to save Missy's life?"

"I never knew that it was going to be necessary to save her life."

"What was your state of mind when you heard Missy scream?"

"I was confused and scared. I can't explain how I was thinking."

"Why were you scared at this point when you heard Missy scream?"

"Why was I scared? Just . . . I was frightened. I heard her scream. I don't know, I can't explain."

"What kind of a scream was it?"

"Like a scream for help and gasping for air."

"And when you and Laura were driving down the hill, did she indicate to you that she was sorry she killed Missy?"

"No. She said that Missy deserved it for screwing her boyfriend."

"And later, before you came to the police, were you concerned about anything?"

"Yes, I was concerned that I might be in trouble for withholding evidence."

"But even with that concern, why were you willing to tell the police what you knew?" Tamia's voice was barely more than a whisper.

"Because I couldn't hold this inside of me any longer. I wanted to go on with my life."

"Did you have any trouble taking a shower after October 1, 1985?"

"Yes." Cindy closed her eyes for a moment. "I guess because I knew what they had done to her."

And that was all. Judge Tso dismissed the courtroom and told all parties to return the next day. The Avila family looked exhausted when they left the court building that afternoon, but none of them were as tired as Cindy Silverio. Her ordeal was nearly done, but not quite.

The next morning Thomas had another opportunity to question her, and this time he wasn't even careful about sounding nice. He questioned whether she had or hadn't seen a knife in Karen's or Laura's hand before chunks of hair fell to the ground that October first. Cindy was having a hard time remembering.

"So, this statement in this earlier report that you saw Karen and Laura take a knife and cut her hair is a bold-faced lie, isn't it?"

"I'm sorry?"

"Isn't it a lie?"

Tamia would have objected to the way Thomas was yelling at Cindy, but she still believed it would back-fire on him in the end. The jury was looking sympathetically toward Cindy, as if they didn't think anyone should have to bear this kind of inquisition. It was obvious that Thomas's angry questions were confusing Cindy.

"What is a lie?" She wrinkled her brow.

"That you saw them take a knife out and cut her hair?" Thomas slapped the report he was holding against his other hand.

"May I take a second and read that?"

"Oh, sure." Thomas rolled his eyes again. "Take as long as you want. Take three years."

The jurors laughed and Tamia instantly objected.

Judge Tso looked over his bifocals at Thomas and responded in a dry voice, "There is no need for that."

"I apologize, Your Honor." Thomas marched back toward Cindy and handed her the report. But by then Cindy had understood the meaning of the attorney's earlier words and she was crying again.

Thomas sneered at her. "Oh, don't give me the crying routine again," he barked. "There's no picture of Missy in there now, is there?"

Judge Tso took off his glasses and leaned over the bench toward the fiery attorney. "Mr. Thomas, please let the witness read the report. And let's have no more comments like that." Judge Tso was beginning to sound bothered, and a few jurors shook their heads, empathizing with Cindy.

Soon Andrews took another turn. During the course of his questions, in which he jumped from one topic to another in an effort to confuse her, Cindy said that she hadn't told anyone about what had happened on October 1, 1985, until three years later. Only, Cindy had already said during earlier testimony that she had told her fiancé the story hours after it happened. Andrews caught the error and used it like a chess champion declaring checkmate.

"Just a few moments ago, Ms. Silverio, you said that when you went to the police it was the first time you had told anyone about what happened that afternoon. But that was a lie, wasn't it? You had told Steven, didn't you?"

Cindy slumped into the witness box. "I guess it wasn't a true statement."

"Thank you. Nothing further."

Thomas smiled. "Yes. In that light, I also have nothing further."

Tamia jumped to her feet again. "Cindy, what did you mean when you said it was the first time you'd told anyone?"

Cindy was crying again, and she directed her answer toward the judge. "I meant it was the first time I had to sit there and think about the whole incident. I'm sorry I'm not wording things the right way, but I'm trying to remember something that happened more than four years ago. It's hard and sometimes I forget things and I remember them at different times. I'm sorry."

Finally the cross-examination was over and a dejected, beaten Cindy Silverio walked quickly from the courtroom. Outside in the hallway Steven took her into his arms.

"It's all right, baby. It's all right." He stroked her hair and began walking with her toward the elevator. "Let's get you out of here." Steven still had to testify, so he hadn't been allowed in the courtroom during Cindy's testimony. But he had peeked through the courtroom window a few times and he could see that she looked broken.

Back inside the courtroom the judge dismissed the court for the noon break and Tamia left immediately to sift through transcripts and notes in her office.

She made a mental list of the testimony they had already heard. Mark and Irene had done beautifully, and the defense attorneys hadn't been able to mar their testimony. Then they had heard from the forest ranger and he had been perfect: a credible witness.

Cindy had held up as well as could be expected, and by the time she had left the witness stand, Tamia was certain the jury still believed her. Time would tell.

The afternoon went by quickly. After Cindy, Steven had testified and then Jimmy Mitchell. His testimony had been very believable. She suspected that Jimmy, like the group with whom he had run, hadn't been as quiet and poised back in 1985. But he was a different young man now, and it had been important for the jury to see his size. He was only five feet three and much smaller than Karen. He told the jury about the incident at the apartment and how frequently Karen would order him to stay away from Missy.

That same day they heard from the coroner's department. Dr. Eva Heuser testified that Missy's body had had bruises along both arms and on her face as if she had been struck before her death. She also mentioned something that would be crucial in the final arguments.

If her body had been left to float freely in the water before the log was placed on her, she would have had tiny scratches on her face. There were none. Therefore it was easy to conclude that whoever drowned her also put the log on her back. It was a big victory for the prosecution, because the defense was trying to prove that anyone could have come along and put the log on Missy's dead body.

It was a productive afternoon. After the coroner, they heard from Lynne Robbins, who talked about Karen's obsession with Missy's death and her strange habit of dressing up her three-year-old daughter, Andrea, to resemble "Auntie Missy." She also testified about the times when Karen visited the cemetery and felt she was being haunted by Missy's ghost. Then Brian Taylor testified how Karen had begged him and Victor to go kill Jimmy, and how Karen had been certain that Jimmy had killed Missy.

The next day, January 23, Jack Froman testified. Cindy's half brother described his sister's pain when she had come to him that summer evening and told him about the murder. The hiker, Robert Sanders, was next and then the assistant manager at Camp Colby Ranch. Next they heard from Catherine Scott, who described how Laura had changed her story two years after the murder.

A criminologist took the stand next and identified the pieces of hair that had been picked up by detectives near the boulder at the murder site as identical to those taken from Missy's body during the autopsy. Then Christy Crawford testified about the times

Karen had betrayed Missy and how Missy had trusted her through their entire friendship.

When the day ended, there were only two crucial prosecution witnesses left, Victor Amaya and Katy Vincent, who would take the stand January 24, first thing in the morning. Victor's testimony would be the most damaging to Laura Doyle; Tamia knew it would answer any questions the jurors might have about why Laura would want to kill Missy Avila. Tamia's case was in its final stages, and the defense would probably present its case the next day.

Tamia could hardly wait.

47

ON JANUARY 24 Tamia called Victor Amaya to the stand. He testified quietly that he had loved Missy Avila and that she had trusted and confided in him. He told the jury how Laura Doyle had threatened to kill Missy just before her death. There were tears in Victor's eyes as he spoke. If the jurors weren't convinced after Cindy's testimony, they looked certain by the time Victor was finished talking.

The cross-examination of Vic Amaya ended just after two o'clock that afternoon and then the defense attorneys made a motion. They explained to Judge Tso that they had a witness who was unable to return the next day and who needed to be heard now, even though the prosecution still had one more witness. Tamia agreed. After all, she was more curious than anyone in the courtroom to see the first defense witness.

William Andrews stood, walked to the microphone, and called Jessica Randolph to the witness stand.

The bailiff went into the hall and motioned for the girl to follow him. She was petite, with blond hair and fair skin, but something about her was cold as steel. Tamia Hope knew who she was. She had been a close friend of Cindy Silverio's back in the days before Missy's murder and she had known Missy, but not nearly as well as the others had.

Tamia found herself resisting an urge to shrug. What in the world could Jessica Randolph have to say on behalf of Karen Severson?

Jessica took the stand and testified that she had known Cindy and her boyfriend, Steven, since high school. Andrews wasted no time getting to the point. He asked her if she had ever seen Cindy Silverio physically harm Missy Avila.

The approach was beginning to make sense to Tamia, if not to the others in the courtroom. Cindy had already testified that she and Missy were friends, good friends, and that she had never hurt Missy in any way. If she had, clearly the defense would argue that Missy's murder could have been done by Cindy just as easily as by Karen and Laura.

Jessica cleared her throat and answered. "Yes. It was sometime in 1984, maybe late in 1984 or early in 1985. I remember Cindy getting out of her car at a park and telling Missy she didn't want her seeing Steven. Then she threw her on the ground."

There was a stir in the courtroom as people realized this testimony conflicted with that of the prosecution's star witness. Mark Avila, who had finally been allowed back in the courtroom, looked furious, as did the other Avila brothers. None of them remembered Cindy ever being upset with Missy, and now they were afraid this testimony might discredit everything Cindy had said. Andrews asked the girl a few more questions and then stepped aside so Tamia could cross-examine her.

Tamia wasn't concerned. There were several key pieces of information that Jessica Randolph simply hadn't mentioned. By the time Tamia was finished, it was apparent that Jessica did not remember when or why the incident had happened, where it had taken place, or what Missy's reaction had been. The defense attorneys seemed frustrated.

When they dismissed Jessica Randolph, Tamia recalled Cindy Silverio to the stand and asked her if there had been a time when she was jealous because Missy was seeing her boyfriend. Cindy shook her head and a blank look came over her face.

"Missy and Steven never dated," she said simply.

Tamia nodded. "Well, then, was there some other reason why you were angry with Missy and had a confrontation with her in the park?"

Cindy furrowed her eyebrows and shook her head again. "You mean like a fight?"

"Yes, like a fight. Did you and Missy ever have a fight?"

"No. Never."

Tamia was satisfied. The decision was up to the jury. They could believe Jessica Randolph or they could believe Cindy. Clearly, one of the girls was either lying or unable to remember past events correctly.

The next morning the case for the prosecution finished up after the jury viewed a videotape of the crime scene. The tape showed a helicopter view of the winding road that leads up to Camp Colby in the Big Tujunga Canyon area of the Angeles National Forest. The courtroom was eerily silent except for the sound of the helicopter. Fifteen minutes passed before the police began narrating the film. By then they were in the parking lot where the girls had taken Missy Avila that afternoon.

Tamia glanced toward the jury as they watched the tape; she could see it was working. The tape gave

every one of them a chance to think about the deliber-
ateness of the murder. There was something especially cruel about the long execution trail they had
taken Missy on before killing her. At the scene the
videotape showed the length of the path and how long
it took to go from the parking lot to the clearing near
the stream where Missy was taunted and teased and
finally killed. Again, there had been plenty of opportu-
nities for Karen Severson and Laura Doyle to change
their minds. The tape also showed the jury the remoteness of the area. Tamia could feel a knot forming
in the pit of her stomach, and she was certain the
jurors were equally uncomfortable. They were reliving Missy's death march, her last moments.

When the tape was finished, there was silence in the
courtroom. Quietly, Tamia Hope walked up to the
microphone.

"No further questions, Your Honor. The people rest
their case."

Judge Tso dismissed all parties until after the break.
It was three o'clock when the attorneys met back in
the courtroom and William Andrews and David
Thomas made a motion that the case be dismissed for
lack of evidence.

Tamia stood quickly to rebut Andrews's motion, but
it was unnecessary. Judge Tso looked bored with the
request and without glancing up from his bench told
the attorneys that there was enough evidence on
which to try the girls for first-degree murder. Tamia
laughed to herself. Judge Tso never had been one to
waste words. The jury was brought back into the
courtroom, and everyone knew the moment had arrived.

The defense was about to present its case. Anything

could happen. They could spring a surprise witness on them or maybe bring up someone willing to testify that Karen or Laura had been somewhere else the day of the murder. There would probably be a string of character witnesses ready to testify about the sweet nature of both defendants. Tamia sat back while the judge gave the defense their turn.

Andrews stood and presented just one short statement.

"Your Honor, I rest on behalf of Ms. Severson."

Then Thomas stood.

"Your Honor, I rest on behalf of Ms. Doyle."

For what seemed like an eternity no one said a word. In her seat at the attorney's table Tamia couldn't believe it. They were finished. There would be no parade of witnesses, no surprise elements, no phony alibis. No wonder they hadn't made an opening statement. By doing so the defense would have been folding its hand before the game had even started. The defense had produced just one witness between them, Jessica Randolph. Tamia glanced quickly at the jurors and could see how surprised they were.

A murmur ruffled through the spectator section, and the Avilas linked hands. It was too good to be true. Of course, Tamia would be prohibited from mentioning the lack of defense witnesses in her closing argument. She would also not be allowed to point out that Karen and Laura had refused to testify. But these implications didn't need underlining. Karen Severson and Laura Doyle had chosen not to defend themselves, and the jury would have noticed.

Judge Tso gave the attorneys a ten-minute break to prepare their closing arguments, and Tamia went over her notes. Hers would take the remainder of the day. Tomorrow, the defense would give its arguments and she would have a final chance to make an argument before the jury began its deliberation.

When the trial resumed, Tamia took the floor. The Avila family, including Irene, sat in the front row of the courtroom, watching Tamia's every move. They had counted on her for so long, and now her work was ending.

First, Tamia instructed the jury about the differences between first-degree and second-degree murder. She also instructed them on manslaughter.

"But this case is obviously one of first-degree murder." Tamia sounded earnest and sincere as she faced the jury. "In this case Karen and Laura had to drop down to the water. One held Missy's head under the water while the other one held her feet." Tamia pulled out the poster-sized pictures of Missy's dead body and pointed to them. "How do we know that? From Missy's body. Missy's body tells you what happened. Look at her feet, still crossed. Do you think she just lay down and died that way? And look at her arm, twisted behind her back. This is the work of two people, two people holding her down as she drowned. Now, weren't they pausing and reflecting on the consequences of their act? What did they expect to happen when they held Missy's head under eight inches of water? And then, when she goes unconscious, what did they think would happen when they put a log on top of her?"

Several jurors were nodding in agreement. Once again Tamia had transformed the courtroom into her very own living room. Everyone there had fallen under her spell—she was no longer an intimidating public official but just a nice woman telling a shocking but true story to a few close friends.

"The court will instruct you that if you find that a defendant made a willfully false or deliberately misleading statement concerning the crime for which she is now being tried, you may consider that statement in deciding the defendant guilty.

"So, you can consider the false and misleading statements by Laura Doyle when she sent that letter of condolence to Irene Avila after Missy died." Tamia stared at Laura Doyle.

"And then when she first reported back to Irene Avila and said, 'Oh, I left Missy off at the park near two guys with a blue Camaro.' And then two years later when she changed the story. Those are false and misleading statements. Karen made many similar statements by consoling Irene Avila after Missy's murder.

"The people believe in this case that the evidence proves beyond a reasonable doubt that this was a willful, deliberate, premeditated murder; that it was an intentional killing, deliberately arrived at, determined as a result of careful thought and weighing of considerations for and against, and was therefore premeditated.

"If they had just wanted to beat Missy up, or scare her a little, they could have done it at a park. Apparently that kind of thing was done frequently in the Arleta area. Then they would have fought and it would have been over.

"You have heard evidence showing Karen's jealousy of Missy, primarily because of Jimmy Mitchell. She did not want Missy around while she was involved with Jimmy. You have heard Jimmy testify about that. You have also heard that Karen was often physically abusive to Missy. There was the fight at Karen's apartment and then the fight in the park when Christy Crawford came to Missy's defense because Karen was going after her. At that time Karen weighed two hundred pounds. That fight has been corroborated by Cindy's testimony as well.

"What about Laura Doyle? Where is her jealousy? Victor Amaya testified that after he broke up with Laura he was out front of his mother's house with Missy when Laura drove up. At that time she said, 'What's that bitch doing here? I'm going to kill that bitch!' She was referring to Missy. And later, after the murder, Laura tells Cindy as they are driving down the canyon that she killed Missy because Missy deserved it for sleeping with her boyfriend."

Tamia paused and shook her head. For several minutes she began recounting the events of October 1 as they had been portrayed by Cindy Silverio.

"And they cut her hair. Before they killed her they cut off Missy's beautiful long, brown hair. Why did Karen Severson and Laura Doyle do this? To humiliate and degrade Missy before they actually killed her. She was a pretty little girl, and she was a very popular little girl. And perhaps they didn't feel so pretty and certainly they didn't feel so popular. So they wanted to humiliate and degrade Missy Avila as they had felt degraded by Missy's beauty and popularity.

"Then Laura Doyle goes into the middle of the stream and puts her hand in the water and says, 'It's not so deep here, Missy. Why don't you come on in?' " Tamia bent down and held her hand over an imaginary stream as she spoke the words. Suddenly she stood up and looked directly at the jurors.

"Isn't that premeditation and deliberation?"

She paced the length of the jury box before continuing. "Now, Laura goes back for Missy because, for some reason, she isn't taking the invitation." Tamia's voice was sarcastic now. "And then Laura starts leading her back into the stream of water. When she still resists going into the water, Karen Severson gives her a nudge. Then Cindy gets scared and runs. Five minutes later she hears Missy scream, that final, single scream as if she's gasping for air. And then Cindy panics."

Tamia furrowed her eyebrows and paced slowly in front of the jurors, looking each of them in the eye. "Wouldn't you? Think: It's getting late. You're up in this area you haven't been in before. You don't like what you see going on there. You hear a scream and you freeze."

Tamia was motionless for a moment. "You see, Cindy Silverio has a very difficult time dealing with death, with the finality of death. So she doesn't want to see what happened in the stream and she cries and cries. For twenty minutes."

Tamia continued, narrating the details of the rest of the afternoon, including Laura's wild ride down the canyon and Karen's fight with Steven and Troy and Cindy later that night. Then she reminded the jurors about Karen's strange behavior, how she moved in with the Avila family and then orchestrated the search to find and kill Jimmy Mitchell.

"You heard Irene Avila testify that the day of Missy's funeral Karen came into her room and said, 'Now that Missy is gone, I'm here for you.' She was going to help take care of Irene." Tamia had contrived a tone of kindness that disappeared with her next words.

"Ladies and gentlemen, Karen Severson wanted to

take Missy's place and she did, for three years after Missy's death. One thing was certain, Karen Severson was going to know what was happening in the investigation into Michele Avila's death."

Next Tamia refreshed the jury about Karen's role in prompting Laura Doyle to change her story two years after the murder. And as she continued telling the story in chronological order, Tamia was sure to mention the death of Cindy Silverio's brother.

"Now, why did it take Cindy six months to call the police after her brother had died? Have any of you gone through a divorce? Have any of you lost a parent or a sister or wife? Weren't you blinded emotionally by that sense of loss for at least six months? Didn't you find it very hard to function? You know how blinding that kind of pain can be."

As she closed her argument, Tamia told the jury what she truly thought had happened to Missy Avila on October 1, 1985.

"Laura Doyle was jealous of Missy and she couldn't handle it. Karen Severson was also jealous. Together they decided to kill Missy, and so they set her up. Laura went and picked her up, playing all the while like she was her friend. Laura played the role well, agreeing to take her to the park. And then"—Tamia raised her eyebrows—"as luck would have it, they meet up with Karen and Cindy, and Karen and Laura begin to fight.

"At that point Karen tells Cindy that this is all a big sham, because they were really there to get Missy. And they did, ladies and gentlemen. They killed her in cold blood in that shallow water on October 1, 1985. They taught her a final and fatal lesson for being attractive to their boyfriends. Missy never had a chance.

She never even had a chance." Tamia paused and looked like a mother pleading with people who might have held her own daughter captive. "We urge you to find them both guilty of first-degree murder in this case. Thank you."

It was after four o'clock that Thursday afternoon when Tamia Hope finished her closing argument, and Judge Tso adjourned the trial until the following Monday morning.

The weekend seemed to take forever, but finally Monday morning arrived. The defense arguments took very little time to complete.

For the most part the defense did what Tamia had expected them to do—discredit Cindy Silverio and every other witness who had testified on behalf of the prosecution. That tactic was all they had left.

David Thomas gave his closing remarks first.

"Thank you for your time, ladies and gentlemen of the jury. I told you this would be a sad case, and it has been. It's about ugly things in our society—about drinking and sex and lying. But the people's case rests solely on the shoulders of Cindy Silverio.

"Now, she isn't on trial, but if she were my witness, I would not be proud. She is despicable, scum of the earth. She came before the court not long ago at the preliminary hearing and testified differently than she testified in this trial."

Thomas continued by accusing the deputy district attorney of filling her closing argument with mere opinions. Thomas stormed back and forth across the courtroom, attacking point by point what he thought was a lack of evidence in the case and continually calling Cindy Silverio a liar.

"Enough people have been hurt already without

convicting these girls based on the lies of Cindy Silverio, who is in the most precarious position of all. Thank you again. I know that you will decide this case fairly and squarely and that you will let the chips fall where they may."

Thomas sat down and William Andrews took the floor. He began his final remarks by comparing the case to a puzzle.

"The prosecution makes an interesting argument, but it reminds me of a fellow putting together one of those thousand-piece jigsaw puzzles. There are some pieces that just don't fit, so he throws them away, but when he's finished, there's a big hole in the middle. There's something else: In this particular case you have to deal with the cast of characters."

Andrews gave a list of the prosecution witnesses and their shortcomings. He focused especially on the inconsistencies in Cindy's testimony.

"It took Cindy more than six months after her brother's death to come forward. Now, we all have trouble with death, and a problem when we look at our own mortality. But six months? It doesn't wash.

"And Missy's body may tell you what happened to her, but it doesn't tell you who killed her, or when the log was placed across her back."

Finally, Andrews asked the jurors not to base their decision on sympathy.

"We can all sympathize with the Avila family. They lost their girl. But if you decide this case on that emotion and ignore the facts, you will have to live with yourselves, knowing you fell short of your duties."

Tamia listened to their arguments, feigning disinterest as she reread her notes. She had prepared for these tactics. In her final closing argument Tamia told the jurors why they should believe Cindy Silverio. She told them that Cindy had had no reason to come forward after all the time that had passed. If she was guilty or somehow responsible, she would have kept silent. After all, no one was accusing her of the murder. The knowledge was simply something she couldn't live with anymore.

She refreshed their memories about what the coroner had said. Missy's face had borne no scratches, so the log had almost certainly been placed on her back immediately after or just before her death.

"Both these women used cold and calculated judgment to arrive at the decision to kill Missy Avila. The pieces of the jigsaw puzzle fit. The evidence shows beyond a reasonable doubt what happened to Missy Avila. Her best friends drowned her in eight inches of water. Both Karen Severson and Laura Doyle are guilty of murder in the first degree. I urge you to submit that verdict. Thank you."

As they left the courtroom, Tamia wondered how quickly the jury would be able to decide a verdict. Normally, the quicker they made a decision, the better.

But David Thomas had been right about one point: The case for the people rested solely on the shoulders of Cindy Silverio and everyone knew it.

48

IT WAS NEARLY midnight on Tuesday, January 30,
and Irene Avila was having trouble sleeping. Tamia
had told her earlier that day that the verdict could be
in as early as the next morning. The jury had already
spent four hours earlier that afternoon in deliberation
and by now they had probably selected a foreman and
taken their first vote. If it was unanimous, the verdict
would be given first thing in the morning.

Irene rolled from one side of the bed to the other
thinking about Missy and all that had taken place since
1985. Sometimes it was hard to believe that Missy had
been gone for more than four years. Who would ever
have thought, back ten or fifteen years earlier when
Karen and Missy strolled to school arm in arm, that
their destinies would come to this trial?

Arleta was a rough place to raise children, the kind
of place where parents felt doomed. Inevitably, their
children would run into gang members and fellow
students who dropped out of school and had babies
before their sixteenth birthdays. In Arleta, Irene was
like any other mother raising her children with a father no longer living in the house. She wanted to believe that she could love her children through the hard
times and steer them around the rougher kids who

might be a bad influence. Irene fell asleep thinking
about how, in Missy's case, her efforts hadn't worked.

As Irene left the house for Pasadena the next morning, she realized that it was January 31—Andrea's
birthday. Just seven years before, Missy was at Karen's
side in a hospital room where Karen had given birth to
Andrea. And now, when the two friends should have
been celebrating the child's seventh birthday, Karen
Severson was about to be convicted of killing Missy. It
was all so crazy.

Two hours later Tamia Hope was in her office when
she received the message from the court clerk in Department J. The verdict was in. It would be read in one
hour, at 10:30. Tamia quickly dialed the numbers of
several print and television news reporters who had
asked to be included. The Avilas were already there;
they had been notified by one of the bailiffs. Suddenly,
Tamia began to feel sick to her stomach.

What if the verdict came back not guilty? What if
the jury hadn't believed Cindy's testimony? What if
they felt sorry for Karen and Laura? Tamia closed her
eyes. There was no time to worry. She gathered her
files and took the elevator to the sixth floor. The Avila
family was huddled in a group near the closed double
doors of the courtroom. Mark Avila looked strong and
handsome and his wife, Shavaun, looked stunning.
Tamia knew Irene would need their strength today.
She walked up to Irene and put an arm around her.

"Try to stay calm." Irene and the others nodded as
Tamia gave them instructions. "When they read the
verdict, no matter what it is, don't shout out or make
any obvious gestures. That could still hurt the case.
Just try to stay as cool and even-tempered as possible."
Tamia paused. "I know it's not going to be easy."

They opened the courtroom doors, and the Avila family filled the eight front-row seats in the center of the audience. In the second row Ernie Avila sat next to his youngest son, Chris. Missy's father wore a plaid blue-and-white lumberjack shirt and said nothing. He knew they couldn't bring Missy back, no matter what took place in this courtroom today. But he wanted to be there, to see that Karen and Laura got what was coming to them.

It was 10:41 when William Andrews and David Thomas took their seats next to Karen Severson and Laura Doyle. Tamia sat at the other end of the same table and put her head in her hands. For a brief moment her hands shook. Then she steadied herself, looked up toward the judge's door, and waited his arrival.

Irene sat between Mark and Katy Vincent. Like Jimmy, Katy was a Christian now and had taken it upon herself to stay near Irene and support her through the trial. The two had become quite close during the past three weeks, and now Katy talked quietly to Irene, telling her to be strong.

But Irene was having trouble. She could feel herself growing light headed and prayed that she wouldn't faint. Mark took her hand and squeezed it just as his mother began to cry. Then he noticed it: a beautiful gold anklet chain wrapped around his mother's fingers.

Irene closed her eyes and whispered the words.

"It's Missy's. The one they found on her body that day. I keep it with me always." Irene held it tighter, and Mark nodded as tears welled up in his eyes too.

On the other side of the courtroom Barbara Doyle and Paula Severson sat side by side. They were outcasts; the seat beside them was the only empty one in the courtroom. There were people who would rather stand than sit next to them. The women had drawn, pinched faces, and both held their purses tightly on their laps. It was 10:50, when the television cameras were allowed into the courtroom, and Paula Severson began to cry. Through the entire trial Paula had maintained that her daughter was innocent. After all, Paula Severson, like other parents with spoiled children, never believed her daughter could do wrong.

At that moment the defense attorneys stood and handed both women notes from their daughters. Irene saw them do it and thought bitterly that no one would be handing her a note from Missy.

At exactly 11:00 A.M. Judge Jack Tso entered the courtroom, and the electricity was palpable. In the front row the Avila family joined hands and waited breathlessly.

The court clerk took the verdicts from the foreman of the jury and, in a plain and monotonous tone of voice, began to read them.

"The people find defendant Laura Doyle guilty of murder in the second degree," she said, and read the other details associated with the conviction.

A small gasp escaped from Irene, and she lowered her head into her hands. Second degree. It was a crushing disappointment. The jury hadn't been able to see that Karen and Laura had planned to kill Missy. Irene closed her eyes and listened as the court clerk read the verdict on Karen.

"The people find defendant Karen Severson guilty of murder in the second degree."

They had convicted them of the same thing. Murder

in the second degree. They didn't believe her murder had been premeditated. Mark and Shavaun started crying now, and quietly Ernie Avila Sr., rose from his courtroom seat and left.

At the attorney's table Tamia Hope let her head drop slowly. She felt terrible. Somehow they hadn't understood, hadn't seen the most obvious element of the case. Of course it was premeditated. However, the verdict could have been worse. In fact, her colleagues would certainly credit her with a victory for getting any kind of conviction at all based on circumstantial evidence on a case five years old. Nevertheless, the decision wasn't fair to the Avilas, and that bothered Tamia most of all as she lifted her head and rose to find them.

Roger Simons watched the Avila family, and his heart went out to them. He knew that the difference between the penalties associated with first- and second-degree murder was ten years. And now, with good behavior, it was possible the girls could get out in just seven or eight years. Simons hoped they would have to serve more time than that. It just didn't seem right. He thought back to their conversations during deliberation. Several of the jurors had doubted Cindy's testimony. They thought she had been more involved than she'd admitted. Those jurors remembered clearly Cindy's statement that Karen and Laura had just wanted to scare Missy, not kill her. And so they didn't think there was enough evidence to prove premeditation.

In the front row of the courtroom Irene's head was swimming. The nightmare was never going to end. She looked up and watched as William Andrews gave

Karen Severson a victorious hug. Irene thought she was going to throw up, and she motioned for Mark and the others to help her into the hallway. But before they stood, Karen turned toward her mother and Irene saw that she was crying.

For the first time since the trial began, Karen Severson was crying. Irene guessed her tears weren't for Missy but for her own plight.

Beside her, Laura Doyle wore her same cold stare. The girl showed no emotion, no concern. Laura had probably expected this verdict since the first day of the trial. She straightened her black skirt and stood to leave the courtroom alongside the bailiff. She would serve her time and get on with life.

Outside in the hallway Mark began to cry, and his voice was filled with anger when he walked up to Tamia and asked her why they hadn't been convicted of first-degree murder.

The jurors were leaving and one of them walked by Mark and Tamia.

"Why second degree?" His voice was resigned and tears slid down his cheeks as he waited for her answer. "Didn't you believe us? Everything we told you was the truth. And she could kill again. Believe me, Karen Severson could kill again."

Mark had wondered how he and his family would ever feel safe again if Karen and Laura were released in just seven or eight years. The Avilas would live in constant fear.

The juror answered him quietly. "I just didn't believe Cindy. I would have believed first degree if she had told us more about what happened. A few of us thought she was holding something back for her own protection." The juror started walking away but stopped suddenly. "Anyway, it's in the past now," she said. "And there has to be something other than speculation to go on."

Mark's face grew sadder as he responded. "Speculation? My sister's legs were crossed and her arm was held behind her back. It takes seven or eight minutes to drown someone and only one minute to prove premeditation. The district attorney told you that, but you still couldn't see it. I don't understand."

The juror was insistent, defending her opinion. "There was no one there to say what their state of mind was at the time they were holding her down. We just couldn't convict them of first degree without knowing for sure."

Mark shook his head as reporters gathered around, listening to their dialogue. "It was planned. They met at the park at a set time. They didn't want to hurt her, they wanted to murder her."

Mark walked away slowly with Shavaun at his side. Together they went into the first-floor lobby alongside Tamia and found Irene surrounded by reporters. One reporter asked her if she had ever suspected Karen. She looked out the window and shook her head, wiping the tears that slid down her cheeks.

"No. Never. If Cindy hadn't come forward, they would have gotten away with it. I'm glad to have the trial over, but it's never going to be over for us. I'll never see my daughter again. Those other mothers can visit their daughters in prison, but my Missy is gone forever."

Irene began to sob, and Mark slowly pulled her away from the reporters. But before she got away, they heard her say one last thing, which they would include in their stories. It summed up the desperately sad nature of the case.

"If only I could have said good-bye!" she cried, and Mark put his arm around her. "I never got to tell my little girl good-bye."

49

ON FEBRUARY 8, eight days after the verdict was announced, Missy would have celebrated her twenty-second birthday. In years past Irene, her sons, and their wives had visited the cemetery and spent the day quietly, each remembering in their own way the beautiful girl who had been taken from them.

This time they threw a party. It was an event Missy would have loved, and it was attended by all her friends and relatives. The only person who wanted to be there and couldn't was Jimmy Mitchell, who had returned to his home in Seattle immediately after the trial.

Before he'd gone home, the Avilas had each thanked him for flying down and testifying. They also apologized for ever having doubted him. He knew he would never be sorry for having called Irene after reading about Missy's murder. Now he could get on with his life and let the past rest.

In the weeks after the party Irene spent more of her time with the support group for parents of murdered children. She wanted to start a chapter of the group in the San Fernando Valley. By now there were nearly 1.5 million people in the Valley and the nearest support group meeting was over the hill in West Los Angeles. The gang violence had increased in the San Fernando Valley, especially in Arleta and its neighboring communities. The areas that thirty years ago had been ideal for raising children were now rough and violent cities with too many people and too many murders. Each week more mothers and fathers were added to the list of parents whose children had been taken from them, and Irene wanted to help.

She began to put together literature about the support group and meet with the group leaders for advice. If everything went well, she would start the meeting at a Valley location before the beginning of summer. Irene knew how important it was for people to share grief.

At these meetings there was a bond that formed instantly among parents who had known such a tragedy. Everyone had the same nightmares, the same constant ache for the child who would never come home. Next to her family the support group was Irene's best outlet for her sorrow and anger.

Irene's sons were glad she had plans. Now that the trial was over, there would have been a huge void in her life without the support group.

On March 9 Irene went one last time to Pasadena's Superior Court to see Karen Severson and Laura Doyle sentenced. By then the support group had advised her to round up people to write letters to the judge. The letters would be included in a file that would be brought out each time the girls came up for parole. This was an important tactic for keeping the convicted behind bars, and Irene made sure that the letters were written. She had worked on her speech as well. The sentencing was the only opportunity for relatives of the victims to address the court and the defendants.

It was Irene's chance to tell Karen and Laura to their faces what they had taken from her.

At 9:00 A.M. Irene was pacing in the court hallway several feet away from Department J. The media circus that day made the trial coverage look sparse. All the networks, newspapers, and several television crime-show reporters had shown up for the sentencing. It seemed that over the course of the trial, more and more people had come to realize the horror of the crime. No one wanted to miss Judge Tso's sentencing Missy's best friends to prison for killing her.

Irene stayed away from the media crowd. She couldn't talk to reporters. She needed to steady herself for her speech. It was her last, final act of love for Missy, and there was nothing that would stop her from giving it her all.

At 10:00 A.M. the doors were opened, and within minutes the audience section was overflowing with spectators and cameras and reporters. The bailiffs had never seen so many people pack into one courtroom for a sentencing hearing, and they quickly opened the jury box for all media. But even then there were people lined two deep along the back wall of the courtroom when Judge Tso entered the chamber.

Irene was struck by how calm the judge appeared. He was about to sentence her daughter's killers, but it was just another day at the office for him. Tamia liked that about Judge Tso. It helped him to resist the emotional pleas of defense attorneys and hand out fair sentences.

Tamia looked uneasy as she waited for the judge to speak. It was during the sentencing that defense attorneys often asked the judge to declare a mistrial. This request could be based on a lack of evidence or on the behavior of witnesses outside the courtroom. Tamia knew there was a strong chance the attorneys would request a mistrial, since they had nothing to lose now that their clients had been convicted. What unnerved her was the slight possibility that the judge would grant it.

The judge cleared his throat and told those in the courtroom that he had read the probation reports for both defendants. Tamia had read them also and been disgusted by them. The reports were written by a sheriff's deputy and included each defendant's life history, statements and letters from the defendants regarding the crime, as well as character references from family and friends. In these reports the girls begged the judge to be lenient with them because of their age. They promised that given a chance they would get jobs and eventually become fine productive citizens. For the Avila family's sake Tamia was thankful the reports wouldn't be read aloud in court.

Then it happened. William Andrews stood up and addressed the judge.

"I'd like to ask Your Honor to declare a mistrial because of lack of evidence." He sounded every bit the gentleman.

"There will be no mistrial," the judge said flatly. "I have told you before and I stand on the opinion that there was more than enough evidence to try the defendants on murder charges."

Then something happened that Judge Tso had almost never seen in a courtroom. The entire audience, with the exception of Paula Severson and Barbara

Doyle, erupted into applause. As it grew, Judge Tso pounded his gavel on the bench.

"There will be none of that in this courtroom," he said, looking astonished. The audience quieted immediately. The applause had been purely spontaneous, and signaled relief as well as approval. After all, everyone in the room knew that anything was possible during the sentencing phase of a trial. The judge could release the defendants on probation. He could throw out the trial. He could sentence them to a lighter prison term. Or he could hand them the maximum penalty attached to second-degree murder: fifteen years to life.

When the judge was satisfied that order had returned to the courtroom, he asked Tamia to present any family members who wished to address the court. Tamia was more than happy to go on with the proceedings now that the judge had denied a mistrial.

Irene Avila stood first and approached the witness box. She had lost weight and looked ten years younger as she took the stand, her hands shaking. The time had come to tell Karen and Laura how she felt.

Both Karen and Laura glanced furtively at Irene as she began to speak.

"Your Honor, I am hoping and praying that my family will see justice done once and for all in this case. Missy's brothers will never know what their sister could have been, we will never watch her grow into a beautiful young woman, never know what she could have contributed to this society.

"My daughter was stripped of her dignity and human rights, she was left to die in that mountain stream like an animal. And I know in my heart that they planned it.

"Who was there to protect my little girl? What must she have gone through?" Irene's voice cracked and she began to cry. She continued reading the letter. "Did she call out for me?" Irene turned and looked at Karen and Laura, but both girls kept their heads turned away.

"Your Honor, these are heartless girls. I ask you to use them as an example so that the same horrible nightmare doesn't happen to another family. We need to see that the justice system doesn't just work for the accused. Thank you, Your Honor."

Irene took her seat next to her daughter-in-law and watched as Mark took the stand.

"When I look around this courtroom," Mark began, "I see Karen Severson and Laura Doyle as judge and jury who convicted my sister to death. All because they were jealous of her. And now, twelve total strangers have had the chance to convict Karen and Laura. Somehow it doesn't seem fair. No matter what the sentence is, nothing will justify what they did to my sister. But I ask you, Your Honor, to hand them the stiffest penalty possible. Thank you."

Ernie Avila, Jr., took the stand then and told Judge Tso that he was certain rehabilitation would not work on Karen Severson and Laura Doyle.

Finally, Tamia rose and told the judge that she thought one thing peculiar about the entire proceeding.

"Karen and Laura never once showed any remorse. There was no remorse in the letters they wrote to the court and none at any time during this hearing today.

"Your Honor, the people's real concern is that Karen Severson and Laura Doyle still do not appreciate the real, serious nature of the crime they committed. For that reason I believe they should be sentenced to the maximum penalty."

William Andrews and David Thomas argued on behalf of their clients that leniency should be given because it was best to forgive and forget.

"In a perfect world there would be perfect justice," Andrews said calmly as the Avila family members hung their heads and held hands. "But this is not a perfect world. So we do our best, given our human frailties."

Thomas said, "Almighty God himself cannot ease the pain of Missy's family and friends without the passage of time. But as difficult as it is, we must forgive and forget. We must move on." Then he turned toward the Avilas and spoke directly at Irene. "I won't insult you by trying to minimize what has happened here. She was a beautiful young girl cut down in her prime. . . . But the past will in time be forgotten. Not the precious memories, but in time we must go on."

Irene was crying angry tears as Thomas spoke, and she shook her head. There would be no forgetting. No forgiving. Not for Irene Avila.

Thomas finished his statement by saying, "Miss Doyle does apologize. I know it means nothing to you now, but know that she does apologize from the bottom of her heart."

Mark Avila watched Laura Doyle's reaction as her attorney made the emotional plea. Her expression remained unchanged. He knew that the attorney was only saying what he was paid to say.

The judge had heard it all.

He summed up the case and said that in his days as a judge he had never seen such ruthless force used unnecessarily. He was appalled that the girls had been so cruel to someone who had trusted them, with whom they had been friends.

"I have considered the nature and seriousness of the crime and the circumstances of that crime. I have considered the particular vulnerability of the victim and the fact that the crime involved great violence to the victim.

"The circumstances of the crime have been stated time and time again. It seems to have been an act of revenge on the part of the defendants toward the victim. Then there was this charade after the killing of Ms. Avila by the defendants.

"The vulnerability of the victim is shown by her small physical stature and the remoteness of the area where she was killed. The court does take notice that the defendants were much larger physically than their victim.

"What troubles the court is the particular violence to the victim. This violence indicates cruelty and viciousness. One does not have far to look for evidence of this extreme cruelty—the remoteness of the area, the bruises and trauma the victim suffered to her face, ears, and neck, and evidence of the victim's hair being hacked off.

"I am satisfied that probation for both defendants should be denied."

Irene Avila bent her head to contain her emotions as she squeezed her son's hand.

Finally, he shuffled the papers on his bench and prepared to hand out the sentences. Irene closed her eyes. It had all come down to this one moment. After this they would go on. They would find a way to make a new life for themselves. Missy was gone. She would live with them in their hearts forever, but it would be time to go on. Irene prayed that the judge would sentence them to the maximum penalty. Anything less would be devastating after all they'd been through.

The judge cleared his throat.

"This court sentences Laura Doyle to fifteen years to life for murder in the second degree. She will serve the time in California's Department of Corrections state prison."

Irene squeezed Mark's hand and waited breathlessly for the judge to read Karen's sentence.

"And this court sentences Karen Severson to fifteen years to life . . ."

Irene didn't hear the rest. They had won. Karen Severson and Laura Doyle were going to prison.

Tamia watched Irene's reaction and for the first time all day the district attorney smiled. For more than a month she'd worried about the sentence Judge Tso would hand out in this case. There was no question that Karen and Laura had killed Missy, and even though she hadn't proven it to the jury, Tamia was certain the murder was premeditated. But that didn't tell anyone how it had actually happened. Because Cindy had left the scene before Missy was killed, there was no way of knowing what really took place that afternoon. The lack of specific details surrounding Missy Avila's last twenty minutes had eaten away at Tamia since the verdict had been read. What if the judge had taken that into consideration and given both girls lighter sentences? Tamia shuddered at the thought and watched as the bailiffs fastened handcuffs on Karen and Laura. Missy's friends were quickly escorted away as newsmen filmed highlights for the evening news.

The reporters began moving in, and Irene knew it

would be an hour before the interviews would end and she and her family could go home. Now, before she did anything else, she had to talk to Missy.

She picked up the picture of Missy she had brought to the hearing. It was the framed eight-by-ten taken just before her death. Irene stared into her daughter's eyes and pulled the picture to her, hugging it tightly and closing her eyes.

Quietly, so that no one could hear her, Irene said good-bye to her only daughter.

"It's over, darling," Irene whispered, her eyes still tightly shut. "You don't have to be afraid anymore. No one will ever hurt you again. Sleep in peace now, Missy. Good night, sweetheart. I love you."

When Irene opened her eyes, Karen Severson and Laura Doyle were gone. For the first time in months Irene noticed the beauty of the sunny day. She walked out of the courtroom flanked by her sons. They would live with Missy's absence and the truth about what had happened to her for the rest of their lives. But tonight, for the first time since October 1, 1985, they would all sleep peacefully.

Epilogue

THROUGHOUT THE TRIAL several things remained unclear about Missy's murder. For one thing, the proceedings never proved which of the girls had actually held Missy's head down in the stream. There was also no way of determining whether both girls were equally in control while the murder was taking place or if, as so many other times before, one of them was barking commands and the other simply following orders.

Also, the transcripts fail to show whether the murder truly was something masterminded by Karen Severson and planned ahead of time, or whether—as the defense attorneys suggested—it had been a situation that simply got out of hand.

Of course, since Karen and Laura refused to testify and since Cindy didn't watch the actual murder, it is possible nobody but the two murderers will ever know what really happened.

Many of the people who read about or attended the trial agreed with the prosecution and the Avila family that most likely the murder was planned and orchestrated by Karen Severson. In fact, spectators noted the smug look Karen Severson had plastered on her face throughout the proceedings.

After all, she had eliminated her single source of frustration, her competition, the one shadow from which she had never been able to emerge. Missy was gone now, she might have reasoned, and if that meant spending another seven or eight years in prison, well, then, she would have to pay that price.

After all, when her sentence was served, Karen Severson would still have another thirty years or so to enjoy herself—maybe for the first time.

Laura Doyle was someone entirely different. People saw her as a disturbed young lady who had mixed with the wrong crowd and allowed her emotions to dictate her actions. She was jealous, she was tired of being second fiddle, and she was easily persuaded by someone like Karen Severson.

Laura never looked quite as smug as Karen during the court proceedings and, when the sentencing was read, betrayed no feeling whatsoever. Her mother, Barbara Doyle, sat in the courtroom dabbing at her wet, puffy eyes. Where had they gone wrong? What had the daughter they'd raised become capable of?

Although she never showed signs of remorse or sorrow during the proceedings, people could detect a hint of anger as Laura adjusted the silly pink bow that pulled her red hair back from her face. They thought it must have been anger at Karen Severson, who had somehow gotten her involved in this killing. In any case, Laura Doyle was every bit as guilty as Karen Severson, and she would pay for it in prison. Most likely—Tamia Hope figured—by taking computer courses.

Another unanswered question was the exact role Cindy Silverio had played in the setting up and killing of Missy Avila. She drove up the mountainside with the girls, but her statements in court indicated that Cindy was something of a dumb brunette—somebody who went along for the ride and whom the killers never thought much about as they drove up the mountainside to murder Missy.

But most people realized there had to be more to her story than that.

The Avilas figured that Karen Severson must have told Cindy some of the same ugly lies about Missy that she had told Laura Doyle. That way, if Missy became suspicious and resisted, Cindy might have been willing to help lead her on the death march to her execution. But somewhere along the way, somewhere between the name calling and trickery and the actual murder, Cindy grew scared and changed her mind. She turned and ran back to the cars, frightened and shaking until Karen and Laura had killed Missy. Nobody actually thought Cindy took part in the drowning, but they were pretty certain that she must have been more than an accidental spectator.

In any event, none of those speculations was answered in court. After the trial Cindy and Steven relocated to an undisclosed location as far from Arleta as they could get.

While there was no way for anyone to learn Cindy's exact involvement, the probation reports filed with the court gave some insight into Karen and Laura's roles.

Tamia Hope kept a copy of each report in her office. The reports were ludicrous and sickening, and she wanted to have them ready to read whenever either girl might come up for parole. Although Tamia arranged for the Avila family to have a copy of the trial transcripts—nearly five thousand pages of testimony

—she never gave them copies of the probation reports, because she didn't think the family could handle reading them.

Appropriately, Laura Doyle's report wasn't as descriptive as Karen Severson's, because under the section of the report that allows the defendant to write her version of the story, Laura had very little to say:

> The defendant stated that she went to a teenage party in an outside area in the mountains around 4:00 P.M. She stated that there was just the four of them—herself, codefendant Severson, the victim, and a girl named Cindy. The defendant stated that the victim did go out with her boyfriend before and after she went out with him. She broke up with him in 1985.
>
> The defendant said that Severson told her that the victim was going out with Severson's boyfriend and that the victim had gone out with Laura's boyfriend when the defendant was going out with him. The defendant said that Cindy cut the victim's hair [This was never discussed by either side during the trial, apparently dismissed because it was not believed to be true] and that Karen [also] cut her hair. And then Laura pulled her off the rock and pushed her. Laura said she drank four to five beers within an hour and a half before the incident and that she drove the victim in her car and the victim was also drinking beer. Laura said that Karen pushed Missy into the water.
>
> The defendant [Doyle] said that the lesson she learned was her abuse of drug and alcohol and she thanks God for being in jail. She said it

*stopped her drug and alcohol use and she has now
graduated. She said she will continue her education.*

*The defendant stated that she had a best friend
—Chris—and that the victim would also go out
with Chris's boyfriend. The defendant stated that
she did not like that. She stated that the victim
would go out with anyone and sell her body for
drugs.*

This portion of the probation report was followed by
a letter from Barbara Doyle, Laura's mother. The letter was summed up by the probation officer:

*Mrs. Doyle writes to the court and says that the
defendant has always been kind and considerate,
helpful and understanding. She says that her
daughter had a hard childhood and states that
the defendant went through school with good
grades, went to modeling school, but didn't have
the money to continue her training. Laura worked
at Vons at least five years and had a brand-new
car, but was a scared and confused girl.*

*She states [in the letter] that she takes part of
the blame because she was not strong enough to
get her out of the environment she was growing
up in. She states that she and her husband fought
all the time and that Laura would try to help her
but it would just make matters worse for Laura.
Her daughter turned to drugs for help. She states
Laura is a good girl and does not believe she has a
mean bone in her body. She says that because of
her home life and drugs, Laura was in trouble.
She states that while in jail, her daughter has*

*gotten her high-school diploma and her general
education diploma and she wants to get into com-
puters. She says that they love one another very
much and have learned a very hard lesson.*

And that, Tamia Hope decided, was just too much
for someone like Irene Avila to read.

Karen Severson's probation report was even worse.

Because Karen Severson believed she could express
herself better through writing, she mailed a letter to
the judge. The probation officer summed up Karen's
letter this way:

*Karen Severson says the whole incident has left
a major impression on her and that it will take
some time to adjust to and live with.*

*She thanks the judge for his fairness in the trial
and feels comfortable knowing that the judge
takes time to consider every angle. She says, "Unfortunately, you did not have the opportunity to
hear my side of the story due to the fact that I did
not testify. . . . I hope it's not too late to tell you
how I feel. . . ."*

*She goes on to say there is not a day that goes by
that she does not think about the victim—Missy.
She said that she was faced with an opportunity
to save the victim's life and failed and will have to
live with that for the rest of her life. She says that
she often questions herself as to why she did not
help but at the time of the incident she was
stunned, shocked, and literally paralyzed by
what she witnessed.*

*She states she had no idea a murder was going
to take place. She states the reason she told no one*

about the murder was because she and her daughter's life would have been threatened. She says she deserves to be punished as an accessory, but to be punished for a murder she did not do is overwhelming.

She says she will have an opportunity to reveal her testimony on appeal but no matter what the outcome is she will suffer from this incident for the rest of her life. She says that she is extremely sorry for what happened and prays that one day the Avila family can, in their own way, forgive her for betraying them. Just as she has forgiven them for betraying her on the witness stand.

She says that she regrets what happened and would do it differently if it happened again and that she can only try to better herself and learn from this terrible mistake. She says that she has learned the value and true meaning of life through this tragedy. She says she has begun changing her life by taking different courses in county jail and has completed a parenting class and several Christian Bible study courses. She states that she has her GED [high-school equivalency degree] and her manicuring license as well as an application for a correspondence course in journalism.

She is engaged to be married to (a man) who has been by her side before and during the last two years. Their plan is to live out of state when she is released. She says that she has associated with the wrong crowd and intends to move away and start over with a new outlook on life—"drug and alcohol free!"

She pleads with the judge for mercy, stating

*that she has a daughter and a family and a fiancé
who need her. And she needs them.*

The interviewing probation officer wrote this about
Karen's oral statement:

> *Karen said that since 1984 the victim had been
> sleeping with boys who had girlfriends, and also
> that she was sleeping around for drugs.*
> *She also stated that she witnessed the codefend-
> ant [Laura Doyle] hold the head of the victim
> underwater and she is truly sorry she stood by
> and did nothing.*

Karen Severson was quoted as expressing remorse
over Missy's murder:

> *"If one can suffer from a memory, then I will
> suffer for this for the rest of my life."*

But then she says this:

> *"Don't get me wrong. My life will go on, and
> through the changes that are occurring in me, I
> will no doubt live a more stable, peaceful life."*

Tamia believed that self-satisfied paragraph gave a
truer picture of Karen Severson than all the rest of her
statements put together.

As with most murder cases the picture of Michele
Yvette Avila grew and stretched during the trial until
in the end she came out looking larger than life. She
was the prettiest girl in Arleta. The girl every boy
wanted. Sweet and innocent. Shining green eyes.

Had she lived, Missy Avila probably would never have made headline news. She would have grown up in Arleta and, like the others she ran with, no doubt would have outgrown her experimentation with drugs. She would have gone to college and gotten a job as a physical therapist, perhaps working with children. She probably would have led a quiet life, maybe married Victor Amaya or someone like him and settled in Arleta. Certainly, she would have grown into a beautiful woman, because Missy Avila was nothing if not pretty.

Because of that, Karen and Laura had been murderously jealous, with a jealousy that grew like a deadly cancer, consuming their hearts, minds, and souls. In a statement she made about Missy's death, Karen mentioned neither remorse nor regret, but only this: "Missy wasn't as innocent as everyone thinks."

Missy wasn't innocent because she was too pretty and too popular. She cast a flirtatious eye too often toward the wrong boys, and so Karen and Laura found her guilty and sentenced her to death.

But when Karen and Laura killed Missy Avila, they made her someone the entire country sympathized with, someone who will always be remembered for being more beautiful, more desirable, than either of them. By killing Missy they immortalized her, and that was the last thing they wanted to do when they held her facedown in eight inches of water that October day.